Heroine of the

Harlem Renaissance

and Beyond

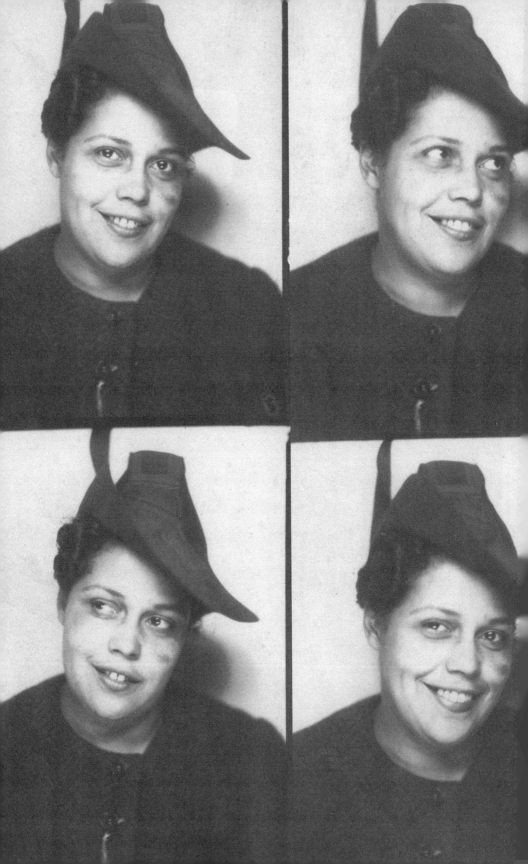

Heroine of the Harlem Renaissance and Beyond

Gwendolyn Bennett's Selected Writings

Edited by Belinda Wheeler
and Louis J. Parascandola

The Pennsylvania State University Press
University Park, Pennsylvania

Unpublished materials held at the Schomburg Center are © Schomburg Center for Research in Black Culture, The New York Public Library.

Historical photographs of Gwendolyn Bennett appear courtesy of the Photographs and Prints Division, Schomburg Center for Research in Black Culture, The New York Public Library, Astor, Lenox, and Tilden Foundations.

Frontispiece: Photo booth portraits of artist and writer Gwendolyn Bennett, circa 1930s. Photo © The New York Public Library.

Untitled [*River Landscape*] reproduced courtesy of Swann Auction Galleries.

Opportunity cover art reproduced courtesy of the National Urban League, *Opportunity: Journal of Negro Life*.

The authors thank the Crisis Publishing Co., Inc., the publisher of the magazine of the National Association for the Advancement of Colored People, for the use of the image first published in the March 1924 issue of *Crisis*.

Library of Congress Cataloging-in-Publication Data

Names: Bennett, Gwendolyn, 1902–1981, author. | Wheeler, Belinda, 1974– editor. | Parascandola, Louis J., 1952– editor.
Title: Heroine of the Harlem Renaissance and beyond : Gwendolyn Bennett's selected writings / edited by Belinda Wheeler and Louis J. Parascandola.
Description: University Park, Pennsylvania : The Pennsylvania State University Press, [2018] | Includes bibliographical references and index.

Summary: "Explores the role of writer Gwendolyn Bennett as an important contributor to the Harlem Renaissance. Includes Bennett's published and unpublished poetry, fiction, essays, diaries, letters, and artwork"—Provided by publisher.

Identifiers: LCCN 2018001477 | ISBN 9780271080963 (cloth : alk. paper) | ISBN 9780271080970 (pbk. : alk. paper)
Subjects: LCSH: Bennett, Gwendolyn, 1902–1981—Criticism and interpretation. | Harlem Renaissance. | LCGFT: Poetry. | Fiction. | Essays. | Diaries. | Personal correspondence.
Classification: LCC PS3503.E5474 A6 2018 | DDC 818/.5209—dc23
LC record available at https://lccn.loc .gov/2018001477

The Pennsylvania State University Press is a member of the Association of University Presses.

It is the policy of The Pennsylvania State University Press to use acid-free paper. Publications on uncoated stock satisfy the minimum requirements of American National Standard for Information Sciences—Permanence of Paper for Printed Library Material, ANSI Z39.48–1992.

Contents

Foreword by Maureen Honey x
Acknowledgments xv
Note on the Text xvii
Bennett Timeline xviii

Introduction *1*

PUBLISHED WORK

Poetry
Introduction *21*
Nocturne (1923) *24*
Heritage (1923) *24*
To Usward (1924) *25*
Song (1925) *26*
Street Lamps in Early Spring (1926) *27*
Hatred (1926) *28*
Lines Written at the Grave of Alexander Dumas (1926) *28*
Moon Tonight (1926) *29*
Dear Things (1926) *30*
Advice (1927) *30*
Fantasy (1927) *31*
Quatrains (1927) *32*
Secret (1927) *32*
To a Dark Girl (1927) *33*
Epitaph (1934) *34*

Art
Introduction *35*
Painting
    Untitled [River Landscape] (1931) *39*

Magazine Covers
>   *Pipes of Pan* (March 1924)   *40*
>   *Untitled* (January 1926)   *41*
>   *Untitled* (July 1926)   *42*

Short Stories
Introduction   *43*
Wedding Day (1926)   *46*
Tokens (1927)   *53*

Editorials
Introduction   *58*
The Ebony Flute (August 1926)   *62*
The Ebony Flute (April 1927)   *67*
The Ebony Flute (July 1927)   *68*
The Ebony Flute (September 1927)   *71*
The Ebony Flute (April 1928)   *71*

Reviews
Introduction   *75*
Heartbreak and North Carolina Sunshine: *The Lonesome Road*—
>   by Paul Green (1926)   *77*
Blue-Black Symphony: *Home to Harlem*, by Claude McKay (1928)   *79*
Banjo, by Claude McKay (1929)   *82*
Plum-Bun, by Jessie Redmon Fauset (1929)   *84*
The Emperors Jones (1930)   *86*

Cultural and Social Articles
Introduction   *89*
The Future of the Negro in Art (1924)   *92*
The American Negro Paints (1928)   *94*
The Plight of the Negro Is Tragic (1934)   *96*
I Go to Camp (1934)   *98*
The Harlem Artists Guild (1937)   *102*

UNPUBLISHED WORK

Poetry

Introduction *107*

Two Poems (1925) *111*

Thin Laughter (1928) *111*

Train Monotony (1928) *112*

Dirge for a Free Spirit (1933) *112*

Fulfillment (1935) *113*

[Give me your hand, beloved] (1935) *114*

I Build America (1938) *115*

Sweat (1938) *117*

Wise Guys (1938) *119*

The Hungry Ones (1938) *125*

Threnody for Spain (1939) *127*

[Across a room when other ones are there] (n.d.) *129*

[Rapacious women who sit on steps at night] (n.d.) *129*

[So this is how it is] (n.d.) *130*

Unfinished Novel

Introduction *132*

Chapter Outline for the Unfinished Novel *The Call* (n.d.) *133*

Excerpts from *The Call* (1928–1932) *134*

Essays

Introduction *142*

My Father's Story (n.d.) *147*

[Ward Place] (1941) *151*

Lancaster, Pa. (n.d.) *153*

Let's Go: In Gay Paree! (n.d.) *156*

25 (n.d.) *158*

[Life as a Javanese] (n.d.) *159*

[Ku Klux Klan Rides] (n.d.) *162*

Last Night I Nearly Killed My Husband! (n.d.) *166*

[Harlem Reflection] (n.d.) *171*

Diaries

Introduction   *175*

France

    June 26, 1925   179

    July 26, 1925   179

    August 2, [1925]   180

    August 8, [1925]   181

    September 27, [19]25   182

    September 28, 1925   183

    April 29, 1926   184

United States

    [April 7,] 1936   186

    April 8, 1936   187

    April 9, 1936   188

    April 18, 1936   188

    May 7, 1936   189

    January 3, 1937   190

    June 19, 1958   190

Correspondence

Introduction   *192*

Literary Friends

    To W. E. B. Du Bois (January 19, 1925)   197

    To Countee Cullen (August 28, 1925)   197

    To Langston Hughes (December 2, 1925)   198

    To Countee Cullen (January 14, 1926)   200

    To Harold Jackman (February 23, 1926)   201

    To Langston Hughes (1926)   203

    To Claude McKay (February 25, 1937)   204

    To James Weldon Johnson (January 4, 1938)   205

    To Alain Locke (May 11, 1939)   208

    To Richard Wright (March 3, 1940)   209

    To Alain Locke (November 30, 1941)   210

    To Langston Hughes (May 13, 1942)   212

Family and Associates

To Joshua Bennett and Marechal Neil Bennett (January 5, 1925)   213

To Marechal Neil Bennett (March 24, 1925)   215

To Joshua Bennett (May 17, 1925)   215

To Marechal Neil Bennett (July 27, 1928)   217

To James Vernon Herring (September 9, 1937)   219

To Mayme (Abernathy) Pizarro (August 31, 1938)   222

To Flora Dugan (October 6, 1947)   223

To Everyone (September 27, 1968)   227

Notes   229

Bibliography   243

Index   245

Foreword

It is fitting that this first collection of Gwendolyn Bennett's published and unpublished work is appearing ninety years after Bennett left Harlem in 1928, when her spectacular rise in the firmament of literary stars known as the Harlem Renaissance ended. Bennett had been a central part of young artists making a big splash in Jazz Age New York, such as Countee Cullen, Langston Hughes, and Aaron Douglas, who joined more senior colleagues Claude McKay, Jessie Fauset, Zora Neale Hurston, Nella Larsen, James Weldon Johnson, and many others to create the most powerful black arts movement ever seen up to that point. Despite her star power in the 1920s, as Belinda Wheeler and Louis J. Parascandola make clear in their splendid introduction, Bennett was completely forgotten by the time of her death in 1981, and it has taken nearly four decades to recover the lost poetry, fiction, visual art, literary columns, and social activism that she contributed to this flowering of modern African American culture in the age of Jim Crow. Confined to the small body of work published in her lifetime and challenged by archival material scattered throughout several libraries, scholars have struggled to develop critical models that adequately describe Bennett's artistic vision. Among the most successful of these critics are Sandra Govan, Cheryl Wall, Nina Miller, Mark Saunders, Michael Chaney, Theresa Leininger-Miller, Denean Sharpley-Whiting, and Belinda Wheeler herself.

Thanks to this scholarly attention, Gwendolyn Bennett's poetry and fiction are now included in major anthologies of the Harlem Renaissance, and she is commonly profiled in biographical entries, but we badly need *Heroine of the Harlem Renaissance and Beyond: Gwendolyn Bennett's Selected Writings*. Without it, we are looking through a glass darkly. When I put together my anthology of women poets from this era, *Shadowed Dreams* (2006), it was clear that the quality of Bennett's poetry put her in the top category of New Negro artists along with Angelina Weld Grimke, Helene Johnson, Georgia Douglas Johnson, and the male pantheon of writers with whom we are familiar, but biographical sketches of Bennett only hinted at what inspired her work. As well, little did most people know that she had written over twice as much unpublished poetry as she had published while she soldiered through the dark days of the Great Depression. Only when I tackled a literary biography of Bennett for *Aphrodite's Daughters* (2016) did I read through the treasure trove of over fifty typed poems in her archive at the Schomburg Center for Research in Black Culture. These riveting pieces, along with her diaries from 1925 and 1936 and her autobiographical essays, fleshed out a lyrical poet whose haunting published verses were both beautiful and sharp-edged. Love, longing, hatred, and bitterness lay at the heart of these lyrics, yet their source was deeply buried in writings that never saw the light of day. Here, Wheeler and Parascandola have made available, along with much other material, fourteen of the unpublished poems, nine of the autobiographical essays, and fourteen of the diary entries written in Paris while she was on an art scholarship in 1925 and in Harlem as she struggled to put her life together a decade later.

Bennett's twenty-three published poems from 1923 to 1928 (with one appearing in 1934) were praised in her own era for their luminous portrayal of black women as beautiful, powerful, passionate, sensual, and proud. "To a Dark Girl" will always be one of the period's most well-known calls to never forget a dual heritage of greatness and enslavement. "Street Lamps in Early Spring" will likewise forever shimmer as a glorious portrait of night as an alluring dark goddess of queenly power. This edition includes these two along with thirteen of Bennett's best-known pieces, most of them from *Opportunity* and Countee Cullen's 1927 anthology *Caroling Dusk*. The youthful poet with her love of romance and fantasy who published these verses would give way to a mature woman unafraid to voice her deepest desires for erotic transport or her bitter disillusionment at love lost in later poems that never saw the light of day. "Train Monotony," "Dirge for a Free Spirit," and "Thin Laughter" are among the many unpublished poems that describe the deterioration of Bennett's marriage to Alfred Jackson, her tumultuous love affair with painter Norman Lewis, the traumatic loss of her father in what was likely a suicidal leap into the path of a subway car on a hot August day in 1926, and other painful disruptions Bennett kept out of the news. The editors have included this biographical information in their introductory material, some of which comes down to us from the black press. This kind of historical and biographical framing is key to unlocking the mystery of Gwendolyn Bennett the artist.

The diary entries included in this volume illuminate the poetry, as do Bennett's memoir essays written largely in the 1930s when she looked back at her childhood and adolescence. We learn a great deal about her parents from these essays, especially her father, who grew up in a small Texas town right after the Civil War and survived its cotton fields only to find himself working as a janitor after earning a law degree in Washington, DC, and evading the authorities. Bennett's parents were teachers whose intelligence could not insulate them from the tightening restrictions of segregation even in the nation's capital, nor from the disintegration of their marriage. Bennett learned firsthand as a child the difficulties of earning a middle-class standard of living even as an educated African American in the early twentieth century. She also learned to construct elaborate fairylands of romance to protect herself from some of life's harsher edges: the splintering of her family, the extramarital dalliances of her father, his futile efforts to establish a successful law practice, his many brushes with the law. The diary entries reflect these challenges and financial worries Bennett faced trying to survive as a student and artist in Jim Crow America. We see in the diaries as well her painful struggles to form stable intimate relationships, having been estranged from her mother, subjected to the violent loss of her father at age twenty-four, and trapped in a failed marriage to an alcoholic womanizer. The beautiful lyric voice Bennett found in her published poetry is rooted in emotional terrain, both public and private, that these materials describe with rare candor and raw passion. Here we see the strength it took for Bennett to believe in herself as an artist, writer, and woman worthy of love. The sunny smile so often seen in photographs of Bennett is a sign of this fortitude as well as a reflection of her incredible resilience.

Heroine of the Harlem Renaissance and Beyond not only draws back the curtain on Bennett's challenging life while adding to our appreciation of her art, it shines a light on her abiding commitment to "uplift the race" in the words of New Negro activists. Sandra Govan resurrected Bennett with her 1980 dissertation, *Gwendolyn Bennett: Portrait of an Artist Lost*, when she reminded us that this powerful poet was equally a central player in creating the Harlem Renaissance through her editorial work, her literary column "The Ebony Flute," and her public readings. Govan later spotlighted Bennett's organizing activity during the 1930s when she wrote essays for the Welfare Council of New York, directed the Harlem Community Art Center, and co-founded the George Washington Carver

School for Democracy. Bennett was a writer-activist par excellence and a precursor to community organizers in the 1960s and beyond. The selection of editorials, book reviews, and articles, many of them published for the first time here, reflect that activist who was looking to strengthen Harlem's community, forge ties between artists and students, bring art into the lives of ordinary people, and fight back against the exploitation of workers and the ravages of unemployment.

Bennett's activism surfaces in her creative work, too, and by including the unpublished pieces in their collection along with the published ones, the editors make clear that Bennett kept a firm grip on attacking sexism, racism, and class exploitation in all the genres within which she operated. Her two published short stories, "Wedding Day" (1926) and "Tokens" (1927), focus on down-and-out black men in Paris who are eaten alive by racism and succumb to its ravaging force. The unpublished poems "I Build America," "Sweat," "Wise Guys," "The Hungry Ones," and "[Rapacious women who sit on steps at night]" showcase a poet who was comfortable with the sweeping story mode of a folk ballad, the proletarian sensibility of a Steinbeck or Dos Passos, the unvarnished vernacular of working-class laborers, the desperate poverty of children and prostitutes, and the gnawing hunger of people in breadlines. She never wavered in her commitment to making these people on the bottom visible, or calling out the callous system that used and discarded them. Bennett's courageous radicalism drew the attention of right-wing politicians, and she was forced out of the Carver School only to come back to life working in the Consumers Union until her retirement in 1968. We see from her example, along with those of Dorothy West, Langston Hughes, Claude McKay, Richard Wright, W. E. B. Du Bois, and others, how inextricably linked were the artistic and political goals of the New Negro movement and how radically its leaders deconstructed American capitalism's racist scaffolding.

Wheeler and Parascandola have given us a tremendous gift with all this primary material and more: a chapter of an unfinished novel hardly anyone knew existed, twenty letters to family and friends, visual art (including a painting Wheeler discovered that survived the fire destroying nearly all of Bennett's art), and essays describing Paris from the vantage point of a black woman artist at the height of modernism, Harlem in the depths of the Depression, and a terrifying night with the Klan in Florida. As they say in their introduction, "Together these works compose the single volume that Bennett never completed in her lifetime. Collectively, these writings will add depth of appreciation to those admirers of Bennett's work during the Harlem Renaissance as well as those interested in the period in general. They also will aid our understanding of radical politics within the African American community in the 1930s." For a collection to offer all of that is truly a landmark moment in Harlem Renaissance, feminism, and modernism studies. We will all benefit from having Gwendolyn Bennett's multifaceted talent, courage, and vision put on full display in *Heroine of the Harlem Renaissance and Beyond.* I am tremendously grateful for it and look forward to the much-needed scholarship that will undoubtedly follow in its wake.

MAUREEN HONEY
University of Nebraska–Lincoln
September 2017

Acknowledgments

We would like to thank the team at Penn State University Press, including Kathryn, Kendra, and Hannah; the copyeditor, Nicholas Taylor; the anonymous reviewers for their helpful suggestions; Louis's grad assistant, Leah Jones; and the staff at the Moorland-Spingarn Research Center at Howard University; the Amistad Research Center at Tulane University; the Schomburg Center for Research in Black Culture (NYPL), particularly Thomas Lisanti; and the James Weldon Johnson Collection at the Beinecke Library at Yale University, especially Rebecca Aldi.

Individually we would like to thank the following important people.

Louis. My former graduate students at LIU, Brooklyn: Malik Crumpler, Sarah Francois, Tiani Kennedy, Yani Perez, and Rajul Punjabi; vice president of academic affairs Gale Stevens Haynes; former VPAA Jeff Kane; Dean David Cohen; my chair in English, Vidhya Swaminathan; the LIU Faculty Development Fund for support; Belinda Wheeler, my co-editor, who has been a tower of strength throughout this process; my brother, John Parascandola; the Nero family; my wife, Shondel Nero, to whom this volume is dedicated—your love and support has sustained me through this and many other projects.

Belinda. Various organizations provided generous funding and/or access to materials at different times during my Bennett research (2009–16), including UNCF/Mellon, New York University's Faculty Resource Network, and Emory University's Travel-to-Collections research grant. Drs. Ed Brunner, Bob Fox, Jeremy Wells, and Liz Klaver provided critical feedback regarding my Bennett research while I was completing my dissertation. Bennett's relatives provided, and continue to provide, invaluable knowledge about Bennett that is not contained in archives. Sandy Govan's continuing support of my work and Maureen Honey's words of encouragement have helped sustain all of my Bennett projects. A special thanks has to go to my colleague and collaborator, Louis, who first contacted me about this project in 2014. There were times when I needed to step away from the project, and Louis was always there during those key moments.

As always, Jen has been a source of strength during every journey I take—no words can ever thank you enough for your support. Finally, I would like to dedicate this book to my grandfather, Frank Wheeler. Without his patience, unwavering support, and love, I never would have overcome many obstacles, including a severe stutter as a child, to become a professor and conduct research on extraordinary people like Gwendolyn Bennett.

Note on the Text

Bennett's work was published in a variety of places, each with its own editing policies. The unpublished work, often typed, contains a number of obvious errors (e.g., "balck" for "black"). We have retained the original texts for all material but silently corrected obvious errors, including in Bennett's sometimes erratic spelling. We have retained, however, her idiosyncratic use (or nonuse) of apostrophes in contractions, particularly "don't," which she consistently spells "dont." We have annotated the text when Bennett's meaning may be unclear to many modern readers.

Bennett was prone to underline words for emphasis in much of her work, whether published or unpublished. Although the practice today might be to italicize, for the sake of authenticity we are staying true to her wishes and keeping all corresponding text underlined.

In the case of ellipses, depending on the publication sometimes four ellipses were used, sometimes three, sometimes three and four in the same publication. For consistency throughout all materials, we have opted to use three ellipses.

We have also tried to omit material as little as possible. In some rare cases where she is repetitive or the context did not seem of interest to modern readers, we have omitted by using an ellipsis in brackets [. . .].

Some of the unpublished work is untitled. In such cases, we have indicated our title in brackets.

Bennett Timeline

1902   Bennett born in Giddings, Texas (July 8).

ca. 1906   Following her parents' divorce, Bennett is kidnapped by her father, Joshua, from her mother, Mayme. Bennett and her father remain on the run for several years. Bennett has no interaction with her mother for more than fifteen years.

1906-7   Bennett and her father live in Washington, DC.

1914   Joshua Bennett marries Marechal Neil (June 3).

1918-21   Bennett attends Brooklyn Girl's High School.

1921   Bennett graduates from Brooklyn Girl's High School (January).

1921-22   Bennett studies at the Fine Arts Department of Teachers College, Columbia University.

1923   Bennett's first magazine cover, "Christmas Carols," is published in *Crisis* (December).

"Heritage" (poetry) published in *Opportunity* (December).

1923-24   Bennett transfers to the Pratt Institute and completes her studies in art and drama.

1924   New York Civic Club function (March 21). Bennett reads "To Usward" (poetry), which is later published simultaneously in *Crisis* and *Opportunity*.

Bennett becomes a faculty member of fine arts at Howard University, Washington, DC (Fall). She teaches design, watercolor, and crafts.

Bennett is awarded a $1,000 scholarship from Delta Sigma Theta Sorority for continued study of art abroad (December).

1925   Bennett takes leave from Howard and travels to Paris to begin her scholarship (June).

1926   Bennett returns to the United States (Summer).

Bennett's father dies (August).

Bennett returns to Howard (Fall).

Bennett becomes the assistant to the editor at *Opportunity* and starts publishing "The Ebony Flute" (column).

Bennett is on the editorial board of *Fire!!* along with Wallace Thurman, Langston Hughes, Zora Neale Hurston, Aaron Douglas, John P. Davis, and Richard Bruce Nugent.

1927 ○ Controversy surrounds Bennett's engagement to a Howard University student (Alfred Jackson); she resigns from Howard and works at a batik factory.

Bennett and Aaron Douglas invited to study with Dr. Albert C. Barnes at the Barnes Foundation in Marion, Pennsylvania.

Jackson completes his internship at Freedman's Hospital, moves to Eustis, Florida, and starts his own practice.

1928 ○ Bennett marries Dr. Alfred J. Jackson (April 14).

"The Ebony Flute" concludes (May).

Bennett teaches art at Tennessee State College over the summer and then moves to Eustis, Florida.

Bennett teaches art and Spanish at Curtright High School in Eustis, Florida.

1930 ○ Bennett visits New York and participates in library program (December).

1931 ○ Bennett creates painting *Untitled* [*River Landscape*]. To date it is the only Bennett painting in existence.

Bennett travels to New York.

ca. 1932 ○ Bennett and Jackson move from Florida to Long Island, New York, where her husband starts his practice.

Bennett begins work at the W. C. Handy Music Publishing Company.

1933 ○ Bennett works at the Hempstead YMCA.

1934 ○ Bennett starts working as a journalist for the Department of Information and Education of the Welfare Council of New York.

Jackson's health continues to deteriorate.

ca. 1935 ○ Bennett maintains a separate residence from Jackson in a boarding house in Harlem. Norman Lewis also has a room at the same boarding house. The following year, Bennett begins a three-year relationship with Lewis.

1935–41	Bennett works on the New York City Works Progress Administration Federal Arts Project.
1936	Bennett reads with Countee Cullen and Claude McKay in New York (February).
	Jackson dies (May 12).
1937	Bennett directs the Harlem Artists Guild.
1938	Bennett accused of Communist affiliation at the Harlem Art Center by the House Un-American Activities Committee.
1938–41	Bennett serves as director of the Harlem Community Art Center (the largest of the Federal Art Projects), taking over from Augusta Savage.
1939	Bennett submits a manuscript of poems to Dr. Frank Horne at the U.S. Works Progress Administration (February).
	Bennett and eleven other African American women honored as "Distinguished Women of Today" at the World's Fair in New York.
	Harlem Community Art Center supports Bennett despite the Communist charges against her.
1940	Bennett marries Richard (Dick) Crosscup (June 26).
	Bennett serves as a panelist at the National Negro Congress conference.
1941	Bennett is suspended as the director of the Harlem Community Arts Center (June 30).
1941–42	Bennett teaches at the School for Democracy.
1943	George Washington Carver School opens. Bennett is a founding member and serves as its director.
1947	George Washington Carver School closes.
1948	Bennett is hired by Consumers Union.
1968	Bennett resigns from Consumers Union.
1970	Bennett and Crosscup move to Kutztown, Pennsylvania, and open an antique store, Buttonwood Hollow Antiques.
1980	Dick Crosscup dies (January 9).
1981	Bennett dies in Reading, Pennsylvania (May 31).

When considering the writers associated with the Harlem Renaissance, one usually thinks of Langston Hughes, Countee Cullen, Zora Neale Hurston, Nella Larsen, Dorothy West, and Claude McKay. While those names deserve their canonical position within that pivotal literary and arts movement, there remain a number of figures whose contribution is only recently being fully realized. One previously understudied figure from this period is Gwendolyn Bennett (1902–1981), a significant writer and artist during the early days of the Harlem Renaissance, and one who remained a powerful advocate for African Americans living in and around Harlem well into the 1930s and 1940s. Bennett's name is increasingly referenced in books that cover the Harlem Renaissance largely due to her brief, yet prolific, literary and artistic output from approximately 1923 to 1928. During that time Bennett published over forty poems, reviews, articles, and short stories in notable African American magazines and anthologies, including Alain Locke's *The New Negro* (1925), William Stanley Braithwaite's *Anthology of Magazine Verse for 1927*, and Countee Cullen's *Caroling Dusk* (1927); her artwork adorned several magazines, including *Crisis: A Record of the Darker Races* and *Opportunity: Journal of Negro Life*; her literary column, "The Ebony Flute," was published monthly in *Opportunity*; and she worked as an editor or assistant editor of several important periodicals, including *Opportunity*, *Black Opals*, and *Fire!!* Bennett's diverse talent in the fields of poetry, short story writing, journalism, art, and editorial work had previously made it difficult for scholars to pigeonhole this dynamic woman into one genre, arguably contributing to her marginalization. Bennett herself said, "I'd feel that if I'd been either an artist, a graphic and plastic artist, or a writer, I might have had a single mind" (qtd. in Govan, *Gwendolyn*

Bennett 204). However, as Douglas Mao and Rebecca Walkowitz state in *Bad Modernisms* (2006), new modernism studies have "extended the designation 'modernist' beyond" canonical authors, expanded the modernist time period beyond the 1920s, and "embraced less widely known women writers, authors of mass cultural fiction, makers of the Harlem Renaissance, artists from outside Great Britain and the United States, and other cultural producers hitherto seen as neglecting or resisting modernist innovation" (1). These developments have been achieved through "two significant enterprises": reconsidering the "definitions, locations, and producers of 'modernism'" and applying "new approaches and methodologies to 'modernist' works" (1). The Harlem Renaissance is now regarded as an artistic movement that was heterodox in its multiple interests, including its many definitions of art. Bennett's ability to maneuver successfully between a "constellation of ideas, movements, publishing venues, and artistic communities" at the beginning of the Renaissance makes her one of the youngest leaders of this movement (Sanders 129).

Much of the scholarship about Bennett has focused on her literary output from 1923 to 1928. This is not surprising given that most published pieces by Bennett cease after she moved to Florida with her first husband, Alfred J. Jackson, in the late 1920s. As more archival research has been conducted, however, we are starting to see Bennett's significance move well beyond 1928. The recovery of over fifty unpublished poems, many of which were written in the 1930s; numerous diary entries throughout different parts of her career; several autobiographical essays; correspondence between Bennett and canonical figures from the Harlem Renaissance from the 1920s to the 1940s; reviews and newspaper articles Bennett wrote in the 1930s; the first recovered painting by Bennett created in the early 1930s; and a book project initiated in the 1930s, illustrate that Bennett continued to be highly productive well after the 1920s. Recently, Cary Nelson (2015) chose to highlight three of Bennett's previously unpublished poems that Belinda Wheeler recovered in the recently published second edition of *Anthology of Modern American Poetry*: "Dirge for a Free Spirit," "I Build America," and "[Rapacious women who sit on steps at night]." Nelson claimed that taken together "this group of three poems alone mandates a revised understanding of Bennett's career" (629). Sandra Govan, Michel Fabre, and Maureen Honey have also used some archival material to push Bennett's artistic timeline beyond 1928. The comprehensive material provided in this collection, including some never-before published and analyzed material, further highlight Bennett's significant contribution to the Harlem Renaissance and beyond.

This volume seeks to claim Bennett's spot beside the names of Hurston, Hughes, McKay, Cullen, Larsen, and West, among others. Bennett's diverse literary output; the social circles in which she played a central role; her critiques of Harlem and elsewhere in her correspondence, reviews, articles, and "The Ebony Flute" during the 1920s; and her staunch radical political voice (particularly in her 1930s work), make her an important figure who deserves more attention.

Rationale for Our Editorial Selections

At first glance, the body of Bennett's work appears slim. She never published a volume of her own work, so her writings have been spread over numerous periodicals and literary anthologies. She is known mostly for her short lyrics published between 1923 and 1928, two short stories, and the highly entertaining literary column "The Ebony Flute" that she wrote for *Opportunity*. Even this relatively small corpus has earned her a place within the Harlem Renaissance. However, what she wrote during her lifetime comprises a much larger body of work. For this reason, we have divided Bennett's works by genre, since she worked in many forms, and broken the work into two sections: works published and unpublished writings. It is necessary to understand both sections in order to appreciate fully this multifaceted artist.

After she fell out of the Harlem Renaissance spotlight, Bennett continued to write voluminously. This anthology is designed to extend our understanding of Bennett and her work beyond the six-year window in which she is often considered. She published many reviews as well as literary and political essays, commenting on significant cultural and social events within the African American community. Unfortunately, many of these works have been lost to modern readers, as they were published in obscure periodicals housed only in research institutions. More important, she did not publish the bulk of her writings, so the works remain locked away in library archives. Her diary entries during her early years in Paris and in Harlem during the post-Depression era provide key firsthand perspectives that add insight into the author's own life, and into what it was like for African Americans living in those exciting, turbulent places and times. In addition, she penned poignant material about such subjects as her troubled marriage, life in the Jim Crow South, and her being forcibly separated from her mother at an early age. These pieces, arguably wrenching to write and read, add greatly to our understanding of this highly talented, but largely overlooked, woman. A sampling of Bennett's correspondence, all previously unpublished, helps explain her troubled family dynamics, and letters to literary luminaries such as Alain Locke, Countee Cullen, Claude Mc Kay, Richard Wright, W. E. B. Du Bois, and Langston Hughes situate her within the Harlem Renaissance and beyond. We also include a chapter from an unfinished novel begun during her Harlem Renaissance years, which sheds light on a little-known aspect of her writing. Finally, we have added several poems from her oeuvre. It was for poetry that Bennett was best known during the Harlem Renaissance, and she continued writing in this medium throughout her life. Many of these poems continue the lyric tradition begun in her younger age, but her later work also added an overt, socially conscious perspective generally lacking in her earlier writings. We include a representative sampling of both published and unpublished work, fiction, nonfiction, and poetry on a range of subjects. We offer a generous array of the earlier works for which her reputation has been established, we include many of her now obscure published reviews and essays, and we provide access to her other unpublished writings now contained only in research libraries.

Together these works compose the single volume that Bennett never completed in her lifetime. Collectively, these writings will add depth of appreciation to those admirers of Bennett's work during the Harlem Renaissance as well as those interested in the period in general. They also will aid our understanding of radical politics within the African American community in the 1930s. In addition, they will serve to introduce Bennett to a new generation of readers and scholars.

Early Life

In order to appreciate fully Bennett's overall contribution to the Harlem Renaissance, one must first understand her roots. The road from Texas to New York, and the center of the Harlem Renaissance, was not without incident for Gwendolyn Bennetta Bennett, who was born to Joshua Robin

Bennett and Mayme Abernathy Bennett on July 8, 1902, in Giddings, a small (1,200 people in 1900) cotton-growing community about sixty miles east of Austin. Her father, Bennett recalled years later, had a "sensitive mouth," "innocent eyes," "clear laughter," and "quick brain," and he worked hard as the youngest of eight children and son of a Texas barber to become a teacher and later a lawyer ("My Father's Story"). Also a teacher, Mayme, in Bennett's words, had beautiful skin that was "the color of ivory," and her "straight and black [hair was] like her grandmother's, a thorough-bred Indian." When Bennett was still an infant, the family moved to Nevada and her parents taught on an Indian reservation. Although Bennett was very young when she lived on the reservation, she fondly remembered "from some where in the dim recesses of my baby subconscious mind the nights when the Indians reached back into their past and donned their war paint and danced the dances of the tribes." To Bennett, "nothing but beauty had touched their [her parents'] lives and mine in those days" ("My Father's Story").

A few years later Bennett's parents moved to Washington, DC, and the beauty Bennett had recalled earlier ended. In Washington, Bennett's father worked as a government clerk while also completing a law degree at night from Howard University. The harder Bennett's father worked to juggle multiple responsibilities, the further apart he grew from his wife. "His bright spirit had been toughened with the endless struggle to get ahead. I don't know what had happened to him," recalled Bennett, "but something hard began to creep into his nature" ("My Father's Story"). Before long Bennett's father began an affair with a fellow night school student. Bennett vividly recalls witnessing her parents' querulous relationship as one of her first memories: "I don't know how I came to know or understand that my father had what was called in those days, an affinity. And yet know it I did and well enough to inject myself into their bitter argument" ("[Ward Place]"). The hostility between Bennett's parents grew and the two divorced when Bennett was approximately four years old. For a time, Bennett lived with her mother and saw her father during regular Sunday visits. Bennett alluded to feelings of great hurt toward her father years later when she wrote about her time with him, "There are still places that have not healed with time." However, when she talked about her earliest memories living with him they were generally pleasant. Recalling her Sunday visits with her father, Bennett said that "we did all the things that were fondest to

FIG. 1   Gwendolyn Bennett (*center*) with a group of male friends (*left to right*): Charley Boyd, Hoggie Payne, Jayfus Ward, "The Fat One" Hoffman, and "Bon Bon" Simmons, circa 1920s. Schomburg Center for Research in Black Culture, The New York Public Library.

my heart. [. . .] We went to the theatre, to restaurants for dinner [. . .] we went for long car rides and to all sorts of places for amusement, we laughed and played together." Life between two households continued for Bennett until her father, as Bennett put it, "found himself fed up with his freedom and wishing that he too might have a part in the fashioning of my life." In 1910, when Bennett was still very young, her father "hit upon a plan to have me all for himself" and on one of their Sunday visits took his daughter and never returned. Bennett would not see her mother "until some sixteen years later" ("My Father's Story"). Bennett and her father—along with his new wife, Marechal Neil—lived on the run, regularly moving between the District of Columbia, Pennsylvania, and New York to avoid detection. This dislocation is at the center of much of Bennett's writing, creating a lifelong search for stability and a deep-seated desire for a sense of home and family.

Though Bennett and her father and stepmother often moved regularly to avoid being located by authorities, they did enjoy periods of normality, such as the pleasant times she recalls spent visiting the theater with a young friend while living in the Elite Hotel in Lancaster, Pennsylvania (see "Lancaster, Pa."). Bennett completed much of her elementary education in Harrisburg, Pennsylvania, as well as several years at Harrisburg's Central High. Gwennie (as she was often known) also developed a close bond with her stepmother. However, these periods of respite seldom lasted long. Bennett's father took a position in Brooklyn and soon moved Gwendolyn and Marechal there. Gwendolyn attended Brooklyn's Girls' High School, where she excelled, particularly in the areas of art, literature, creative writing, and drama. She was the first African American student to be elected into both the Girls' High School's drama and literary societies. In addition, Bennett received commendations for her graphic art and her writing skills. Despite these achievements, Bennett and other African American students also encountered racial prejudice, as is evidenced in Eric Walrond's sketch about an incident his friend Gwennie may well have experienced, "Cynthia Goes to the Prom."[1] Bennett took the skills she had acquired with her to Teachers College at Columbia University, where she enrolled in the Fine Arts Department. Bennett did well at the college but transferred to the Pratt Institute after two years, citing the "racist atmosphere on campus" (Langley and Govan 7). At Pratt, Bennett's love of art and drama grew.

Howard University and Paris

After graduating from Pratt in 1924, Bennett was hired to teach art at Howard University. During the 1924–25 academic school year, she taught courses in watercolor, design, and crafts. Bennett's brief time at Howard from 1924 to 1927 was filled with turbulence. It was a coup for someone her age to be hired in one of the most prestigious African American institutions of higher learning in the country, although the art program was a fledgling one, having been established only in 1923 (Govan, *Gwendolyn Bennett* 66). However, she was unhappy at Howard being away from the excitement and sense of community she had begun to establish in New York. In a letter to her parents (5 Jan. 1925) she described Washington, DC, as a "God-forsaken place" with "quiet streets [and] no elevators nor subways." She is even more revealing in a letter to Carl Van Vechten: "I am in a dry place where no water is . . . barren fields are dry as dust here" (qtd. in Govan, *Gwendolyn Bennett* 108).[2]

FIG. 2 Portrait of Gwendolyn Bennett, circa 1920s. Schomburg Center for Research in Black Culture, The New York Public Library.

In December 1924 Bennett was awarded a $1,000 scholarship from Delta Sigma Theta Sorority to study art in Paris. She took a one-year leave from Howard to begin her scholarship in the summer of 1925. She was one of the earliest African American visual artists to arrive in Paris, and she soon became familiar with the relatively small community, including Meta Warrick Fuller, Laura Wheeler Waring, and Henry O. Tanner. In addition, she studied art at the Académie Coloressi, the Académie Julien, the École de Panthéon, and the Académie de la Grande Chaumière and French literature at the Sorbonne (Sharpley-Whiting 94–101). She also met such writers as Gertrude Stein and Ernest Hemingway at Sylvia Beach's famed bookstore Shakespeare and Company (Honey 99). In addition, she visited many of the nightclubs, even seeing a dance revue starring Josephine Baker (see "Let's Go: In Gay Paree!"). Despite her normally gregarious nature, Bennett took some time to acclimate to Paris, often feeling lonely and detached, which is reflected in her letters and diary.

Although Bennett was happy to return to the United States and resume her life in DC, she soon became embroiled in controversy after becoming engaged to a Howard medical student, Alfred Jackson. Such fraternization was highly frowned on by the deeply conservative school, and she announced her resignation in 1927. Bennett accepted an invitation to study art along with Aaron Douglas at the prestigious Albert C. Barnes Foundation in Merion, Pennsylvania in the fall of 1927. Leaving Howard left her in a precarious financial situation, one that would continue for much of her adult life; after finishing her time at the Barnes Foundation she was forced to seek employment as a Javanese woman in order to get a job in a batik factory (see "[Life as a Javanese]").

Bennett's Life and Work During the Harlem Renaissance Years

While working at Howard, Bennett made periodic visits to New York and simultaneously began publishing some of her own work in African American periodicals and establishing friendships with a number of people who would become important Harlem Renaissance figures. Bennett knew that African American magazines were an excellent way to contribute to her community and further promote racial progress; share her ideas with an informed and interested audience, including fellow writers and other potential publishers; and generate some additional, albeit minor, income.

Crisis and *Opportunity* were two of the largest African American magazines during the mid-1920s, with circulations of sixty-five thousand and eleven thousand, respectively. *Crisis*, headed by W. E. B. Du Bois, was the official publication of the NAACP, and *Opportunity*, headed by Charles S. Johnson, was sponsored by the National Urban League (Wheeler, "Gwendolyn Bennett" 204). The exchange of ideas in most magazines, including African American periodicals, "fostered surprising alliances, encouraged dialogue among opposing points of view, and promoted cooperation among writers from competing artistic and political camps" (Churchill and McKible 13). Additionally, African American magazines in particular "served as essential vehicles for sustained culture building, both in keeping artists' work before the public and in continuously theorizing the relations among aesthetics, race, and racial progress" (Nina Miller qtd. in Wheeler, "Gwendolyn Bennett" 204). Before long, Bennett had published her first poem, "Nocturne," in *Opportunity*'s November 1923 issue, and her first magazine cover adorned the December 1923 issue of *Crisis*.

Bennett's publications in these issues of *Crisis* and *Opportunity* had ripple effects on the young girl's career. Ernestine Rose, the head librarian at the 135th Street Library, recognized the talent in the area and promoted regular "poetry readings, book discussions, and general library activity" (Levering-Lewis 105). Countee Cullen was a frequent reader of poetry (both his own and that of others) at the local library branch, as was Bennett. On Friday, January 18, 1924, at a nearby Brooklyn YMCA, Bennett and Cullen read a selection of their poetry during the center's book lovers' hour. Before long, Bennett befriended a number of artists and writers, including Cullen, Jessie Redmon Fauset, Alain Locke, Regina Anderson, Eric Walrond, Aaron Douglas, and Langston Hughes. In his autobiography *The Big Sea*, Hughes writes of meeting literary and artistic figures, including Bennett, when he began forming his "first literary and artistic friendships" (173).

With the help of Bennett, Fauset, and Anderson, Charles S. Johnson organized a Civic Club dinner for March 21, 1924, to announce to the wider community that a new wave of artists, the New Negro, had arrived. In a letter to Ethel Ray, his secretary, Johnson described the event:

> This past week [. . .] I was arranging for the "debut" of the younger Negro writers. It was a most unusual affair—a dinner meeting at the Civic Club at which all of the younger Negro writers—[Countee] Cullen,

Walter White, [Eric D.] Walround [*sic*], Jessie Fauset, Gwendolyn Bennett, Alain Locke, M[ontgomery] Gregory, met and chatted with the passing generation—[Du Bois, James] Weldon Johnson, Georgia Douglas Johnson, etc. and with the literary personages of the city: Carl Van Doren, editor of the *Century*, Frederick Allen of *Harper's*, Walter Bartlett of *Scribner's*, [. . .] Paul Kellogg of the *Survey*, Horace Liveright of Boni, Liveright Publishers, etc.—about 100 guests and tremendously impressive speaking [. . . The evening] served to stimulate a market of the new stuff which these young writers are turning out. The first definite reaction came in the form of an offer of one magazine [*Survey Graphic*] to devote an entire issue to the similar subjects as treated by representatives of the group. A big plug was bitten off. Now it's a question of living up to the reputation. (24 Mar. 1924)

The Civic Club dinner would later be "widely hailed as a 'coming out party' for young black artists, writers, and intellectuals whose work would come to define the Harlem Renaissance" (McHenry 383n100). The final speaker of the event was Bennett, who presented her poem "To Usward." It was at that moment that Bennett and many of her young colleagues were ready to take the literary world by storm. As fate would have it, Bennett's artistic talent led her to the aforementioned trip to France to study art. As Bennett's unpublished letters and diary entries that appear in this collection show, being away from Harlem's literary scene in those early months was difficult for her, but she was still able to publish.

Shortly after her return from Paris, on August 13, 1926, Bennett's father died at the age of forty-six in a subway incident, likely a suicide because of shame over business scandals and an affair with Clara Hicks, his secretary, who was also a former student of Bennett's. Even more traumatically, Gwendolyn and her stepmother, at least according to one news account, witnessed his death ("Eastern" 2). Such a blow must have been devastating to Bennett, who was always close to her father. His frequent infidelities to Bennett's mother and stepmother deeply pained her. In addition, the charges against him for fraud and embezzlement shamed her. Nevertheless, no matter his failings, Bennett's father deeply loved his daughter, and she maintained bittersweet memories of him throughout her life. As Honey astutely observes, "Bennett had a complex relationship with her father that was compounded by his shocking early death" (126).

Despite the personal setbacks, Bennett published over twenty poems in the 1920s, many of which are anthologized today. Her mastery of various poetic forms and subjects that crossed racial, class, and gender lines allowed her to expand the modernist base at a key moment in the development of the Harlem Renaissance. Two notable strengths of Bennett's early poetry were her ability to create dynamic anthems of racial uplift and pride for the African American community, and to link youthful imagery with the senses in both traditional and nontraditional forms. In the selections contained in this collection we have assembled a range of her poems.

In addition to Bennett's poetic contribution, her artwork was also sought after early in her career. Bennett studied art in the United States alongside notable Harlem Renaissance figures like Aaron Douglas, and her paintings were well regarded in the artistic community. Unfortunately, much of it was destroyed in two fires. One fire occurred at Bennett's mother-in-law's home in Washington, DC, in 1926 (Langley and Govan 8). A second fire occurred at Bennett's stepdaughter's home after Bennett's death in the early 1980s (Tanner). Up until 2012 it was believed that none of Bennett's artwork had survived. The discovery by Wheeler of *Untitled* [*River Landscape*] from 1931, therefore, provides us with the only known painting by Bennett to be in existence today.[3] Though almost all of Bennett's paintings have been lost or destroyed over the years, her graphic art remains. Bennett's artwork adorned several issues of *Crisis*, *Opportunity*, and *Messenger* as well as several books. The artwork chosen for magazine covers emphasized youth and racial and gender equality, making them important pieces at the beginning of the Harlem Renaissance.

Bennett also wrote fiction, though only three pieces survive: two short stories, "Wedding Day" and "Tokens"; and the start of a novel, *The Call*. Both short stories are set in Paris and focus on the U.S. expatriate experience abroad and racial inequality, making them an important part of Bennett's oeuvre. The former story was published in the landmark experimental journal *Fire!!* (1926), which Bennett co-edited. The latter was also published in an important venue, *Ebony and Topaz: A Collectanea* (1927), edited by Charles S. Johnson. The publication in our anthology of a chapter from her unfinished novel *The Call*, set in the rural South and written in dialect, will add greatly to an appreciation of her skills as a fiction writer.

In addition to Bennett's poetry, art, and fiction, she also wrote one of the most highly regarded literary columns of the day, "The Ebony Flute," which appeared in *Opportunity* from August 1926 until May 1928. Bennett's growing reputation and commitment to the movement no doubt motivated Charles S. Johnson to invite Bennett to design and edit a weekly literary column. Though *Opportunity* was officially an "organ of the National Urban League," Elizabeth McHenry points out that Johnson's "particular interests" largely "dictated that the content of the magazine would include aspects of the cultural side of Negro life that had long been neglected" (291). Johnson welcomed Bennett's column in his August 1926 *Opportunity* editorial: "The growth of Negro literature groups throughout the country and their manifest concern about the activities of other writers prompts the introduction this month of a column carrying informal literary intelligence. It begins under the hand of Gwendolyn Bennett, one of the most versatile and accomplished of our younger group of writers. She is in a position to provide interest in plenty for those who enjoy the lighter side of Negro letters" (241). Though Johnson's editorial suggests that Bennett would be focusing on "the lighter side of Negro letters," Bennett's column was a delicate blend of communal literary society and outspoken critique of important literary and artistic events taking place inside and outside of Harlem.

Similar to "The Ebony Flute," Bennett's book and theater reviews and her articles on art and social issues provide readers with a critical analysis of leading plays and books being published during the Harlem Renaissance as well as important social issues the community was facing. Even though Bennett was away from Harlem during the time she wrote several reviews, her knowledge of the material and her experience with columns such as "The Ebony Flute" more than qualified her to write them.

Married Life in Florida and the Return to New York

Bennett married Alfred J. Jackson on April 14, 1928. Although an article in the *Pittsburgh Courier* touted it as a perfect marriage of art and science, unfortunately the reality was quite different (Dutrieuille 6). Jackson established a medical practice in Eustis, Florida, and Bennett soon relocated there. She had to give up her literary column, since she no longer had direct access to Harlem, and she essentially stopped publishing (though not writing) for several years. She tried to keep active in Eustis, teaching art and Spanish at a high school in the area and becoming involved in local issues, but the overt racism she and her husband faced (see "[Ku Klux Klan Rides]"), coupled with the Depression and the Mediterranean fruit fly, which devastated crops in the area, placed a major strain on the couple. Jackson turned to alcohol. The largely autobiographical piece "Last Night I Nearly Killed My Husband!" vividly details the troubled marriage. In desperation, Bennett convinced her husband in 1932 to return to the New York City suburb of Hempstead, where she would be close to her beloved Harlem.

Harlem Work, Investigations, Remarriage, and a Final Sense of Peace

The early 1930s was an extremely difficult financial period for Bennett. In addition to the Great Depression, her husband's health continued to deteriorate and his medical practice failed. Bennett managed to piece together short jobs to earn some money: six months at the W. C. Handy Music Publishing Company; a little over a year as director of the Hempstead YMCA; almost two years at the Welfare Council of New York City's Department of Public Information and Education (Govan, "After the Renaissance" 29). Her unstable income and unhappy marriage left her mentally, physically, and emotionally exhausted. These positions, according to Bennett, provided little pay, no permanent job security, and required that she work an "ungodly number of hours" (Bennett letter to Horowitz). It left her little time or space to do creative work, and virtually nothing from these years was published (an exception is the bleak "Epitaph" [1934], her last published poem). Despite these challenges, Bennett had a major impact on Harlem arts organizations. In many ways, she sacrificed her own artistic talents in order to further the advancement of others. Bennett held a post from 1935 to 1941 working for the Works Progress Administration Art Project. She also directed the Harlem Artists Guild in 1936 and was connected with the Harlem Art Center. There was an intimate connection between the artists and Harlemites. Noted artist Romare Bearden stated that "Gwen took a leading part in [the Harlem Artists Guild] from its inception" (Govan, "After the Renaissance" 29–30). Well-known artist Jacob Lawrence was one of the students at the Harlem Art Center (30). Unfortunately, these organizations, as with other Works Project Administration groups, came under increasing scrutiny by the House Un-American Activities Committee for allegedly having Communist links. Although these charges were never proven, Bennett was suspended from her job in 1941.

FIG. 3   Group portrait of Harlem Community Art Center instructors, circa 1930s. Front row, *left to right*: Zell Ingram, Pemberton West, Augusta Savage, Robert Pious, Sarah West, and Gwendolyn Bennett. Back row, *left to right*: Elton Fax, Rex Gorleigh, Fred Perry, William Artis, Francisco Lord, Louise Jefferson, and Norman Lewis. Schomburg Center for Research in Black Culture, Jean Blackwell Hutson Research and Reference Division, The New York Public Library.

Despite continuing scrutiny from the government, Bennett persevered in her quest to advance what Brian Dolinar terms "the black cultural front." She participated in a "cultural session at the 1940s conference of the National Negro Congress" (Dolinar 3) and championed the need for the organization to spend "more time, space, and effort on the cultural front" (Bennett qtd. in Dolinar 3). She became a founding member of Harlem's George Washington Carver School in 1943, which was attended by approximately seven hundred students, mostly poor African Americans. She said she established the school to "help Negroes to see the whole world and where they fit into it" (Bennett qtd. in Conrad 9). Unfortunately, the school was forced to close because of continued charges of Bennett's perceived links to Communism in 1947. FBI records show that Bennett remained under investigation well into the 1950s.[4] While the FBI finally concluded that Bennett was not guilty of any crimes, its frequent accusations took their emotional toll on her and devastated her career. Eventually, she was able to channel her desire to help others in a less politically charged position, working for Consumers Union from 1948 to 1968.

Not unlike her professional career during the post-Renaissance era, Bennett's personal relationships endured highs and lows. The first significant relationship Bennett had after her first husband was with the African American artist Norman Lewis, beginning in 1936 and lasting approximately three years. It was a highly volatile relationship that left Bennett emotionally scarred, as evidenced by many of the diary entries we have included in the collection. On the other hand, the relationship she had with a white, Harvard-educated, politically active teacher, Richard Crosscup, which culminated in their marriage in 1940, seems to have brought her, by all accounts, much peace (Honey 150–52). She writes of the relationship in some detail in a letter to her aunt Flora Dugan. When Bennett retired from Consumers Union in 1968, the couple moved to Kutztown, Pennsylvania, where they set up an antique store, Buttonwood Hollow Antiques (see "To Everyone"). The couple lived there happily until Crosscup died suddenly of a heart attack in 1980. Bennett remained in Kutztown until her death on May 30, 1981. She died in Reading, Pennsylvania, was cremated, and her ashes were scattered in her beloved gardens at her family home (Tanner).

Bennett's tranquil final few years seem fitting for someone who had such a hectic life. Though it was filled with many rewards, she had much sorrow in her employment and especially in her relationships with her family and her significant others. In these last two decades of her life, she found a contentment and a stability that had never existed previously. It seems appropriate that her life ended in Pennsylvania, a state where much of her childhood and youth were spent. Perhaps her undated poem "Fulfillment" reflects this time of her life with Crosscup: "To be with you is to know peace again, / And the deep understanding of things."

By the time of Bennett's death, she was largely forgotten as a literary or artistic figure. Most of her Harlem Renaissance friends were dead, too, and her writings were no longer in vogue. A sign of her neglect is evidenced by the scant recording of her death. There is only a small mention of her passing in the *New York Amsterdam News*, stating that she was "a figure in the Harlem Renaissance Movement in the 1920s" ("Gwendolyn Crosscup Dies" 22).

Though Bennett's work remained dormant for some time, in the past few decades her writing and art has gained growing recognition. This began with the groundbreaking study by Sandra Govan, who completed a doctoral dissertation on Bennett in 1980. Since that time, Bennett's literary and artistic endeavors have continued to gain critical attention, and she is appearing in an increasing number of anthologies. We feel that the best way to add to this interest in Bennett is to provide a more complete portrait of this unique artist, by discussing her unpublished and published writings. It is our hope that this collection will provide new information, add to the growing reclamation of this highly talented woman, and restore her to her proper place in the Harlem Renaissance and beyond.

Published Works

Introduction

As mentioned in the general introduction, Bennett published over twenty poems during the 1920s. Two notable strengths of Bennett's early poetry were her ability to create dynamic anthems of racial uplift and pride for the African American community, and to link youthful imagery with the senses in both traditional and nontraditional forms. Poems contained in this collection that fall into this category include "Heritage" (1923), "To Usward" (1924), and "To a Dark Girl" (1927). In "Heritage," the speaker dreams "to see," "to hear," "to breathe," "to feel" her ancestral home. The poem is composed of six stanzas—each comprising three lines and each containing nineteen syllables—and the end of every second stanza ends with an ellipsis. Each stanza begins with the emphasis clearly on the gender-neutral speaker—"I want to see," "I want to hear," "I want to breathe," and "I want to feel"—but her quick reference to nature, people, and sounds shows her deep commitment to connecting with her past. As the speaker moves through the list of sights, sounds, smells, and feelings, the reader also understands that while the speaker may begin by romanticizing the past, she is aware of how white influence has disrupted their lives. As William J. Maxwell and Joseph Valente describe it, "Snippets of modern longing for Africa, imagined as the classical cradle of black historical becoming, are spliced to derive a liberated but indefinite racial future."[1] The poem begins with a picturesque scene, but the concluding image of the minstrel smile points to a sad past. Minstrelsy was a brutal form of racial domination that reflected the "hostility of a [white] working-class audience towards

African Americans" (Stott 378). As Scott Herring states in his article "Du Bois and the Minstrels," during the mid to late nineteenth century, African Americans were stereotyped as "a demonized group of self-sacrificing Uncle Toms and Mammys; they seen as embodying a sexual potency and promiscuity secretly envied by whites," or "represented as primitive, laughable clowns" (3). The "smiling" mask was an image Langston Hughes and Paul Laurence Dunbar famously used in their poems. The reference to this dominating image shows that racial prejudice still affects African Americans today, but the speaker's decision to emphasize the beautiful images, sounds, feelings, and smells reminds African Americans that they can still connect with their ancestral past and imagine a bright future.

Bennett's "To Usward" (1924), as Wheeler has written elsewhere ("Gwendolyn Bennett"), was a racial anthem that Bennett read at the aforementioned March 1924 Civic Club dinner. She dedicated the poem "to all Negro Youth known and unknown who have a song to sing, a story to tell or a vision for the sons of the earth." In her poem, Bennett begins by praising the elders in the African American community who had paved the way for people like her by quietly "pushing [. . .] our growth" and recognizing the "strength in entity." Immediately after, however, Bennett makes a case for the New Negroes who also "have a song to sing." The New Negroes' song may be "different from the rest," but Bennett implores the older members of her audience to "let them sing / Before the urgency of Youth's behest!" Although there are differences between the two groups, Bennett asks for all parties to come together and "break the seal of years / With pungent thrusts of song / For there is joy in long-dried tears / For whetted passions of a throng!" Bennett's poem was warmly received at the event and was simultaneously published in *Crisis* and *Opportunity*'s May 1924 issues.

Another Bennett poem that is often anthologized is "To a Dark Girl" (1927). Throughout the poem, the theme of building connections within the race and developing the race in the larger community is evident, particularly through Bennett's use of an androgynous speaker. The verse comprises three stanzas that contain four lines each. With its lyrical form, strong racial pride, and validation of the African American female— physically and emotionally—Bennett's poem reminds readers of past and present obstacles African American women faced in the 1920s, dissolves class boundaries, and promotes African American males and females working together and respecting each other in order to show how that joint initiative can lead to the betterment of their race.

In addition to promoting racial uplift and pride, Bennett appealed to a broad audience by combining youthful imagery and the senses in traditional and nontraditional forms. In his critique of Bennett's lyric poems, James Weldon Johnson wrote, "Miss Bennett is the author of a number of fine poems, some of them in the freer forms, but she is [at] her best in the delicate, poignant lyrics that she has written" (241). Bennett's sensory poems make a valuable contribution to the Renaissance generally, but they are also an excellent example of her connecting often disparate ideas or images together in order to build on her youthful and vibrant aspirations for her race.

A number of Bennett's poems, written in traditional and nontraditional forms—such as "Quatrains" (1927), "Nocturne" (1923), "Secret" (1927), "Street Lamps in Early Spring" (1926), "Song" (1925), and "Dear Things" (1926)—delicately interweave sound and sight as a way to discuss an array of topics that affect a diverse readership. In "Quatrains," for example, Bennett re-creates the creative process many eclectic artists go through as they seek inspiration. In the first quatrain, the speaker combines concrete images of brushes, paints, a copper jar, and a green bowl with the sounds of music and silent laughter. The rhyming lines, composed of eight, eight, eight, and ten syllables, respectively, further add to the poem's lyric nature, yet the silent laughter in the poem's third line adds to the quietness of the scene and the painter's growing frustration. In the second quatrain, the speaker plays with alliteration, sibilant sounds, and rhyming lines comprising six, six, eight, and six syllables, and comes to a deeper understanding of the surrounding sounds. In this quatrain, the painter realizes for the first time that the beauty in sounds is not that "strange" after all, and decides not to limit one's creativity to painting alone. There are some things, notes the speaker—such as the singing grass and the soft, slow falling snow—that cannot be captured in a static image like a copper jar or a pale green bowl, and would be better expressed in a youthful, lyric poem. Finally, the mellifluousness throughout the second quatrain shows a level of mastery that suggests the speaker has come into his or her own as a poet.

Nocturne

Crisis, Nov. 1923, 20

This cool night is strange
Among midsummer days . . .
Far frosts are caught
In the moon's pale light,
And sounds are distant laughter
Chilled to crystal tears.

o   o   o

Heritage

Opportunity, Dec. 1923, 371

I want to see the slim palm-trees,
Pulling at the clouds
With little pointed fingers . . .

I want to see lithe Negro girls,
Etched dark against the sky
While sunset lingers.

I want to hear the silent sands,
Singing to the moon
Before the Sphinx-still face . . .

I want to hear the chanting
Around a heathen fire
Of a strange black race.

I want to breathe the Lotus flow'r,
Sighing to the stars
With tendrils drinking at the Nile . . .

I want to feel the surging
Of my sad people's soul
Hidden by a minstrel-smile.

To Usward

Crisis, May 1924, 19

Opportunity, May 1924, 143–44

> *Dedicated to all Negro Youth known and unknown*
> *who have a song to sing, a story to tell or a vision for the sons of*
> *earth. Especially dedicated to Jessie Fauset upon the event of her*
> *novel, "There is Confusion."*

Let us be still
As ginger jars are still
Upon a Chinese shelf.
And let us be contained
By entities of Self . . .
Not still with lethargy and sloth,
But quiet with the pushing of our growth.
Not self-contained with smug identity
But conscious of the strength in entity.
If any have a song to sing
That's different from the rest,
Oh let them sing
Before the urgency of Youth's behest!
For some of us have songs to sing
Of jungle heat and fires,
And some of us are solemn grown
With pitiful desires,
And there are those who feel the pull
Of seas beneath the skies,
And some there be who want to croon
Of Negro lullabies.
We claim no part with racial dearth;
We want to sing the songs of birth!
And so we stand like ginger jars
Like ginger jars bound round
With dust and age;
Like jars of ginger we are sealed
By nature's heritage.

But let us break the seal of years
With pungent thrusts of song,
For there is joy in long-dried tears
For whetted passions of a throng!

o   o   o

Song

The New Negro: Voices of the Harlem Renaissance, ed. Alain Locke,
225 (New York: Boni and Liveright, 1925)

I am weaving a song of waters,
Shaken from firm, brown limbs,
Or heads thrown back in irreverent mirth.
My song has the lush sweetness
Of moist, dark lips
Where hymns keep company
With old forgotten banjo songs.
Abandon tells you
That I sing the heart of a race
While sadness whispers
That I am the cry of a soul . . .

A-shoutin', in de ole camp-meetin' place,
A-strummin' o' de ole banjo.
Singin' in de moonlight,
Sobbin' in de dark.
Singin', sobbin', strummin' slow . . .
Singin' slow; sobbin' low.
Strummin', strummin', strummin' slow . . .

Words are bright bugles
That make the shining for my song,
And mothers hold brown babes
To dark, warm breasts
To make my singing sad.

A dancing girl with swaying hips
Sets mad the queen in a harlot's eye.
    Praying slave
    Jazz band after
    Breaking heart
    To the time of laughter . . .
Clinking chains and minstrelsy
Are welded fast with melody.
    A praying slave
    With a jazz band after . . .
    Singin' slow, sobbin' low
Sun-baked lips will kiss the earth.
Throats of bronze will burst with mirth.
Sing a little faster,
Sing a little faster,
Sing!

o   o   o

Street Lamps in Early Spring

Opportunity, May 1926, 152

Night wears a garment
All velvet soft, all violet blue . . .
And over her face she draws a veil
As shimmering fine as floating dew . . .
And here and there
In the black of her hair
The subtle hands of Night
Move slowly with their gem-starred light.

Hatred

Opportunity, June 1926, 190

I shall hate you
Like a dart of singing steel
Shot through still air
At even-tide.
Or solemnly
As pines are sober
When they stand etched
Against the sky.
Hating you shall be a game
Played with cool hands
And slim fingers.
Your heart will yearn
For the lonely splendour
Of the pine tree;
While rekindled fires
In my eyes
Shall wound you like swift arrows.
Memory will lay its hands
Upon your breast
And you will understand
My hatred.

o   o   o

Lines Written at the Grave of Alexander Dumas

Opportunity, July 1926, 225

Cemeteries are places for departed souls
And bones interred,
Or hearts with shattered loves.
A woman with lips made warm for laughter
Would find grey stones and silent thoughts
Too chill for living, moving pulses . . .

And thou great soul, would shiver in thy granite shroud,
Should idle mirth or empty talk
Disturb thy tranquil sleeping.

A cemetery is a place for shattered loves
And broken hearts . . .
Bowed before the crystal chalice of thy soul,
I find the multi-colored fragrance of thy mind
Has lost itself in Death's transparency.

Oh, stir the lucid waters of thy sleep
And coin for me a tale
Of happy loves and gems and joyous limbs
And hearts where love is sweet!

A cemetery is a place for broken hearts
And silent thoughts . . .
And silence never moves, nor speaks
Nor sings.

o   o   o

Moon Tonight

The Gypsy, Oct. 1926, 13

Moon tonight,
Beloved . . .
When twilight
Has gathered together
The ends
Of her soft robe,
And the last bird-call
Has died.
Moon tonight—
Cool as a forgotten dream,
Dearer than lost twilights
Among trees where birds sing
No more.

Dear Things

Palms, Oct. 1926, 21–22

Some things are very dear to me—
Such things as flowers bathed by rain
Or patterns traced upon the sea,
Or crocuses where snow has lain . . .
The iridescence of a gem,
The moon's cool opalescent light,
Azaleas and the scent of them,
And honeysuckles in the night.
And many sounds are also dear—
Like winds that sing among the trees,
Or crickets calling from the weir,[1]
Or Negroes humming melodies.

But dearer far than all surmise
Are sudden tear-drops in your eyes.

o   o   o

Advice

Caroling Dusk: An Anthology of Verse by Negro Poets, ed. Countee Cullen, 156–57 (New York: Harper and Row, 1927)

You were a sophist,
Pale and quite remote,
As you bade me
Write poems—
Brown poems
Of dark words
And prehistoric rhythms . . .
Your pallor stifled my poesy
But I remembered a tapestry
That I would some day weave
Of dim purples and fine reds
And blues

Like night and death—
The keen precision of your words
Wove a silver thread
Through the dusk softness
Of my dream-stuff . . .

o   o   o

Fantasy

Caroling Dusk: An Anthology of Verse by Negro Poets, ed. Countee
Cullen, 158 (New York: Harper and Row, 1927)

I sailed in my dreams to the Land of Night
Where you were the dusk-eyed queen,
And there in the pallor of moon-veiled light
The loveliest things were seen . . .

A slim-necked peacock sauntered there
In a garden of lavender hues,
And you were strange with your purple hair
As you sat in your amethyst chair
With your feet in your hyacinth shoes.

Oh, the moon gave a bluish light
Through the trees in the land of dreams and night.
I stood behind a bush of yellow-green
And whistled a song to the dark-haired queen . . .

Quatrains

Caroling Dusk: An Anthology of Verse by Negro Poets, ed. Countee Cullen, 155 (New York: Harper and Row, 1927)

1

Brushes and paints are all I have
To speak the music in my soul—
While silently there laughs at me
A copper jar beside a pale green bowl.

2

How strange that grass should sing—
Grass is so still a thing . . .
And strange the swift surprise of snow
So soft it falls and slow.

o   o   o

Secret

Caroling Dusk: An Anthology of Verse by Negro Poets, ed. Countee Cullen, 155–56 (New York: Harper and Row, 1927)

I shall make a song like your hair . . .
Gold-woven with shadows green-tinged,
And I shall play with my song
As my fingers might play with your hair.
Deep in my heart
I shall play with my song of you,
Gently . . .
I shall laugh
At its sensitive lustre . . .
I shall wrap my song in a blanket,
Blue like your eyes are blue
With tiny shots of silver.
I shall wrap it caressingly,
Tenderly . . .
I shall sing a lullaby

To the song I have made
Of your hair and eyes . . .
And you will never know
That deep in my heart
I shelter a song of you
Secretly . . .

o   o   o

To a Dark Girl

Opportunity, Oct. 1927, 299

I love you for your brownness,
And the rounded darkness of your breast;
I love you for the breaking sadness in your voice
And shadows where your wayward eyelids rest.

Something of old forgotten queens
Lurks in the lithe abandon of your walk,
And something of the shackled slave
Sobs in the rhythm of your talk.

Oh, little brown girl, born for sorrow's mate,
Keep all you have of queenliness,
Forgetting that you once were slave
And let your full lips laugh at Fate!

Epitaph

Opportunity, Mar. 1934, 76

When I am dead, carve this upon my stone:
Here lies a woman, fit root for flower and tree,
Whose living flesh, now mouldering round the bone,
Wants nothing more than this for immortality,
That in her heart, where love so long unfruited lay
A seed for grass or weed shall grow,
And push to light and air its heedless way;
That she who lies here dead may know
Through all the putrid marrow of her bones
The searing pangs of birth,
While none may know the pains nor hear the groans
Of her who lived with barrenness upon the earth.

Introduction

As listed in the general introduction and noted in Bennett's timeline, much of her post-1928 career was devoted to the arts, particularly in the administration of arts programs and schools. Bennett was even honored as one of the "Distinguished Women of Today" at the 1939 World's Fair in New York, in large part because of her contribution to the arts. When it came specifically to artwork, oil paintings and graphic art were two mediums Bennett was known for throughout her career.

Given that only one oil painting by Bennett has been recovered to date, Bennett's *Untitled* [*River Landscape*] (1931) (see fig. 4), it is hard to categorize to what themes or styles she was attracted. The only other Bennett painting to be cataloged to date was her *Winter Landscape* (1936) in Alain Locke's *The Negro in Art*, though the physical painting has yet to be recovered. It is hoped that more of Bennett's work will be rediscovered (in catalogs or physical canvasses) and scholars will be able to determine whether her artwork's themes in the 1920s are different from or similar to those in her artwork from the 1930s onward. Time will tell.

While Bennett's oil paintings are currently scarce, fortunately there is a nice sampling of her graphic artwork on hand. Bennett created several magazine covers for *Opportunity* and *Crisis* in the early-to-mid 1920s, and some of her smaller pieces appeared in *The Messenger* and several books. Bennett's magazine covers are by far the most striking of her graphic art pieces on offer today, and scholars such as Cary Nelson, Caroline Goeser, Sandra Govan, and Belinda Wheeler have discussed them at length. For the purposes of our anthology, we have selected three of Bennett's five covers: March 1924 *Crisis*, January 1926 *Opportunity*, and July 1926 *Opportunity*.

When it came to themes, Bennett's cover designs were always heavily enshrined in racial topics and youthful representations of African Americans, not unlike her poetry. Along with the appearance of women in each of the magazine covers, which could also suggest the magazines' desire to reach out to an underrepresented section of the African American community, four of Bennett's five covers also have blacks and whites, males and females, mingling together. Though each of the five magazine covers are line drawings composed in ink, the distinction between races and genders is not always clear, forcing Bennett's audience to consider the scene from multiple perspectives. Bennett's commitment to crossing racial, gender, and class lines in her magazine art, like her poetry, allowed her to further illustrate how art can break down barriers and foster alliances between diverse groups of people.

In Goeser's description of Bennett's March 1924 *Crisis* cover (see fig. 5), she astutely observes Bennett inserting "an African presence into a scene based on ancient Greek mythology in her *Pipes of Pan*" (106). In this outdoor scene Pan, the Greek god of woods and flocks, is represented as a youthful black shepherd, rather than the more common image of half-man, half-goat. Pan appears to have drifted off to sleep as he listens to the nearby black and white satyrs and nymphs who are dancing or playing various musical instruments. In her examination of Bennett's image, Goeser correctly notices Bennett tracing "a comparative link between the youthful Greek god and young African American musicians of the 1920s on the forefront of the jazz revolution," with Pan therefore "becoming a kind of cultural progenitor of African American music" (107). The nymphs' long flowing hair, the long curvy lines depicting the grass and the tree bark, and the fluffy clouds in the background combine to further enhance this relaxing scene. As Wheeler has written elsewhere, "In Bennett's cover no gender is favored, no species—human, satyr, or nymph—is superior, no race is regarded as better than the other; instead, all beings come together in this beautiful, peaceful location to enjoy the natural surroundings and one another's company" ("Gwendolyn Bennett" 209–10). The combination of Pan's connection with music and nature, and the importance of the prefix "pan," meaning "whole" or "all," enables Bennett to present her dark-skinned Pan as "an ancestor for all of humanity, not just the white western world" (Goeser 107), thereby reinforcing her commitment to minimizing divisions between diverse groups.

Bennett's January 1926 *Opportunity* cover (see fig. 6) celebrates the last day of the Christmas season, Epiphany, or Three Kings' Day. Bennett reenacts this historic moment with a twist by having three ambiguously gendered "kings" pay homage to the Caucasian Virgin Mary and baby Jesus while offering gifts of gold, frankincense, and myrrh. The dark-skinned, athletic figure in this cover image is positioned away from his or her two colleagues, kneels directly beneath Mary and baby Jesus, and wears a common, cotton-like garment with no headdress, revealing an Afro and large hoop earrings. The two other kings, in contrast, wear traditional robes and coverings on their head. Though the youthful black figure is quite distinctive, when seen next to the four white individuals (two other kings, Mary, and baby Jesus) the feeling of community is just as apparent. All three kings are of the same rank, despite their different clothing; all have wealth that they are willing to offer up; and all are present to worship the Virgin Mary and baby Jesus.

Bennett's most famous cover adorned the July 1926 issue of *Opportunity* (see fig. 7). Unlike Bennett's other covers, "this is the only image where no males are present and where the African American experience—past and present—is graphically represented" (Wheeler, "Gwendolyn Bennett" 210). Govan finds parallels between McKay's "Harlem Dancer" and Cullen's "Heritage," and connects African American writers with artists, but omits how this cover is parallel with Bennett's work, thereby minimizing her ability to influence other artists and expand the base of modernism. "This line drawing represents many of the themes Bennett expresses in her poetry including past and present obstacles African Americans," particularly women, faced (210). "The picture's middle panel with its palm trees, a hut, and a bright sun, gives the picture a tropical or Mediterranean feel," not unlike the image Bennett presents in her poem "Heritage" (210). Next to these images, three youthful dark-skinned African American women dancing in the sunlight are in silhouette. The progression of the women's poses, coupled with their developing clothing (from naked, to wearing banana skirts [as famously fashioned by Josephine Baker], to wearing fabric skirts), helps trace the development of African American women's history (210). The idea that the background panel could be representing African American women's past is strengthened when the viewer examines the foreground image of the new, light-skinned, young, modern woman. The woman's fashionable clothing, her tilted head and raised shoulder, her slightly closed eyes, and relaxed arms and fingers, could suggest the woman is dancing slowly—"a dancing girl with swaying hips" ("Song")—or that she is walking with a "lithe abandon" ("To a Dark Girl") (210). Bennett's decision to contrast the background and foreground, black and white, past and present, dark and light skin tones, modest and elegant clothing, and simple to sophisticated body postures, creates a poignant piece of artwork that traces African American women's history—their clothing, their dance, their body image, and their beauty—and further illustrates many of the themes discussed in her poetry (210).

FIG. 4   *Untitled* [*River Landscape*], 1931. To date, this is the only known painting by Bennett in existence. It was located by Belinda Wheeler in 2012.

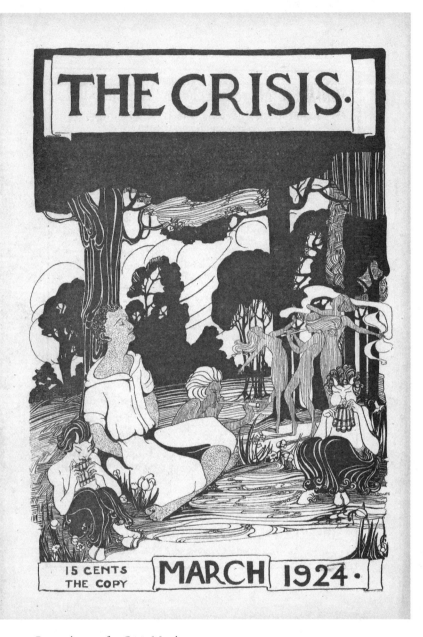

FIG. 5   Bennett's cover for *Crisis*, March 1924.

FIG. 6　Bennett's cover art as it appeared on the front cover of *Opportunity: Journal of Negro Life*, January 1926. Schomburg Center for Research in Black Culture, Jean Blackwell Hutson Research and Reference Division, The New York Public Library. The New York Public Library Digital Collections.

FIG. 7   Bennett's *Opportunity: Journal of Negro Life* cover, July 1926. Schomburg Center for Research in Black Culture, Jean Blackwell Hutson Research and Reference Division, The New York Public Library. The New York Public Library Digital Collections.

Introduction

Bennett's only published short stories, "Wedding Day" (1926) and "Tokens" (1927), chronicle, in part, the U.S. expatriate experience and racial inequality abroad, specifically Paris, making them an important part of her oeuvre, particularly given her experiences in Paris in the mid-1920s. Bennett's "Wedding Day"[1] centers on Paul Watson, an African American expatriate musician and former boxer, whose hate for white Americans and reluctance to connect with his new French homeland (either the people or the language) adds to his isolation. After shooting two white American sailors who call him "nigger," and spending the rest of his jail sentence serving with the French in the Great War, Watson returns to Paris, where he falls for a white American prostitute and plans to marry. On his "wedding day," the socially and culturally awkward Watson learns that his white fiancée, despite her low profession, cannot bring herself to marry a black man, further exacerbating his poor opinion of whites and increasing his feeling of solitude. This controversial story was seen by some readers as an act of disloyalty by Bennett and the radical, young authors and editors of *Fire!!* The magazine's editorial staff—Wallace Thurman, Langston Hughes, Zora Neale Hurston, Aaron Douglas, John P. Davis, Richard Bruce Nugent, and Bennett—wanted to challenge the status quo in their attempt to elevate the race. Rather than providing a feel-good type of racial uplift, the authors desired to be brutally honest about matters such as sexuality and violence, as is evidenced in even more shocking work contained in *Fire!!*, such as Zora Neale Hurston's one-act play on black self-loathing

Color Struck and Wallace Thurman's story of a prostitute, "Cordelia the Crude." Bennett and the other *Fire!!* authors/editors believed that African Americans could face harsh aspects of black life and set about addressing it. This meant not only writing about themes like the editors did but also presenting that information in different ways to their audience. As Martha Jane Nadell explains, "Thurman and his peers were trying to do more than push the boundaries of acceptable representations. They were trying to fashion a new, modern African American aesthetic that included the colloquial language and imagism of Hughes, the dialect accounts of working-class life of Hurston, the themes of sex, interracial romance, urban ennui, and drugs that pervade the poetry, drama, and short stories" (78). The editors' approach called on older African Americans and others who may have been shocked by their honesty to allow those who "have a song to sing / That's different from the rest" to be permitted the freedom to do just that (Bennett, "To Usward").

Bennett's second published short story, "Tokens," has received little critical attention. Also set in France, "Tokens" centers on another African American male, Jenks Barnett, who had a successful career as a singer whose voice was "so rare [. . .] in range and quality" that no one dreamed that his career and life would be cut short by tuberculosis. Just like Watson, however, Barnett's life comes crashing down when a woman he loves, "Tollie Saunders with her golden voice and lush laughter," dumps him in favor of a chance to sing in the United States. His career was suffering before her departure, but blinded by love Barnett continued to buy her tokens of her affection until, "before the pinch of poverty," she leaves, taking everything with her. Like Watson's fiancée, Saunders left "no farewell." Devastated, Barnett spirals out of control. Binge drinking for three days, Barnett ends up in a "dingy, damp Parisian jail with a terrific pain in his back." Moved from one prison to another, Barnett receives no treatment for his symptoms for over eighteen days, and as a consequence he becomes a terminal patient at the Merlin Hospital. While the Seine, "mute river of sorrows . . . grim concealer of forgotten secrets . . . endlessly flowing . . . touching the edges of life . . . moving purposefully along with a grey disdain for the empty, foolish gaiety of Seraigne or the benign dignity of Merlin Hospital," rolls along, Barnett's tongue lashes all who come before him, including doctors, nurses, and his good friend Bill Jackson. Unlike Watson, however, Barnett is able to find closure near the end of his life. Barnett asks

Jackson to leave two "tokens" to the people who have meant something to him during his life, Tollie and a young girl who used to visit. Though Jackson notes, "Funny how the first kind thing Jenks [Barnett] had done for anybody since Tollie left him should be done for a person who was dead [the young girl had since died, but Barnett was unaware]," Barnett is grateful "to be out here once more looking at the Seine and the world where people lived and breathed." In the end, though, just as Watson is a cog in the machine that is life for an African American man in France, so, too, is Barnett. As the narrator states at the conclusion of the story, "*High on the bluff of Saint Cloud stands the Merlin Hospital, immaculate sentinel of Seraigne . . . with its crazy houses and aimless streets, scrambling at the foot of Saint Cloud's immense immutability. Row on row the bricks of the hospital take dispassionate account of lives lost or found.*"

Bennett's published short stories provide portraits of two shattered African American men who lost themselves in France. There were times during Bennett's year in Paris when she, too, faced racial inequality and felt isolated from her home country (see her diaries or letters). However, unlike Watson and Barnett, Bennett was able to regroup, connect with other expatriates living in France, and continue to work successfully before returning to the United States.

Wedding Day

Fire!! Nov. 1926, 25–28

His name was Paul Watson and as he shambled down rue Pigalle[1] he might have been any other Negro of enormous height and size. But as I have said, his name was Paul Watson. Passing him on the street, you might not have known or cared who he was, but any one of the residents about the great Montmartre district of Paris[2] could have told you who he was as well as many interesting bits of his personal history.

He had come to Paris in the days before colored jazz bands were the style. Back home he had been a prize fighter. In the days when Joe Gans[3] was in his glory Paul was following the ring, too. He didn't have that fine way about him that Gans had and for that reason luck seemed to go against him. When he was in the ring he was like a mad bull, especially if his opponent was a white man. In those days there wasn't any sympathy or nicety about the ring and so pretty soon all the ringmasters got down on Paul and he found it pretty hard to get a bout with anyone. Then it was that he worked his way across the Atlantic Ocean on a big liner—in the days before colored jazz bands were the style in Paris.

Things flowed along smoothly for the first few years with Paul's working here and there in the unfrequented places of Paris. On the side he used to give boxing lessons to aspiring youths or gymnastic young women. At that time he was working so steadily that he had little chance to find out what was going on around Paris. Pretty soon, however, he grew to be known among the trainers and managers began to fix up bouts for him. After one or two successful bouts a little fame began to come into being for him. So it was that after one of the prize-fights, a colored fellow came to his dressing room to congratulate him on his success as well as invite him to go to Montmartre to meet "the boys."

Paul had a way about him and seemed to get on with the colored fellows who lived in Montmartre and when the first Negro jazz band played in a tiny Parisian cafe Paul was among them playing the banjo. Those first years were without event so far as Paul was concerned. The members of that first band often say now that they wonder how it was that nothing happened during those first seven years, for it was generally known how great was Paul's hatred for American white people. I suppose the tranquility in the light of what happened afterwards was due to the fact that the cafe in which they worked was one in which mostly French people drank and danced and then too, that was before there were so many Americans visiting Paris. However, everyone had heard Paul speak of his intense hatred of American white folks. It only took two Benedictines[4] to make him start talking about what he would do to the first "Yank" that called him "nigger." But the seven years came to an end and Paul Watson went to work in a larger cafe with a larger band, patronized almost solely by Americans.

I've heard almost every Negro in Montmartre tell about the night that a drunken Kentuckian came into the cafe where Paul was playing and said:

"Look heah, Bruther, what you all doin' ovah heah?"

"None ya bizness. And looka here, I ain't your brother, see?"

"Jack, do you heah that nigger talkin' lak that tah me?"

As he said this, he turned to speak to his companion. I have often wished that I had been there to have seen the thing happen myself. Every tale I have heard about it was different and yet there was something of truth in each of them. Perhaps the nearest one can come to the truth is by saying that Paul beat up about four full-sized white men that night besides doing a great deal of damage to the furniture about the cafe. I couldn't tell you just what did happen. Some of the fellows say that Paul seized the nearest table and mowed down men right and left, others say he took a bottle, then again the story runs that a chair was the instrument of his fury. At any rate, that started Paul Watson on his siege against the American white person who brings his native prejudices into the life of Paris.

It is a verity that Paul was the "black terror." The last syllable of the word, nigger, never passed the lips of a white man without the quick reflex action of Paul's arm and fist to the speaker's jaw. He paid for more glassware and cafe furnishings in the course of the next few years than is easily imaginable. And yet, there was something likable about Paul. Perhaps that's the reason that he stood in so well with the policemen of the neighborhood. Always some divine power seemed to intervene in his behalf and he was excused after the payment of a small fine with advice about his future conduct. Finally, there came the night when in a frenzy he shot the two American sailors.

They had not died from the wounds he had given them hence his sentence had not been one of death but rather a long term of imprisonment. It was a pitiable sight to see Paul sitting in the corner of his cell with his great body hunched almost double. He seldom talked and when he did his words were interspersed with oaths about the lowness of "crackers."[5] Then the World War came.

It seems strange that anything so horrible as that wholesale slaughter could bring about any good and yet there was something of a smoothing quality about even its baseness. There has never been such equality before or since such as that which the World War brought. Rich men fought by the side of paupers; poets swapped yarns with dry-goods salesmen, while Jews and Christians ate corned beef out of the same tin. Along with the general leveling influence came France's pardon of her prisoners in order that they might enter the army. Paul Watson became free and a French soldier. Because he was strong and had innate daring in his heart he was placed in the aerial squad and cited many times for bravery. The close of the war gave him his place in French society as a hero. With only a memory of the war and an ugly scar on his left cheek he took up his old life.

His firm resolutions about American white people still remained intact and many chance encounters that followed the war are told from lip to lip proving that the war and his previous imprisonment had changed him little. He was the same Paul Watson to Montmartre as he shambled up rue Pigalle.

Rue Pigalle in the early evening has a somber beauty—gray as are most Paris streets and other-worldish. To those who know the district it is the Harlem of Paris and rue Pigalle is its dusky Seventh Avenue. Most of the colored musicians that furnish Parisians and their visitors with entertainment live somewhere in the neighborhood of rue Pigalle. Some time during every day each of these musicians makes a point of passing through rue Pigalle. Little wonder that almost any day will find Paul Watson going his shuffling way up the same street.

He reached the corner of rue de la Bruyere and with sure instinct his feet stopped. Without half thinking he turned into "the Pit." Its full name is The Flea Pit. If you should ask one of the musicians why it was so called, he would answer you to the effect that it was called "the pit" because all the "fleas" hang out there. If you did not get the full import of this explanation, he would go further and say that there were always "spades" in the pit and they were as thick as fleas. Unless you could understand this latter attempt at clarity you could not fully grasp what the Flea-Pit means to the Negro musicians in Montmartre. It is a tiny cafe of the genus that is called *bistro* in France. Here the fiddle players, saxophone blowers, drumbeaters and ivory ticklers gather at four in the afternoon for a porto or a game of billiards. Here the cabaret entertainers and supper musicians meet at one o'clock at night or thereafter for a whiskey and soda, or more billiards. Occasional sandwiches and a "quiet game" also play their parts in the popularity of the place. After a season or two it becomes a settled fact just what time you may catch so-and-so at the famous "Pit."

The musicians were very fond of Paul and took particular delight in teasing him. He was one of the chosen few that all of the musicians conceded as being "regular." It was the pet joke of the habitues of the cafe that Paul never bothered with girls. They always said that he could beat up ten men but was scared to death of one woman.

"Say fellow, when ya goin' a get hooked up?"

"Can't say, Bo. Ain't so much on skirts."

"Man alive, ya don't know what you're missin'—somebody little and cute telling ya sweet things in your ear. Paris is full of women folks."

"I ain't much on 'em all the same. Then too, they're all white."

"What's it to ya? This ain't America."

"Can't help that. Get this—I'm collud, see? I ain't got nothing for no white meat to do. If a woman eva called me nigger I'd have to kill her, that's all!"

"You for it, son. I can't give you a thing on this Mr. Jefferson Lawd[6] way of lookin' at women.

"Oh, tain't that. I guess they're all right for those that wants 'em. Not me!"

"Oh you ain't so forty.[7] You'll fall like all the other spades I've ever seen. Your kind falls hardest."

And so Paul went his way—alone. He smoked and drank with the fellows and sat for hours in the Montmartre cafes and never knew the companionship of a woman. Then one night after his work he was walking along the street in his queer shuffling way when a woman stepped up to his side.

"Voulez vous."

"Naw, gowan away from here."

"Oh, you speak English, don't you?"

"You an 'merican woman?"

"Used to be 'fore I went on the stage and got stranded over here."

"Well, get away from here. I don't like your kind!"

"Aw, Buddy, don't say that. I ain't prejudiced like some fool women."

"You don't know who I am, do you? I'm Paul Watson and I hate American white folks, see?"

He pushed her aside and went on walking alone. He hadn't gone far when she caught up to him and said with sobs in her voice:—

"Oh, Lordy, please don't hate me 'cause I was born white and an American. I ain't got a sou to my name and all the men pass me by cause I ain't spruced up. Now you come along and won't look at me cause I'm white."

Paul strode along with her clinging to his arm. He tried to shake her off several times but there was no use. She clung all the more desperately to him. He looked down at her frail body shaken with sobs, and something caught at his heart. Before he knew what he was doing he had said:—

"Naw, I ain't that mean. I'll get you some grub. Quit your cryin'. Don't like seein' women folks cry."

It was the talk of Montmartre. Paul Watson takes a woman to Gavarnni's every night for dinner. He comes to the Flea Pit less frequently, thus giving the other musicians plenty of opportunity to discuss him.

"How times do change. Paul, the woman-hater, has a Jane now."

"You ain't said nothing, fella. That ain't all. She's white and an 'merican, too."

"That's the way with these spades. They beat up all the white men they can lay their hands on but as soon as a gang of golden hair with blue eyes rubs up close to them they forget all they ever said about hatin' white folks."

"Guess he thinks that skirt's gone on him. Dumb fool!"

"Don' be no chineeman. That old gag don' fit for Paul. He cain't understand it no more'n we can. Says he jess can't help himself, every time she looks up into his eyes and asks him does he love her. They sure are happy together. Paul's goin' to marry her, too. At first she kept saying that she didn't want to get married cause she wasn't the marrying kind and all that talk. Paul jus' laid down the law to her and told her he never would live with no woman without being married to her. Then she began to tell him all about her past life. He told her he didn't care nothing about what she used to be jus' so long as they loved each other now. Guess they'll make it."

"Yeah, Paul told me the same tale last night. He's sure gone on her all right."

"They're gettin' tied up next Sunday. So glad it's not me. Don't trust these American dames. Me for the Frenchies."

"She ain't so worse for looks, Bud. Now that he's been furnishing the green for the rags."

"Yeah, but I don't see no reason for the wedding bells. She was right—she ain't the marrying kind" . . . and so Montmartre talked. In every cafe where the Negro musicians congregated Paul Watson was the topic for conversation. He had suddenly fallen from his place as bronze God to almost less than the dust.

The morning sun made queer patterns on Paul's sleeping face. He grimaced several times in his slumber, then finally half-opened his eyes. After a succession of dream-laden blinks he gave a great yawn, and rubbing his eyes, looked at the open window through which the sun shone brightly. His first conscious thought was that this was the bride's day and that bright sunshine prophesied happiness for the bride throughout her married life. His first impulse was to settle back into the covers and think drowsily about Mary and the queer twists life brings about, as is the wont of most bride-grooms on their last morning of bachelorhood. He put this impulse aside in favor of dressing quickly and rushing downstairs to telephone to Mary to say "happy wedding day" to her.

One huge foot slipped into a worn bedroom slipper and then the other dragged painfully out of the warm bed were the courageous beginnings of his bridal toilette. With a look of triumph he put on his new gray suit that he had ordered from an English tailor. He carefully pulled a taffeta tie into place beneath his chin, noting as he looked at his face in the mirror that the scar he had received in the army was very ugly—funny, marrying an ugly man like him.

French telephones are such human faults. After trying for about fifteen minutes to get Central 32.01 he decided that he might as well walk around to Mary's hotel to give his greeting as to stand there in the lobby of his own, wasting his time. He debated this in his mind a great deal. They were to be married at four o'clock. It was eleven now and it did seem a shame not to let her have a minute or two by herself. As he went walking down the street towards her hotel he laughed to think of how one always cogitates over doing something and finally does the thing he wanted to in the beginning anyway.

Mud on his nice gray suit that the English tailor had made for him. Damn—gray suit—what did he have a gray suit on for, anyway. Folks with black faces shouldn't wear gray suits. Gawd, but it was funny that time when he beat up that cracker at the Periquet. Fool couldn't shut his mouth he was so surprised. Crackers—damn 'em—he was one nigger that wasn't 'fraid of 'em. Wouldn't he have a hell of a time if he went back to America where black was black. Wasn't white nowhere, black wasn't. What was that thought he was trying to get ahold of—bumping around in his head—something he started to think about but couldn't remember it somehow.

The shrill whistle that is typical of the French subway pierced its way into his thoughts. Subway—why was he in the subway—he didn't want to go any place. He heard doors slamming and saw the blue uniforms of the conductors swinging on to the cars as the trains began to pull out of the station. With one or two strides he reached the last coach as it began to move up the platform. A bit out of breath he stood inside the train and looking down at what he had in his hand he saw that it was a tiny pink ticket. A first class ticket in a second class coach. The idea set him to laughing. Everyone in the car turned and eyed him, but that did not bother him. Wonder what stop he'd get off—funny how these French said descend when they meant get off—funny he couldn't pick up French—been here so long. First class ticket in a second class coach!—that was one on him. Wedding day today, and that damn letter from Mary. How'd she say it now, "just couldn't go through with it," white women just don't marry colored men, and she was a street woman, too. Why couldn't she have told him flat that she was just getting back on her feet at his expense. Funny that first class ticket he bought, wish he could see Mary—him a-going there to wish her "happy wedding day," too. Wonder what that French woman was looking at him so hard for? Guess it was the mud.

Tokens

Ebony and Topaz: A Collectanea, ed. Charles S. Johnson, 149–50
(Manchester, NH: Ayer Co. Publishing, 1927)

High on the bluff of Saint Cloud stands the Merlin Hospital, immaculate sentinel of Seraigne . . . Seraigne with its crazy houses and aimless streets, scrambling at the foot of Saint Cloud's[1] immense immutability. Row on row the bricks of the hospital take dispassionate account of lives lost or found. It is always as though the gay, little town of Seraigne were thumbing its nose at Saint Cloud with its famous Merlin Hospital where life is held in a test-tube, a thing to be caught or lost by a drop or two of this or a pellet of that. And past the rustic stupidity of Seraigne's gaiety lies the wanton unconcern of the Seine. The Seine . . . mute river of sorrows . . . grim concealer of forgotten secrets . . . endlessly flowing . . . touching the edges of life . . . moving purposefully along with a grey disdain for the empty, foolish gaiety of Seraigne or the benign dignity of Merlin Hospital, high on the warm cliffs of Saint Cloud.

A trim nurse had drawn Jenks Barnett's chair out onto one of the balconies that over-looked the Seine. Listlessly, aimlessly he turned his thoughts to first one aspect and then another of the Seine, Merlin Hospital, the cliffs of Saint Cloud, Seraigne . . . over and again . . . the Seine, Merlin Hospital, the cliffs . . . of . . . Saint . . . Cloud . . . silly, little Seraigne. It was a better way—that Seine business. Just swallow up life and sorrow and sadness . . . don't bother about the poor fools who are neither dead nor alive . . . just hanging on to the merest threads of existence . . . coughing out one's heart and yet somehow still keeping heart. Purposeless thoughts these as one just as purposelessly fingers the blanket that covers one's emaciated, almost lifeless legs. But the Seine goes on, and Seraigne continues to be happy, and the pain in one's chest grows no easier.

It so happened that at this particular time there were a number of colored patients at the Merlin Hospital. Most of them were musicians who had remained in Paris after the World War. Two of them had come to London and thence to Paris with Will Marion Cook in the Negro entertainer's heyday.[2] Jenks was one of these. He had been a singer in those days. His voice was now spoken of in the hushed tones one uses when speaking of the dead. He had cherished great plans for himself in those days and no one dared hope otherwise, so rare was his voice in range and quality. That was all changed now . . .

Merlin Hospital had won nation-wide fame as a haven for patients suffering from tuberculosis. An able staff of doctors and nurses administered daily hope of recovery to broken bodies or perhaps kindly, although inadequate, solace to those whose cases were hopeless. Jenks Barnett had been there five weeks. His case was one of the hopeless ones. The tale of his being there did not take long in the telling. Shortly after the success of Cook's orchestra with its inimitable "singing trombonist" Tollie had come—Tollie Saunders with her golden voice and lush laughter. From the very first she and Jenks had hit it off well together. It was not long before he was inextricably enmeshed in the wonder of her voice and the warm sweetness of her body. Dinner at Les Acacias . . . for Tollie . . . a hat for her lovely head . . . that dress in Chanel's window . . . she wanted one of those large opal rings . . . long nights of madness under the charm of her flute-sweet voice. His work began to suffer. Soon he was dismissed from the orchestra. Singing *soirees* didn't pay too well. And then one day before the pinch of poverty came Tollie had left him, taking with her all the pretty things he had given her . . . leaving no farewell . . . her chance had come to sing in an American production and she had gone. No word of their plan to startle the singing world with their combined talents; no hint of regret that she was leaving . . . just gone. Three nights on a gorgeous drunk and he had awakened to find himself in a dingy, damp Parisian jail with a terrific pain in his back . . . eighteen days in which he moved from one prison-house to another . . . sunshine and air again when his friends had finally found him and arranged for his release . . . sunshine lasts but a short time in Paris . . . endless days of splashing through the Paris rain in search of a job . . . always that pain between his shoulder-blades . . . then night upon night of blowing a trombone in a stuffy little *Boite de Nuit*³ during which time he forgot the pain in his back . . . and drink . . . incessant drink . . . one more drink with the fellows . . . and after the job cards and more drink. One came to Merlin after one had been to the American Hospital. One came to Merlin after one had been to every other hospital round about Paris. It does not take long to become accustomed to the turning knife in one's chest. It is good for a hopeless case to watch the uncurbed forgetfulness of the Seine.

Spring had sent ahead its perfume this day. It was as though the early March air were powdered with the pollen of many unborn flowers. A haze settled itself in the air and on the breast of the river. Jenks forgot for a moment the relentless ache in his bosom and breathed deeply in sheer satisfaction. In the very midst of this gesture of aliveness the tool of death, lodged in his lung, gave a wrench. A hacking cough rose in his throat and then seemed to become stuck there. His great, gaunt frame was shaken in a paroxysm of pain. The fit of stifled coughing over, his head fell back upon the pillow. A nurse hurried to his side. "Guess you'd better go in now. I told you not to move around."

With quick, efficient hands she tucked the cover more closely about his legs, lowered the back of the invalid chair in which he was sitting, and pushed him carefully back into the hospital. As his chair was rolled through the ward it was as though he were running the gamut of scorn. Jenks was not a favorite at the hospital by any stretch of the imagination. Few of the patients there had escaped the lash of his tongue. Sour at life and the raw deal it had dealt him, he now turned his attention to venting his spume on those about him. Nurses, doctors, orderlies, fellow-patients, persistent friends . . . all shared alike the blasphemy of his words. Even Bill Jackson, the one friend who continued to brave the sting of his vile tongue, was not spared. Bill had known him and loved him before Tollie came. It was in this memory that he wrapped himself when Jenks was most unbearable. He accused Bill of stealing his money when he asked him to bring him something from the city . . . There had been many who had tried to make Jenks' last days easier but one by one they had begun to stay away until now there was only Bill left. Little wonder the other patients in the hospital heaped invective upon him as he passed.

So thin he was as he lay beneath the covers of the bed that his knees and chest made scarcely perceptible mounds in the smooth whiteness of the bed. The brown of his face had taken on the color of dried mud. Great seams folded themselves in his cheeks. There he lay, the rotting hulk of what he had once been. He had sent for Bill . . . these waiting moments were so long!

"Hi there, Jenks" . . . it was Bill's cheery voice . . . "thought you'd be outside."

"Can't go out no more. Nearly kicked off the other day."

"Thas all right . . . you'll come around all right."

"For God sakes cut it out. I know I'm done for. You know it, too, damn it all."

"Come on now, fella, be your age. You can't last long if you get yourself all worked up. Take it easy."

"Oh I get so damned sick of the whole business I wish I would hurry up and die. But whose business is that but mine . . . got somethin' to tell you."

"Shoot."

"See I'm dyin' . . . get me. They keep stickin' that needle in me but I know damn well I'm dyin'. Now what I want you to do is this . . . I wrote a letter to Tollie when I first came here . . . it's in her picture in my suit-case . . . you know that silver frame. Well when I die I want you to give it to her, if it's a thousand years from now . . . just a token of the time when we were in love. Don't forget it. Then you remember that French kid that used to be on the ward downstairs . . . she always liked that radium clock[4] of mine. She's been transferred to the Gerboux Sanitarium . . . almost well now. I think they said she would be out in a year. Good kid . . . used to climb up here every afternoon . . . stairs sort of wore her out, too. Give her my clock and tell her I hope she lives to be well and strong 'cause I never'll make it. God, she was an angel if ever there was one . . . she used to sit there on that chair where you're sittin' now and just look at me and say how she wished she could die in my place cause I was such a big man . . . and could sing so . . . I believe she'd like to have something to remember me by. And, Bill, you take . . . that . . . mmmghgummmm . . . mmm . . ."

That strangling cough rose in his throat. His eyes, always cruel, seemed to look out softly at Bill. A nurse hurried swiftly into the room and injected a hypodermic needle into his arm. A tremor went through his body. His eye-lids half closed . . . he slept.

The days dragged out in one week after another. Jenks lingered on like the days. Outside the Seine flowed endlessly on unhindered and free. It was all so futile and strange . . . waiting this way.

June had laid her warm mouth upon the face of the earth. With soft languor the sun slid tenderly over the cliffs of Saint Cloud . . . even tenderly over the grey bricks of Merlin Hospital. Jenks had raged so about not being allowed to lie on the balcony that at last the hospital authorities had relented . . . there was such a short time left for him anyway . . . he might as well have what he wanted . . . this was the first day that had been warm enough. As he lay there he looked out across the cliffs, past the little town of Seraigne, out past the Seine . . . on . . . on . . . immune to life . . .

conversant with death . . . on to the great simplicities. He got to thinking of when he was a boy . . . the songs he used to sing . . . he almost thought he'd try to sing now . . . what did it matter if he got another coughing spell . . . but then the nurses would all be in a flurry. Nice to be out here once more looking at the Seine and the world where people lived and breathed.

Bill sighed as he placed the little clock on the mantle-piece. Funny world, this! The French girl had died in late May. He had better not tell Jenks . . . it might upset him. No-o-ope better just keep the clock here. Funny how the first kind thing Jenks had done for anybody since Tollie left him should be done for a person who was dead.

High on the bluff of Saint Cloud stands the Merlin Hospital, immaculate sentinel of Seraigne . . . with its crazy houses and aimless streets, scrambling at the foot of Saint Cloud's immense immutability. Row on row the bricks of the hospital take dispassionate account of lives lost or found.

EDITORIALS

Introduction

Although Bennett had a growing reputation in the arts in and around Harlem by early 1926, her literary column "The Ebony Flute" in *Opportunity* introduced her to an even wider audience throughout the United States and abroad. By mid-1926 the Harlem Renaissance was expanding beyond its local borders and casting its eye toward the rest of the country and abroad. There was a diverse readership, including African Americans and non–African Americans, older and younger voices, and males and females, engaging in heated exchanges about the New Negro movement, the place of literature and art in the development of the race, and so on. Unlike other columns that focused on one artist or work each issue, "Bennett adopted the 'fragmentation inherent in an interdisciplinary field' (Howsam 75), dividing her column by subject and systematically discussing important topics of the day" (Wheeler, "Gwendolyn Bennett's 'The Ebony Flute'" 745). As someone who was an integral member of various literary communities, including poet Georgia Douglas Johnson's DC-based Saturday Nighters, Bennett established a similar literary society community in each issue.

Each month readers would learn about what was going on in Harlem, around the country, and internationally as it pertained to African American writers, artists, playwrights, singers, and others. Bennett also engaged many of the day's literary discussions, including the infamous debate about Carl Van Vechten's *Nigger Heaven* (1925), a novel that was praised or chastised by literary heavyweights including W. E. B. Du Bois, Marcus Garvey, and Langston Hughes. Bennett "provided her audience with a tailored, yet friendly, discussion that fostered congeniality between diverse groups, offered an alternative viewpoint on controversial figures or topics, updated readers on international and national events or the happenings of prominent African American figures, and promoted reader involvement" unlike what had been seen previously (Wheeler, "Gwendolyn Bennett," 212).

For example, Bennett's July 1927 column is divided into six distinct parts: music (particularly old spirituals); *Opportunity* contest winners getting published; the Saturday Nighters literary group, and news of their recent meeting; updates on current known writers and artists (location and/or current project); African Americans featured in *Carolina Magazine*; and a topic of the day (in this case, Van Vechten defending members of the New Negro movement). The same categories did not always reappear each month, reflecting Bennett's commitment to keeping the column fresh by only discussing the pertinent topics of the day. Though not all of Bennett's columns, particularly her earlier ones, are neatly divided into clear categories, in all nineteen editorials there is still a structure that makes it easy for readers to move from one topic, discussion, or idea to the next, not unlike an agenda for a literary group.

In her first column (Aug. 1926) Bennett sets about building a community between diverse groups by explaining her column's title: "I was struck by the exceedingly great beauty of his [William Rose Benét's] use of the 'ebony flute' [in his poem 'Harlem'] as an instrument upon which one could 'sing Harlem.' [. . .] Ebony, black and of exquisite smoothness . . . And a flute has that double quality of tone, low and sweet or high and shrill, that would make of Harlem or any other place a very human song. No better instrument then for the slim melody of what book one has read or who is writing what new play than an ebony flute." Bennett's ability to align her literary column, a seemingly low art form, with a traditional lyric poem, a high art form, represents her commitment to breaking down barriers between different artistic modes of expression. Additionally, Bennett's praise of a poem about Harlem that was written by a white male poet and published in a theater arts magazine that was edited by a white male editor and for a wealthy audience, is an excellent example of her fostering alliances between black and white artists and editors, males and females, and high and low classes. Bennett further demonstrated that congeniality between blacks and whites was obtainable when she published Benét's note in response to her earlier comments: "I am flattered that you like 'Harlem,' and glad that you should use the term 'The Ebony Flute' for a heading to your column, which column seems to me an excellent idea'" (Sept. 1926, 292). Throughout all her work, including her column, Bennett moved adroitly between discussions of blacks and whites.

Bennett's column also provided her audience with ways to read controversial "texts." She knew that in order to narrate collective history, or in Bennett's case explain complicated texts in the context of the African American tradition, she needed to have "an authoritative knowledge of the past and the means publicly to relate an interpretation of that knowledge" (Maffly-Kipp 237). As someone with a theater background, Bennett felt very comfortable reviewing recent plays, operas, and musicals (theater and recitals); in fact, Bennett devotes a portion of each of her nineteen columns to this artistic form. In her September 1927 column Bennett discusses the Broadway musical *Africana*: "Never have I seen such gorgeous abandon as was exhibited by that chorus nor have I ever seen such a perfectly matched curtain of brownness as hung behind Ethel Waters . . . literally there were the sort of 'brown girls' about which the poets sing. I grow a little tongue-tied when I begin to speak of Miss Waters, herself. She sings to her audience with the same intimacy that one feels sitting in one's own home listening to one's own gramophone." Bennett was aware that "'folks say' *Rag Tang* is a better show" than *Africana*, so she set about explaining her reasons for favoring the latter: "I understand that *Rag Tang* is more after the pattern of the usual Broadway musical show but is that what we want of a Negro revue?" (276). Thus, Bennett encourages her readers to step out of their comfort zone and embrace a controversial musical that is not formulaic like *Rag Tang*. A month later Bennett comments that she did attend a production of *Rag Tang* and was "delightfully surprised" that it was able to live up to all the hype people had given it (Oct. 1927, 128). Though some may see Bennett's admission that the play "was beautiful," as a correction of her previous month's statement, Bennett makes many of the same comments about *Rag Tang* as she did about *Africana*, suggesting she liked the plays equally. Even when an African American play came out that was not well received, Bennett provided her audience with another way to "read" the situation. A drama, *Meek Mose*, by Frank Wilson, received mixed reviews, including one by Bennett: "The plot was hackneyed . . . here and there the acting was superb . . . the music, arranged and directed by Alston Burleigh was beautiful" (Apr. 1928). Though there were some problems with the play, Bennett reminded her audience of the importance of what this production reflected in the African American community: "To us the play in itself and its success or failure was unimportant. We were more concerned with the fact that here had arrived the day when the theatre goers of Broadway were willing to attend seriously to the things that Negroes had to say about their own lives."

Whether discussing various genres, authors, parts of the globe, writing contests, or everyday life, Bennett was truly at home writing "The Ebony Flute." Her enthusiasm for the local, national, and global Renaissance that was taking place, and her desire to make everyone feel like they were part of this revolution, was evident in each issue, no doubt helping to make it one of the most read columns of its time.

The Ebony Flute

Opportunity, Aug. 1926, 260–61

In searching about for a heading that would make a fit label for literary chit-chat and artistic what-not I stumbled upon "The Ebony Flute." So lovely a name it is that I should like to have made it myself, but I didn't. I say "stumbled" advisedly. Reading again William Rose Benet's poem, Harlem,[1] in the *October Theatre Arts Magazine* I was struck by the exceeding great beauty of his use of the "ebony flute" as an instrument upon which one could "sing Harlem." An ebony flute ought to be very effective for most any sort of singing for that matter. Ebony, black and of exquisite smoothness . . . And a flute has that double quality of tone, low and sweet or high and shrill, that would make of Harlem or any other place a very human song. No better instrument then for the slim melody of what book one has read or who is writing what new play than an ebony flute . . . speaking of Benet's *Harlem*, what a lovely thing it is! It opens with:

> *I want to sing Harlem on an ebony flute*
> *While trap-drums ruffle to a crash and blare,*
> *With a clear note*
> *From a sylvan throat*
> *Of a clarinet—of a clarinet!*
> *God and brute, black god and brute*
> *Grinning, brooding in the murk air,*
> *Moons of flame and suns of jet,*
> *Hurricane joy and dumb despair.*
>
> *Vermillion, black and peacock blue,*
> *Pink, plum-purple, zig-zag green—*
> *I want to sing Harlem with a paint-box too,*
> *Shaking out color like a tambourine,*
> *Want a red*
> *Like a furious fire;*
> *Want a black*
> *Like midnight mire;*
> *Want a gold*

Like golden wire;
Want a silver
Like Heaven entire
And God a-playing at his own front door
On a slide trombone with a conical bore!

And on through line on line of beauty that coins a Harlem as a poet would see it, lush and colorful . . . fertile like rich earth. On and on to its close which ends with the crooning of his "Mammy Earth . . ."

O child of the wild, of the womb of the night,
Rest, and dream, my dark delight!

Tropic Death, a book of short stories by Eric Walrond will come out in October. Boni and Liveright are the publishers. I can scarcely wait for this book to be on the market . . . Few of the Negro writers that are being heralded on all sides today can begin to create the color that fairly rolls itself from Mr. Walrond's facile pen. *Tropic Death* ought to have that ripe color that is usually the essence of Mr. Walrond's writing . . . and also a simple forcefulness that the author often achieves . . . A new magazine is added to the Chicago list of Negro publications: *American Life Magazine,* Moses Jordan editing . . . the same Mr. Jordan whose book, *The Meat Man,* was published a few years back.[2] The June issue, Volume One—Number One, carried "From Venice to Vienna" by Jessie Redmon Fauset and "Pale Lady" by Langston Hughes. I have not seen the July issue of this magazine but look forward to seeing the future copies that will come out. . . . Maude Cuney Hare has an article on *Creole Folksongs* in the July number of the *Musical Observer.*[3] Needless to say, Mrs. Hare's article is adequate . . . certainly there are few people more authoritative in their speaking of Creole folksongs than she.

Aaron Douglas is doing the illustrations for Carl Van Vechten's *Nigger Heaven* which will appear August the twentieth. *The Publisher's Weekly* says that Mr. Douglas' advertisement for this book in the current magazines is the best for the month of June . . . but by far the most important thing about Mr. Douglas these days is his new wife. He married Miss Alta Sawyer of Kansas City, Missouri, on Friday, June eighteenth . . . The English edition of Langston Hughes' *Weary Blues* came out on July ninth . . . the second edition of *The New Negro* will be out in the fall . . . The Negro writers must not let the first of September slip up on them without having their manuscripts ready for the Albert and Charles Boni contest.[4] The address for sending the novels to the judges is 66 Fifth Avenue . . . Thinking of novels makes me recall what Simeon Strunsky of the *New York Times Book Review* said not so long ago about beautifully written books . . . "The beautifully written book as a rule is the over-written book. One sinks into beauty ankle-deep." He goes to quite some trouble to poke fun at the elegant conservatism of what is called beautiful prose today. But even in the face of Mr. Strunsky's caustic remarks on the question of beautiful writing, properly so-called, I should be ever so happy to find some of that ankle-deep beauty in the things that come out of the Boni contest . . . what of it, if some Negro should write a *Marie Chapdelaine* with its wistful but perfect simplicity or perhaps an "Ethan Frome . . ."[5] Mr. Strunsky rambles on to the amazing consolation that "We still have our newspapers. In them are the reservoirs of simple health upon which we can draw when the English language threatens to cave in under heavy doses of beauty between bound covers" . . . and we can do little else but wonder how any one can live in New York and see the rife yellow journalism of the daily news sheets and speak of them as the salvation of the English language . . . nor even the aridity of the *New York Times* could be set on the pinnacle that had been built for "beautiful writing."

"George Sand Reigns Again For a Day" in the *Times* for June twenty-seventh made me think of a young newspaper writer I knew in Paris who was always breaking into any conversation that chanced to be going on at the time with the information that he lived in the back part of a house the front part of which had belonged to George Sand . . . and I always think within myself that I could see in that about as much claim to fame as any . . . F. Fraser Bond in reviewing *The Best Love Stories of 1925*: "Something has come over the American love story . . . It seems to have grown up. No longer does it find its chief concern in the billings and cooings of tepid adolescents" . . . he goes on further to observe that "Peter Pan has put on long trousers." Can't you see some E. E. Cummings–John V. Weaver person coming forward with a "Come out of it Lovers" to scare away that something that has "come over" the love story of today . . . [6]

Hall Johnson's[7] Negro operetta, *Goophered*, with the libretto by Garret is to have in it three lyrics by Langston Hughes: *Mother to Son; The*

Midnight Blues; and *Song for a Banjo*. This operetta is for early fall or late summer production. Mr. Johnson is the winner of the third prize of the music section of the OPPORTUNITY Contest . . . and by the way, Zora Neale Hurston and Langston Hughes are collaborating on an operetta the libretto of which is to be by Miss Hurston and the lyrics by Mr. Hughes[8] . . . they are also writing a musical comedy together . . . Mentioning musical comedies of a dusky character reminds me of the ill-fated *My Magnolia* which ran for a single week at the Mansfield Theater.[9]

Jean Toomer, author of *Cane*, is spending the summer at the Gurdjieff Institute[10] in Fontainebleau, France . . . Countee Cullen and his father, Reverend Cullen, are traveling through Europe for the summer months . . . they will make many interesting stops chief among them a pilgrimage to the Holy Land . . . Arthur Huff Fauset[11] whose "Symphonesque" won first prize in the short story section of the OPPORTUNITY contest is to be a member of their party . . . Dr. Rudolph Fisher[12] has very endearingly nick-named his new baby "the new Negro."

Friday, July sixteenth, the annual reception for summer school students was given at the 135th Street Library.[13] Mr. Johnson of OPPORTUNITY spoke on the OPPORTUNITY contests and what they had meant to the younger school of writers. When Mr. Johnson had finished his speech he called on several of the prize winners of the first and second OPPORTUNITY contests who chanced to be in the audience and asked them to read . . . "Golgatha Is A Mountain" was never so lovely for me until I heard Mr. Arna Bontemp[14] [*sic*] read it himself. He reads with a voice as rich in its resonance as his prize-winning poem is in its imagery and beauty. It was good to see so many of the people who are writing and doing things together . . . Zora Neale Hurston, Bruce Nugent,[15] John Davis[16] . . . Langston Hughes who talked a bit about blues and spirituals and then read some of the new ones he had been doing . . . and just before he sat down he read a poem called "Brass Spittoons" . . . as lovely as are many things with much more delectable names.

Horace Liveright is busy casting his play *Black Boy* for its fall production.[17] Paul Robeson is to play the lead which I understand is to be a prize-fighter. I heard Mr. Liveright say the other night that he was having difficulty in finding an actress for the role of Irene who plays in the lead opposite Mr. Robeson. This part is difficult to fill since the heroine is supposed all during the play to be white and is discovered at the end to be a colored girl who "passes." Remembering the harmful publicity that attended the opening of *All God's Chillun*[18] because of a white woman's playing opposite a Negro, Mr. Liveright has been leaving no stone unturned to find a Negro girl who can take the part. There are hundreds who are fitted for the physical requirements of the piece but few whose histrionic powers would measure up to the standard of Broadway production.

Clarissa Scott[19] of Washington dropped into the office the other day on her first trip in the interest of the new social investigation work she is to be doing in New York this summer . . . the same Clarissa Scott whose *Solace* won a prize in the OPPORTUNITY contest for last year . . . and it was good to see her again and to know that she would be in New York all the summer . . . sandwiched between talk of what was happening in Washington and at Howard the question arose as to what was the most beautiful line of poetry written by a Negro . . . her first thought was:

> *Dark Madonna of the grave she rests;*
> *Lord Death has found her sweet.*

from Countee Cullen's *A Brown Girl Dead* . . . strange how discussions of this sort get started, isn't it? I had never thought in terms of the best or most beautiful or the greatest line of Negro poetry before . . . there are several that come in line for the distinction now that I come to think of it . . . without thinking too long my first choice is from Langston Hughes' new blues poem called *The Railroad Blues* . . .

> *A railroad bridge is a sad song in de air*
> or
> *Where twilight is a soft bandanna handkerchief*[20]

. . . or perhaps Lewis Alexander's[21]

> *A body smiling with black beauty* . . .

or Jean Toomer's

> *Above the sacred whisper of the pines,*
> *Give virgin lips to cornfield concubines,*
> *Bring dreams of Christ to dusky, cane-lipped throngs.*[22]

We wonder what William Stanley Braithwaite[23] would say . . . or Claude McKay . . . or Jessie Fauset . . . But all that resolves itself into the hopelessness of deciding what the greatest of anything is . . . nothing is really greatest but greatness itself . . .

o   o   o

The Ebony Flute

Opportunity, Apr. 1927, 123

Dr. [Alain] Locke is preparing a pamphlet on four Negro poets: Jean Toomer, Claude McKay, Countee Cullen, and Langston Hughes . . . This is for Simon and Schuster, publishers of a series of *Pamphlet Poets*—I think Carl Sandburg, Natalie Crane[1] and Edwin Markham[2] are among some of the poets who have already been brought out. [. . .] *Theatre Arts Magazine* is getting out a volume on world drama made up largely of essays having appeared in its issues. Dr. Locke's two articles on the Negro in the field of drama are being welded into one for this volume.

And about Claude McKay:—This quotation from a rather wistful letter written in the sun-drenched South of France:

"I suffered a big loss when my suitcase of manuscripts (containing all of the poems I have written during the last four years, dictionaries, reference books, etc.) was stolen at Marseilles last summer. Luckily I had in a satchel the novel I was writing and some short stories.

"At present I am devoting all my spare time to prose. I find poetry such an inadequate means of saying the things I have to say."

We are ever so thankful for the God-given satchel that saved the novel and short stories, however we cannot but tremble at the thought of the beauty that may have been lost in the ill-fated suitcase. We are a little awed before the immensity of Claude McKay's outlook when he can say poetry is too small a medium for the expression of his thoughts . . . he who has so beautifully wooed and won the Muse of Poetry. [. . .]

Langston Hughes' new book of poems[3] has been receiving very good reviews . . . as an appropriate send-off for the book there comes the announcement of his having been awarded the *John Keats Prize* of twenty-five dollars by *Palms Magazine* for his group of poems, *A House in Taos*. Mark Van Doren was the judge. [. . .]

o   o   o

The Ebony Flute

Opportunity, July 1927, 212–13

At this writing there are many things, there are ever and ever so many things more rare than this particular "day in June" . . . a gentle rain patters its way down upon the city roofs . . . for some unknown reason I am reminded of a spiritual that I heard a young Negro student sing a few nights ago . . . *Keep Your Hand Upon the Plow*[1] . . . for me it was a new spiritual and oh such a beautiful one. In a recent issue of *The Town Crier* there appeared an editorial entitled *Old Spirituals* . . . lavish applause was showered upon the Negro as a songster. The following paragraph carries the gist of the entire article:

> *The Negro is becoming articulate. There was a time when he was known only as the singer of other men's ballads. That was the day of Jubilee Singers,*[2] *long before an Old Spiritual had even a name. Every one went to hear them, much in the same spirit that every one went to see the freaks in the sideshows. Even then the Negro carried himself with a dignity which disarmed the most prejudiced . . . It would seem that they might have a message for the world. It has been sung on the road up from slavery and with a poignancy that has lain beneath an exterior of carefree indolence, now dimly understood as being something in the nature of camouflage. There must have always existed a toughness of fibre which would not permit the surrender of individuality to those who dominated them. In a way, they were captains of their souls if not masters of their fate.*

Edward J. O'Brien, compiler and editor of the best short story series, a volume which is issued annually, has written to Eugene Gordon, the Boston newspaper man,[3] a request for a biographical sketch to be inserted in the *Best Short Stories of 1927*. This means that *Rootbound*, winner of the fourth prize in the short story division of last year's *Opportunity* Contest, has been designated by Mr. O'Brien as one of the stories printed in 1926 which in his opinion may fairly claim a position in American literature, and which is to be listed in the Roll of Honor in his volume. It is also to be indicated in that part of the volume known as the yearbook by three asterisks affixed to its title. Blanche Colton Williams[4] in her *O. Henry Memorial Award Volume of Short Stories for 1926* also picked *Rootbound* as an outstanding story, along with Dorothy West's[5] *The Typewriter*, which with a story by Zora Neale Hurston, *Muttsy*, won second prize in *Opportunity's* contest last year.

The Saturday Nighters of Washington, D.C., met on June forth at the home of Mrs. Georgia Douglas Johnson.[6] Mr. Charles S. Johnson was the guest of honor. It was particularly pleasing to see and talk with Miss Angelina Grimke.[7] She is a beautiful lady with ways as softly fine as her poems. The company as a whole was a charming medley . . . E. C. Williams[8] with his genial good humor; Lewis Alexander with jovial tales of this thing and that as well as a new poem or two which he read; Marieta [*sic*] Bonner[9] with her quiet dignity; Willis Richardson with talk of "plays and things" . . . and here and there a new poet or playwright . . . and the whole group held together by the dynamic personality of Mrs. Johnson . . . some poems by Langston Hughes were read . . . he, by the way, is in the Southland. Dr. Locke tells us that his trip is to cover much of the "Land of Cotton" . . . and while we are tracing our travelogue let us say that Frank Horne[10] is spending the summer in Chicago after a winter in Fort Valley, Georgia . . . Dr. Locke is again returning to Europe . . . Jean Toomer will again be in Fountainbleau, France, at the Gurdjieff Institute . . . Eric Walrond, who has been in Panama, has now returned to New York. And so Negroes go hither and thither and yon, writing about this and that . . .

We have at hand the May number of the *Carolina Magazine*, which is devoted to articles and poems by Negro authors. The magazine is well set up with a noble list of truly artistic contributors . . . Arna Bontemps, Aaron Douglas, Charles S. Johnson, Arthur Huff Fauset, Helene Johnson[11] and Eulalie Spence.[12] If all white colleges were so liberally inclined, the combined artistic expression of the darker and fairer groups might arrive at a truly great Art. This issue of the *Carolina Magazine* was one more brave step toward this Utopian communion of spirit. In accord with this general urge to "render unto Caesar what is Caesar's" *The Midland, A Magazine of the Middle West* carries as the first article in its May issue a piece entitled *The Harlem Poets*.

Recently Mr. Benjamin Brawley,[13] Professor of English Literature at Shaw University, wrote a paper entitled *The Negro Literary Renaissance* which appeared in *The Southern Workman*. Mr. Brawley had little or no high praise to spare for the "younger Negro" . . . there was an almost venomous sting in the severity of his criticism of those young black throats that have dared to sing a new song. I have come by a copy of a letter which Mr. Carl Van Vechten wrote in answer to Mr. Brawley's paper and incidentally in defense of the younger Negro. This question is of too great moment for the letter to be hidden from the public eye and so I shall take the liberty to print it here:

My dear Mr. Brawley:

I have read with interest your paper entitled the *Negro Literary Renaissance*, in the *Southern Workman*. Your opinions are your own, and although I do not share them you are entitled to them. I think, however, that in such a paper, written by a college professor, one might expect a meticulous niceness in regard to matters of fact. You write: "When Mr. [Langston] Hughes came under the influence of Mr. Carl Van Vechten and *The Weary Blues* was given to the world," etc. *The Weary Blues* had won a prize before I had read a poem by Mr. Hughes or knew him personally. The volume, of which this was the title poem, was brought to me complete before Mr. Hughes and I had ever exchanged two sentences. I am unaware even to this day, although we are the warmest friends and see each other frequently, that I have had the slightest influence on Mr. Hughes in any direction. The influence, if one exists, flows from the other side, as any one might see who read my first paper on the *Blues*, published in *Vanity Fair* for August, 1925, a full year before *Nigger Heaven* appeared, before, indeed, a line of it had been written. In this paper I quoted freely Mr. Hughes' opinions on the subject of Negro folk song, opinions which to my knowledge have not changed in the slightest.

I might say a word or two apropos of the quotableness of the verse of Countee Cullen. Suffice to say that the fact is that he is quoted more frequently, with two or three exceptions, than any other American poet. I myself quoted four lines as a superscription to *Nigger Heaven*, and two other lines later in the book, I think the concluding lines of his beautiful sonnet, *Yet Do I Marvel*,[14] I have seen printed more other (in periodicals in other languages than English, moreover) than any other two lines by any contemporary poet.

I beg to remain yours very sincerely,

(Signed) CARL VAN VECHTEN.

. . . And at this juncture I am moved to quote H. G. Wells: *Art that does not argue nor demonstrate nor discuss is merely the craftman's impudence.*[15]

o   o   o

The Ebony Flute
Opportunity, Sept. 1927, 276

[. . .] A few nights ago I went to see *Africana*[1] . . . never have I seen such gorgeous abandon as was exhibited by that chorus nor have I ever seen such a perfectly matched curtain of brownness as hung behind Ethel Waters . . . literally there were the sort of "brown girls" about which the poets sing. I grow a little tongue-tied when I begin to speak of Miss Waters, herself. She sings to her audience with the same intimacy that one feels sitting in one's own home listening to one's own gramophone. The night that I was there the audience clamored for song after song and she delightfully gave them what they knew they wanted. [. . .]

o   o   o

The Ebony Flute
Opportunity, Apr. 1928, 122

We hasten to welcome another group of creative workers to the fold . . . *Book and Bench*, comprising four writers of verse, five prose writers, two composers of music and one painter, has been organized in Topeka, Kansas, since last fall. They plan publishing a year-book, entitled *Urge*, early in May . . . The number grows . . . The Quill Club in Boston[1], The Ink-Slingers in California and Black Opals in Philadelphia[2] . . . to say nothing of the many groups in New York.

Uncle Tom's Cabin, the American cinema featuring James B. Lowe, a Negro, in the part of Uncle Tom, has been enthusiastically received in England.[3] In December it began its run at the *London Pavilion, Piccadilly Circus*. Mr. Lowe appears in person in a prologue to the picture in which there are real Negroes singing spirituals. *The Glasgow Bulletin, The Illustrated Graphic, Cinema, The Daily Chronicle*, and *Reynold's* give unmeasured acclaim to Mr. Lowe's acting. A special benefit performance of this moving picture was held on Sunday, January the twenty-ninth. The proceeds of the performance were given in aid of the Mayor of Westminster's Flood Relief Fund. The program included such internationally known Negro entertainers as The Three Eddies,[4] Noble Sissle, Eubie Blake, The Four Harmony Kings[5] and none other than Josephine Baker who "flew" over from Paris for the occasion.

Lawrence Brown,[6] partner of Paul Robeson and former accompanist of Roland Hayes has left Paris for London where he will give several concerts. Thence he will go to Cannes and Vienna where he will fill several drawing room engagements.

Forbes Randolph's *Kentucky Jubilee Choir*[7] are to be heard with "Roxy" over Radio Station W.J.Z. on Sunday evenings. The jubilee choir is made up of eight male voices that were picked from an audition of five hundred voices from all over the country. It has been said that the audition for the chorus cost about ten thousand dollars. These singers have seventy-five songs in their repertoire . . . *The Dixie Jubilee Singers* under the direction of Miss Eva A. Jessye,[8] author of *My Spirituals*, gave concerts on Saturday, Monday and Wednesday during the week of February eleventh to eighteenth at the Wanamaker Store in New York City. Miss Jessye's book will be remembered with delight by those who have seen it. By the way, *Forty Negro Spirituals* by Clarence Cameron White[9] has been published by the Theodore Presser Company in Philadelphia. This book is well edited and many of the arrangements are more charming than those to which we have become accustomed. Clarence Cameron White has just been awarded First Prize for Distinguished Achievement as a Violinist and Composer by the Harmon Foundation. At the same time Dr. Nathaniel Dett was awarded First Prize for Distinguished Achievement in Music . . ."[10] the two awards were made because there was no musical award made last year. No longer ago than Sunday afternoon, February nineteenth, we had the pleasure of meeting Dr. Dett. It was at the Barnes Foundation in Merion, Pa. . . . Dr.

Albert C. Barnes[11] had invited a small group of people, both colored and white, to the Foundation where he spoke on "African Art." . . . With the beautiful pieces from the Barnes collection as examples of what is best in African art it is quite evident that Dr. Barnes succeeded in convincing his audience that the Africans truly had an art form which bore easy comparison with the best in Greek and Egyptian art. But to go back to our meeting Dr. Dett . . . We had always just missed him on every occasion so that we were delighted to run upon him in this unexpected fashion. He was with Alan Freelon[12] . . . who, by the way, has just completed the illustrations for a score by Dr. Dett . . . and it is to Mr. Freelon that I owe this glad surprise. Dr. Dett has the simplicity that goes with true greatness. Youth pervades his talking and thinking. He was as avid a searcher into the truths and beauties of plastic art as he must be into the hidden mysteries of music. He paid us the pretty compliment of saying, "The Ebony Flute continues in its even dulcet tones" and of course we were friends right off after that. In the course of our tour around the galleries we mentioned the fact that Edmund T. Jenkins[13] had spoken with such respect and admiration for Dr. Dett's work. . . . Dr. Dett then spoke of what a tremendous loss the race had suffered in losing Jenkins, stating that he was perhaps the only Negro that had done any reputable work with symphony composition. I was pleased to know that Dr. Dett had seen and spent a great deal of time with Mr. Jenkins on that last discouraging trip which Jenkins made to America. In so many words Nathaniel Dett, fellow genius and musician, said that Edmund Jenkins bore the stamp of a divine fire and that his great dream was misunderstood and scorned by those who should have been his friends.

Meek Mose, a drama by Frank Wilson[14] [. . .] opened in New York City at the *Princess Theatre*, on Monday, February sixth. [. . .] [A]lthough most of the Quaker City and Gotham dramatic reviewers gave the play a fair break yet it was quite evident that only an unimportant few of them spoke of it as great drama. The plot was hackneyed . . . here and there the acting was superb . . . the music, arranged and directed by Alston Burleigh[15] was beautiful. But to us the play in itself and its success or failure was unimportant. We were more concerned with the fact that here had arrived the day when the theatre goers of Broadway were willing to attend seriously to the things that Negroes had to say about their own lives . . . then too, here were such players as Charles Moore who had played for nine years with *Williams and Walker* in their hey-day, Laura Bowman[16] who has played for years in Negro stock companies, and J. L. Criner[17] long known as one of the Lafayette Players who were in essence the spirit of the old school in Negro acting and yet they were taking a leading part in the new movement towards true Negro expression upon the American stage. So . . . de sun do move . . . *Meek Mose* was produced by Lester Walton[18] of the staff of the *New York World*.

Carl Van Vechten, author of *Nigger Heaven*, is nominated for the Hall of Fame in *Vanity Fair* for February. We are very glad for this for whether you are a person who likes *Nigger Heaven* or not you must admit that this book paved the way for a good bit of the writing that Negroes themselves are doing today . . . and goodness knows that is surely something. But then you see we've always liked *Nigger Heaven* regardless of what many of our friends have said or thought about it.

Introduction

Similar to Bennett's "The Ebony Flute," Bennett's book and theater reviews in publications such as the *New York Herald Tribune*, *Opportunity*, and *Social Work Today* provide readers with a critical analysis of leading plays and books being published during the Harlem Renaissance. Even though Bennett was away from Harlem during the time she wrote several of these reviews, her knowledge of the material and her experience with columns such as "The Ebony Flute" more than qualified her to write them. Bennett's reviews give us a key figure's assessment of works that went on to contribute to the canon, such as McKay's *Banjo*, and other works by African American authors or about African American life that remain marginalized today. Bennett's reviews emphasize place and her knowledge about people from that place. She does not maintain the essentialist perspective that the author has to belong to the group he or she is writing about, but posits that the work will only lack authority if the person does not know the subject group well. It was her lifelong credo that literature should be free of racial propaganda. She views literature more for its aesthetic value than as a forum to discuss racial problems.

In "Blue-Black Symphony," a review of Claude McKay's best-selling novel *Home to Harlem* (1928), for example, Bennett praises McKay's deep knowledge of his subject matter, saying that the author "has written about things that he himself has already experienced." It is a book free of racial "propaganda," a celebration of the life of Harlem inhabitants despite the grittiness that is revealed: "Here is realism, stark, awful but somehow beautiful." She compares the novel with white author Carl Van Vechten's *Nigger Heaven*. Whereas "Van Vechten is a student giving a cursory account of his findings[,] Mr. McKay is the African chief telling the story of his tribe to the children of unborn men."

In her review of another McKay novel, *Banjo* (1929), set on the docks of Marseilles, France, she again praises the author's authenticity. The novel "is no superficial glazing of the surface." The reader can feel McKay's familiarity with both the bistros being described and the language used on the wharves. What makes the novel particularly powerful to Bennett is its description of the Pan-African contact zone that was Marseilles, where Africans, American Negroes, and West Indians all intermingled.

In addition to reviewing authors like McKay, who wrote of the Negro underclass, Bennett also reviewed works by those who expounded on more genteel black life. Her review of Jessie Fauset's *Plum-Bun* (1929), for example, praises the novel's depiction of "the better class of Negroes." She observes that the novel is at its best when describing the lives of black middle-class Philadelphians, a group she knows well.

Bennett also reviewed the work of several prominent white authors. In her review of Paul Green's collection of six plays, *The Lonesome Road* (1926), she says, "It is merely incidental that he writes of Negroes." Green knows well the lives of North Carolina Negroes, but more important, he knows about "life." It does not matter if he is a white Southern man; in plays such as *In Abraham's Bosom* Green "lays a sensitive hand on the very pulse-beat of this warm dark people."

"The Emperors Jones" is an example of Bennett's reviewing of performed dramatic work. She comments on a production of Eugene O'Neill's *The Emperor Jones* performed on May 29, 1929, at the Hedgerow Theatre in Moylan-Rose Valley, Pennsylvania. Despite the out-of-the-way venue, Bennett rates the acting of Wayland Rudd (playing the lead role of Brutus Jones) to be at the level of African American stars Paul Robeson and Charles Gilpin.

Heartbreak and North Carolina Sunshine:
The Lonesome Road—by Paul Green
Opportunity, Sept. 1926, 294

> *Look down, look down dat lonesome road*
> *Whah me and my pardner's got to go . . .*
> NEGRO SONG

There are those who have said and will say that Paul Green knows Negroes and especially North Carolina Negroes. This is most certainly true but I prefer to say that Paul Green knows life and the bitter twists that living can give to simple souls born for laughter. It seems to me that it is merely incidental that he writes of Negroes. However, I think that in itself is a timely and fortunate happenstance. The fact that he sees in the lives of an isolated and frowned-upon people the elements that go to make joy and sadness beautiful is a tribute to his foresight and prophetic judgment. Greater than Paul Green's having caught the spirit and characteristics of the Negroes around him is the fact of his knowing the undercurrents of feeling that surge through peoples living close to the soil and his aptitude in employing everyday words and common phrases to coin an idiom peculiar to the particular group of which he writes.

"The Lonesome Road" is a thin volume of six plays dealing with Negroes. Between the two covers of this book the author has caught with surprising skill the oscillating mirth and sorrow of the black man of North Carolina. He has aptly portrayed the element of merriment that ofttimes suffuses the most dire tragedy—especially in the daily lives of Negroes in the Southland. He has taken individuals rather than types for the action of his plays. As Barrett H. Clark[1] has said in his very able introduction to the volume when he speaks of *In Abraham's Bosom*, the first play in the book—"In this play there is no effort to solve the problem: it is Mr. Green's business simply to state it in terms of humanity." So it is with all his characters. They move and think in the scenes given them for living with fine or evil qualities as the case may be. He has no propaganda to disseminate; his concern is with the sheer artistry and truth of his work.

The six plays cover a wide expanse of human emotions. They are only six in all but myriad in their subject matter. "In Abraham's Bosom"[2] is a poignant little play showing how swiftly the Negro may pass from one emotion to another with but slight demarcation between either one or the other. Abraham MacCranie, a workman, has a dream of becoming so educated as to be appointed teacher for a neighborhood school to be given over to Negro children. He is the object of the ridicule of his fellow workers in the turpentine grove. During one of their lunch hours he is so ired by the arrogance of Lonnie MacCranie, the son of Colonel MacCranie who is also the father of Abe, that he strikes him. To strike a white man in the South is usually a prophecy of certain death. Because of the relationship between the Colonel and Abe, he is let go with only a whipping. Abe passes with lightning change from a feeling of superiority over his comrades to arrogance at a white man's similar attitude . . . cowering fear at the Colonel's wrath to dumb submission under his lash. And finally when the caustic moments are past he is lulled to a blissful abandon by the soft words of his sweetheart Goldie. "White Dresses" tells the tale of how Mary, the grandchild of Granny McClean, is forced to marry Jim Mathews, a very black Negro. Henry Morgan, the owner of their home and Mary's white employer, insists upon this marriage in order to save his son, Hugh, because he foresees love between the two of them. By the coincidence of white dresses given as gifts on Christmas eves, separated by many years, Granny shows Mary the wisdom of Mr. Morgan's plans since he, himself, is her own father. "The Hot Iron" is in the words of Mr. Barrett perhaps "the most affecting one act play I know." Tilsy McNeill works to take care of her three children by ironing day and night. In the midst of an afternoon that had been too full of hard work her worthless husband comes home to resume his usual ill-treatment. In a fit of fury she kills him with the hot iron she has been using for her work. The play ends with Tilsy and her children running across the fields away from the horror that has been committed. "The Prayer Meeting" is a bitter tragedy of an old woman whose two granddaughters "go wrong" while a grandson in whom she believes implicitly is killed by a mob for having knifed a white man. The lighter vein runs through this grim playlette . . . there is ever so much foolish evil in the sham prayer meeting that the two granddaughters hold at their grandmother's home during her absence. Her unexpected return throws consternation into what had been a scene of gaiety and carefreeness. "The End of the Row" portrays Lalie who "would be" educated and Mr. Ed Roberts, a wealthy white man who has helped her and wants her "to stay with him" rather than go away for further training. There is the offbeat of Nora who has "set her cap" for Mr. Roberts; Aunt Zella, Nora's mother, who doesn't approve of "stuck-up niggers"; and Lucille, Nora's friend who accepts many beautiful gifts from "ole black Antney." These three women plague Lalie when they reach "the end of the row" where they are picking cotton. Lalie tells Mr. Roberts that she cannot accept his help any longer and that she is going away but there is that in her voice that makes of her words a lie. "Your Fiery Furnace" . . . Here we have Abraham MacCranie, after years of futile attempting to uplift and educate the Negroes of his community. He is lynched when he goes to deliver a speech in plea for a new school building. He has been betrayed to the mob by his own son who is a vagabond with high aspirations of being a "sport."

These plays are fine substance for little theater movements with unbiased ideals. They are not written for those who see in Negroes only minstrel laughter and cotton picking jokes. Mr. Green catches and holds the wistful quality in Negro laughter. He, strangely enough for a southern man who has spent but three years away from the south, sees the seamy side of the Negro's life in North Carolina. Telling their story he lays a sensitive hand on the very pulse-beat of this warm dark people.

o   o   o

Blue-Black Symphony: Home to Harlem, by Claude McKay

New York Herald Tribune, 11 Mar. 1928, K5

Here is Harlem once more—this time through the eyes of a Negro. Harlem with its laughter, its tears, its working and playing. Here is rich soil which the author ably plows. Claude McKay knows Harlem from the inside. He has gone its mundane ways, one with the black throng that pulsates through his novel.

In this one fact lies the essential difference between this book and *Nigger Heaven*, by Carl Van Vechten, which I am convinced will be for a time at least the criterion by which all novels about Harlem and Negro life in metropolitan cities will be judged. Mr. Van Vechten is a student of research giving a cursory account of his findings; Mr. McKay is the African chief telling the story of his tribe to the children of unborn men. Nor do I mean to make an odious comparison, for each has its place in the American literature of this century. Then too, there are many points of similarity between the two books. Each book is more or less built around the night-life of Harlem, albeit they each depict a different stratum of Negro society. Both books are only sketches of Harlem life, telling in brief that it is a place of color, movement and fever. Each author has taken for his central figure a brown Lothario—Van Vechten's hero a young Negro writer; McKay's Jake, a strapping buck who is a longshoreman.

"Home to Harlem" is the story of Harlem's serving classes. Longshoremen, waitresses, butlers, laundresses, bell-boys, kitchen-workers, maids and servitors of all sorts amble their way through the pages of Claude McKay's book. These cleaners of shoes and passers of foods gyrate and ogle through the Harlem days that followed the World War. This is Harlem before the era of the "gin-mill"—Harlem in those last agonized days before Prohibition. Negroes, dim-brown, clear brown, rich brown, chestnut, copper, yellow, near-white, mahogany and gleaming anthracite in those frantic whisky guzzling days before the subterfuges of Volsteadism[1] set in . . . Negroes who are servers of men, fighting, drinking, laughing, dancing. In the words of the author, "dancing, thick as maggots in a vat of sweet liquor, and as wriggling." Here is realism, stark, awful but somehow beautiful. McKay has left no stone unturned, no detail unmentioned in this telling of things as they are. Yet he has told many of the most sordid truths with the same simplicity that a child tells its mother this or that thing has happened. He has touched many ugly and jagged contours with a naïveté that is surprising. There is no lewdness in his uncovering unpleasant secrets about his people. He simply says, "Here is truth." Then again he says, "This is earthy but withal beautiful." McKay brings all five of his senses to the writing of this book. With sensual accuracy his characters move through the smells, the color, the taste of dark-eyed Harlem, touching life with warm, brown hands.

The plot of the story is thin, unimportant. Just the recitation of the amorous meanderings of one Jake Brown, ex-soldier, stevedore, Pullman porter. Rather a symphonic tone-poem of dark brown workers that here and there resounds with immortal chords of sentiment. Claude McKay sets the major theme for his symphony in the tale of his characters as people of a working class. Actually this is a story of whether or not a man of Jake's personal charm shall haul barrels and sling hash for his living or be a "sweet-man," kept by the earnings of women in whose eyes he has found favor. This is a pæan of foodstuffs carried by Negro soldiers who were trained and taken to Europe with the idea that they were to fight in the World War; of black men who unknowingly are hired to work as scabs on the docks at nine dollars a day; of brown men who stoke furnaces on tramp steamers and sleep in filthy places, rife with foul smells; of dining car waiters who must labor under the tyranny of a Negro cook and who must sleep in overcrowded bunks, infested with vermin . . . all juxtaposed against the Harlem "lounge lizard" who leads a lazy, comfortable life. Interwoven with this major theme is that of these same workers in their search for love. True, this erstwhile lofty passion is found in the midst of much squalor. However, it is rather the aimless wanderings of adventuresome, elemental human beings rather than the misconduct of people who are definitely depraved. Theirs is a venial sin, committed with much hymn-singing and forgotten with clear-eyed alacrity. The major themes are bound together with an occasional melodic run. One of these is Jake's love for "a cute, heart-breakin' brown" he met at the Baltimore cabaret; another is his friendship for Raymond, a Haytian chap who worked on the same dining-car with him. Claude McKay does much playing of cymbals and blowing of loud brasses, but he also plays a fine thread of tune on the violin.

One feels that the author of "Home to Harlem" has written about things that he himself has already experienced. His workers are not mere puppets; they are McKay recast to fit the story. McKay has stoked furnaces and answered to the call of "George."[2] Much of the fervor of this book is born of that fact. Mr. McKay is a poet as well as a worker. Ever and anon this first novel becomes Claude McKay, the poet, laying fond hands upon the shoulders of Claude McKay, the worker. There is a color in Mr. McKay's words at times that is sheer poesy. Then again you feel the sweat trickling down his own back. He bears a firm conviction in his heart that Negroes are beautiful even though their beauty is oft-times bowed beneath heavy burdens. He has given us a new side of Harlem, a side few Negroes would dare or wish to write about. This is the side of the Negro that a white man can never know except by proxy. There is no propaganda in this book unless it is that longshoremen, waitresses, et al. are a joyous people for all their drudgery. Claude McKay is content to let his message be that Harlem is shot with liquor-rich laughter, banana-ripe laughter . . . merging its life into a soft, blue-black symphony.

Banjo, by Claude McKay

Opportunity, Aug. 1929, 254–55

Here is a tale of the breakwater of Marseilles and of that human flot-sam and jetsam that is daily cast upon its shores. Through the pages of Mr. McKay's story move African Negroes, European Negroes, American Negroes, Irishmen, Frenchmen . . . one might even say that the people of the world pass flamboyantly through this new novel from the hand that wrote *Home to Harlem*.

Home to Harlem was the story of Negroes at work in America. Dishwashing, pullman-portering, stevedoring and then the sweet abandon that comes with well-earned rest. On the other hand, *Banjo* is a symphony of vagabondry. Here we have the loafers and other unfortunates who have been cast high on the shores of life by the tides of wandering. With the same palette he used in *Home to Harlem* the author daubs on the same rich colors, paints in the same turbulent stream of living. If there is one conclusion to be drawn from these two books of Mr. McKay's, it is that Negroes are always colorful, always interesting whether they be basking in contented leisure of work finished and coffers full or lying sodden with drink upon the beach of "lost men." It is with an unsullied curiosity that the author looks about him for the little earmarks that make Negroes out-standing in a world where all men are abandoned.

Banjo is longer, more studied than *Home to Harlem*. Yet there is little more plot to this new book than there was to the first novel. It is more the rambling mural of Banjo and his buddies, Malty, Dengel and Ginger than a composite picture. Briefly Lincoln Agrippa Daily, for that is Banjo's real name, has one passion in life and that is his banjo and the sweet, insinuating music his agile fingers make from it. Close to his heart is the dream of having a Negro band to play from cafe to cafe in the gay city of Marseilles. We follow him through the medley of his travels with a small group of musicians. He takes the love that Latnah, the East Indian girl, offers casually . . . in the code of the breakwater. And then Ray of *Home to Harlem* memories comes into the picture and becomes Banjo's fast friend. Jake, whom we knew in the earlier book comes on the scene for a brief moment. The book ends with Ray and Banjo cutting away from the rest of the "gang" to find new ports. Rather than the conventional idea of a solid plot with all events threading up, this book is a series of impressionistic scenes from the lives of several individuals in Banjo's "gang." And yet by some magic the book does not suffer because of this looseness. Perhaps it is akin to impressionism in painting where the aggregate of associated parts becomes a mental and emotional whole. One feels that after all life as a beach-comber would be just a hodge-podge string of events.

Again as in *Home to Harlem*, Mr. McKay is in native waters. This book is no superficial glazing of the surface of beach-life in Marseilles. Most certainly the author knows the lingo first-hand; he must have been in and out [of] the *bistros* he pictures hundreds of times. And who but one of Claude McKay's intellect, adrift in the by-ways of life, could reproduce so poignantly the many nuances of Negro thought and discussion. Here is where the book reaches supreme heights . . . in those heated discussions between Africans, Senegalese and American Negroes. The talk of Marcus Garvey, the blind devotion of his West Indian followers, the endless arguments on which nation is least prejudiced against Negroes—all this is typical to Negroes who at least have speaking intelligence and an abundance of time on their hands. It was the excellence of these scenes in the book that made me wish that there had been no attempt to tell a story but instead a personal treatise from the McKay viewpoint on life in the civilized world, being a Negro, and the conglomerate musings of a cosmopolite. He makes so many priceless observations. Latnah's resentment against Banjo, not because he was untrue to her but because she who was brown was left behind when he went in search of a white woman . . . that devil-may-care loyalty that Negro "hoboes" bear toward each other . . . the fine distinctions between the way African, West Indian and American Negroes acted when they were drunk.

No doubt this book will bring down upon its head the wrath of the circumspect, as did *Home to Harlem*. With this I have little patience. Granted that the book is filled with expressions that are considered risque in "the best" parlor circles. True, that it is for the most part concerned with slices of life that would in social surveys be considered sordid. In spite of these admissions I hazard the guess that Claude McKay was little concerned with the incident he was depicting. To him this tale was life as he saw it about him in Marseilles. There is no snigger of wrong emphasis in his discussion of the most taboo subject. He seems to tell his story with the same naïveté that a child has when it makes some shocking statement with no undercurrent of thought. I wondered as I read the book how the people who will criticize it from a moral standpoint would have written a novel around Marseilles. But I suppose the answer to that is that one should not choose Marseilles for a subject under any circumstances.

Banjo is a full-length novel, rounding out its three hundred some pages with solid writing. It has power and courage. And by a strange twist of life where ugliness may be intriguing, it has beauty.

o   o   o

Plum-Bun, by Jessie Redmon Fauset

Opportunity, Sept. 1929, 287

And now we have another book from the pen that gave us "There is Confusion."[1] This later book, "Plum-Bun," is of a little wider scope than Miss Fauset's earlier book. True, she has started the children who are to be the men and women of her book in the familiar background of Philadelphia; true, that the author is concerned with the same ordinary well-bred Negro of intelligence and education; but on the other hand this last book seems to come to grapple with a larger, more potent element in Negro life—passing for white. For that reason I am prepared to say that the theme of Jessie Fauset's second novel is of more importance in the scheme of Negro letters than her first book.

The story carries us with two sisters, Angela and Virginia Murray, through their childhood, spent in peace and calm in Philadelphia, to their adolescence when they both arrive in New York City—the one passing for white and the other caught in the warm, multicolored whirl of Harlem. The greater portion of the book is given over to the difficulties as well as pleasures that Angela encounters as a Negro who is passing for white. Miss Fauset has approached this problem through the interesting side-light of the opinions of the white people with whom Angela comes in contact. There is Matthew Henson, a Negro, who loves Angela in the old Philadelphia days; Roger Fielding, a Nordic, who loves her in the New York days; and Anthony Gross, who is, himself, a Negro almost forced into *passing*, through whose love Angela finally wins her way back to the race she has deserted.

Many there will be who will quibble over Miss Fauset's fortunate choice of incident by which all her characters and happenings are brought together.

This will not be altogether fair since "Truth is stranger than Fiction."[2] I'll wager that Miss Fauset could match every incident in her book with one from real life. I imagine this book will be even less convincing to members of the white race. They still conjecture over the possibility of a Negro's completely submerging himself in their group without a shadow of detection. But here again Miss Fauset can smile benignly up her writing sleeve and know whereof she speaks.

Most of us will see in many of this book's characters some of the real figures that people our Negro world. [Van] Meier and Miss Powell were fashioned. Then on the other hand most of [us] know a hundred or so charming Virginias. The models have not suffered from Miss Fauset's handling.

The author writes with a quaint charm about Philadelphia. One feels as one reads parts of the book that deal with Philadelphia that the author is with wistful reminiscence looking back into scenes that she, herself, has lived. There is a tenderness of touch that Miss Fauset bestows upon these scenes. I found particular pleasure in her apt, yet subdued, picture of Sunday afternoon in a middle-class Negro home. Her descriptions of New York scenes in the latter part of the book never ring with the same fervor that these earlier scenes do. I should like to see the author take some simple segment of Philadelphia life and write an entire book around that scene. I imagine that it would have all the simple serenity and mellowness that haunts the queer, little narrow streets of that city. Somehow, for all Miss Fauset's cosmopolitan wanderings, I feel that Philadelphia has left an indelible print on her heart.

The author of this story does not seem concerned to a great extent with the inner workings of her characters. In this day of over-emphasis on the mental musings of people and things this may be called a fault but I feel that the author was wise in not delving into the mental recesses of people to whom so much was happening. This is a task for a master psychologist. Who can tell how the minds of white Negroes work? Is it not a problem to stump the best of us that they who are so obviously white should feel a "something" that eventually draws them from the luxury and ease of a life as a white person back to the burden of being a Negro? Miss Fauset tells her story, packed as it is with the drama and happenings of a life of passing for white. It is better for the story that Miss Fauset avoided too much of a metaphysical turn.

When one has finished reading *Plum-Bun* one naturally wonders what Miss Fauset will write next. Most certainly she knows well the better class of Negroes who have been so long an enigma to the reading public at large. I think it fitting that she busy herself about bringing them to light. Books about cabarets, stevedores, et al. are prevalent enough. Why not this gentlewoman's pen that dips so choicely into the lives of black folk who go to school and come home to the simple niceties of living "just like all the white folks do?"

o   o   o

The Emperors Jones
Opportunity, Sept. 1930, 270–71

Now that the Negro as an integral part of the American theatre has come into being there must be standards by which to judge his ability and achievement. There are Barrymores and Sotherns[1] by which to measure a Hampden.[2] There are Marlowes[3] and Modjeskas[4] by which to measure a Cowl.[5] And so we come to the Negro whose outstanding interpretation in drama has been the ill-fated Emperor—that is, until the recent Othello of Robeson matched itself with the famous portrayal by Ira Aldridge.[6] I am willing to wager that for many a round year Negro actors will be spoken of in terms of their ability to do O'Neill's hectored character.

So far as New York columns are concerned we have had to date two outstanding Emperors Jones—namely, Charles Gilpin[7] and Paul Robeson. I had the rare good fortune to see the premiere of what I consider the other outstanding member of this royal family. On May 29, 1929, at the Hedgerow Theatre, in Moylan-Rose Valley, Pa., Wayland Rudd was presented as Brutus Jones.

Philadelphia with all its repressions and quiet dignity had turned out en masse. Inter-racial gatherings in Philadelphia are usually farces except in one or two rare instances. This was one of the rare instances. To speak of a theatrical premiere as an inter-racial gathering seems an anomaly. However, this particular premiere bore all the earmarks of a studied and planned meeting of the proverbial twain. Two bus-loads of colored people had gone from the square at the back of Broad Street station[8] with much ado and laborious checking of those present and much confusion about those not yet arrived. Of course the fine families of Germantown⁹ had driven in their own cars. Arriving, after a beautiful drive, at the theatre one came upon a scene of the most delicious pandemonium I have ever witnessed. It seems that the Negro contingent had come in legion although a much lesser number had been expected. It seems that there had been some understanding between Mr. Jasper Deeter,¹⁰ the spirit of the Hedgerow Theatre, and a little theatre group among colored people with whom he had been working that they were to have complimentary seats. They had paid their bus-fare; there was no returning until the bus returned with the entire group. The powers that were prevailed on Mr. Deeter and finally by some miracle he managed to crowd in everybody who had come at quite a loss to the house and with the same promise of "not soon again." With this fanfare the play was ready to begin . . .

It is difficult to speak of this particular production of the *Emperor Jones* without saying something about the Hedgerow Theatre itself. The movement, for it is a movement, is not new. It seems that it has been on foot some four years or more. Jasper Deeter, who acts as director of the theatre and also plays in the productions there, is really the power behind the throne. He is no long-haired intellectual with a flare for the theatre but a died-in-the-wool trouper whose name makes no small conjure along Broadway. You have but to talk with him to feel the fire and sincerity of the man. Jasper Deeter will always be remembered as the original Smithers,¹¹ a part that he still plays with convincing fervor. Mr. Deeter is well remembered for his superior directing of the original cast of "In Abraham's Bosom." Of this venture a journalist says, "While this play was being performed in the Garrick Theatre the directors of the Theatre Guild saw it, and for their production of 'Porgy' they selected all four of Mr. Deeter's principals, whom he had selected from the comparatively wide theatrical nowhere. One of the principals, Abbie Mitchell¹² was offered a role that was not to her liking, and elected instead of 'Porgy' Jed Harris'¹³ *Coquette*." This gives some idea of Mr. Deeter's ability to choose stars. This seems to have a direct bearing on the fact that he seems to have picked the best of the major three actors of *Emperor Jones*.

For me there was something fearful and contemptible about the Brutus Jones of Charles Gilpin; there was something almost childlike about the rollicking Emperor of Paul Robeson. Wayland Rudd did something that was a combination of both of these with a dash of something so poignant that it wrung your heart as you lived through the part with him. He seemed to give a larger futility to the role. He didn't seem so much a senseless bully caught in the toils of this own folly as a human being crushed by an insurmountable fate. For some reason words seem to fail me in describing just the shade of difference that made this portrayal more artistic to me than the other two.

In stature he is a cross between Robeson and Gilpin. He has that rich dark color that Robeson has. His voice has those organ overtones about which Europeans rave when they are heard in our blues and spirituals. If I seem eulogistic, I may be forgiven by virtue of the excellency of Mr. Rudd's performance.

I can't help wishing that the Hedgerow Theatre were in and around the New York center of drama. Such rare finds as Wayland Rudd should not be hidden even though in the lovely Moylan-Rose Valley. Mr. Deeter says that theirs is a theatre in which an actor may act in accordance with his ability and ambitions not with restrictions because of his type. When last I talked with Mr. Deeter he was planning to present "In Abraham's Bosom." I wonder whether Wayland Rudd played Abe. There are great possibilities before the Hedgerow Theatre. I'm a bit afraid that, although they have secluded themselves the world will make the proverbial beaten track to their door.

Introduction

Bennett's newspaper and journal articles, written in the 1920s and 1930s, are critically important to a broad audience as they discuss African Americans' place in the arts, including painting, music, theater, and literature, and in the community, including health and education. She published articles in a range of publications during this period, such as the *Howard University Record*, *Southern Workman*, *Better Times*, *Art Front*, and *Opportunity*. The focus of her discussion ranged from art and writing and the Negro's place in those forms to timely articles about the health and education of Negroes in the midst of the Great Depression. "The Future of the Negro in Art" is an early piece (1924) written while she was teaching art at Howard University. In it, she expresses pride in the contribution that African Americans have made in art, influencing such European masters as Matisse. She praises the talents of such painters as Henry Ossawa Tanner, Laura Wheeler, Albert (Alexander) Smith,[1] and Augusta Savage, while looking forward to the works that would be produced someday by her own students: "The Negro of ancient Africa has given us a heritage; it is for us who are living and learning in this day and time to guard and cherish the future of the Negro in art." In "The American Negro Paints" (1928) Bennett critiques an art exhibition by American Negro artists that took place between January 6 and 17, 1928, and poses the question "Did this particular exhibition create a wider interest in the work of the Negro artist as a contribution to American culture?" Although the position of the African American artist in Harlem during this period was at an all-time high, Bennett makes the case that with the exception of a few, "many of the pieces were not even of good academic technique." As someone who trained as an artist in the United States and in France, Bennett had a keen eye for artistic technique in various forms, including oils, drawings, and graphic design. Her assessment of the exhibition—sponsored by the Harmon Foundation along with the Commission of the Church and Race Relations of the Federal Council of Churches of Christ in America and on display at the International House on Riverside Drive in New York City—is a timely reminder that all African American artists need to focus on the quality of the work they produce rather than making a quick buck in a fast-moving artistic market. In her article "The Harlem Artists Guild" (1937) Bennett educates uninformed *Art Front* readers of the important work the guild has done since its inception in 1935 and continues to do, and reminds informed readers of how the guild "will continue its fight for the Negro artist's legitimate place as a worthwhile force in the society of which he is a part."

Moving away from art, Bennett also highlighted the everyday struggles people faced during the Great Depression and informed readers of the social welfare programs available to assist members of the community. In her article "The Plight of the Negro Is Tragic" (1934), for example, Bennett reports on the situation that many African American professionals faced as they sought to survive the Great Depression. Doctors, as Bennett and her husband knew too well, were one of the groups hardest hit. Those who sought careers that once seemed to lead to a promising future were now losing their homes, cars, and other assets. So, while a professional such as a doctor or teacher was seen as "a leader among his people," states Bennett, these pillars, too, were struggling. While others have pledged that African American teachers "have felt the effects of the depression less than any other individual in the professional group . . . [because their] salary has been cut only seven and a half percent," states Bennett, "relatives of teachers have been unable to get relief because of there being a teacher in the family. [Consequently, the] burden of supporting entire families has accordingly fallen to the teacher." Even ministers have not fared well in this current environment, states Bennett. With salaries cut by more than 50 percent they are in many cases struggling like their parishioners. While Bennett concludes her piece with one bright spot in the employment field—nursing—which has suffered less unemployment "than in any other professional field in Harlem," the objective of her article is clear. Everyone in Harlem, from the common man to the upper echelon, knew that professionals in many cases were facing a similar or more dire situation than was everyone else in the community. As Bennett states, "The professional group in Harlem [. . .] has been harder hit than any other similar group throughout the city." "The Negro professional man," continues Bennett, "by the very uniqueness of the community in which he lives has always been subjected to more trying conditions than his white associates."

In another example of Bennett's work in the community, she writes about the program for women supported by numerous groups, including the Brooklyn Urban League. In her article "I Go to Camp" (1934) she details the program that allows African American women and their children to travel to camp, relax, enjoy fellowship with others, and eat well-balanced meals each day. As Bennett writes, "For two weeks these women have regular, balanced meals, supervised rest and play. Both they and their children thrive upon the daily routine of fresh air and pure food. Nerves are relaxed and for the time being the worries of meagre home lives are forgotten. Although the June camp was not started as a relief measure for depression-stricken mothers, this project has yet served to carry these Negro women through the past four harrowing years."

The Future of the Negro in Art

Howard University Record 19.2 (Dec. 1924): 65–66

Few of us know that the art of the African Negro is the basic foundation of all the new schools of art in Europe. Since the art of Europe is the mother of American art this of necessity makes African art the parent of American modern art. Most of us think that the new school of art fostering Impressionism and Cubism as advocated by Matisse, Picasso and Cezanne was born of some nebulous idea out of the "infinite" in the minds of some one of these men. The fact is that Matisse and his followers became inspired first by African Sculpture and Modeling and from this inspiration received the impetus from which they evolved this thing they call "Modern Art."

It might be well for us to look into this ancient African art that so completely revolutionized art in the whole world. Clive Bell, one of the foremost art-critics of these times, has said that the Negro sculpture and art of its highest period deserves a place as enviable as that of the art of ancient Rome and Greece. Paul G[u]illaume,[1] at present the greatest living authority on Modern Art, has made the statement that the Negro art as exhibited in some of the sculpture of its best period is more to be praised than either the art of Greece or Rome. A.C. Barnes of Merion, Pa., has spent thousands of dollars in making collections of Negro art. To him belongs the distinction of having today the greatest collection of Negro art in the world. He numbers in his gallery some of the finest expression of a people's soul that was nurtured in the lush richness of the tropical continent of Africa. Masks whose line, imagination and feeling are a challenge to Benda's[2] subtle creation and a joy to the student of art—all a part of Negro art. Figures and figurines that rival all the gods and goddesses of Phidias.[3] Color combinations that are the embryo of modern impressionism. Negro art! The mother of to-day's new ventures into the beautiful—and yet how few of us know of the fact. So few of the people in the world know and concede that the Negro as a race has any heritage in art.

Granted a marvelous heritage from the soul of Africa then let us turn to the Negro in present day art. There is one name with which to conjure, i.e. the name of H. O. Tanner,[4] dean of Negro art and high master in the courts of fame of the world of the white man's art. Tanner with his vision of religious fervor and truth, painting the soul of the Negro love of warm color and deep feeling. Tanner who has caused the prejudice-crazed world to let down the bars of color and let a genius walk through to fame. Tanner has set the mark; it is for the younger and less experienced Negro artist to follow.

There are other names that call up visions of the coming of a real Negro art. Laura Wheeler,[5] winner of a Paris scholarship in 1913–14 and even now at work in France, has her distinctive place in the world of Negro art, a place that is steadily growing in its importance. And side by side with Miss Wheeler stands the figure of Albert [Alexander] Smith whose work in the medium of Etching has given him a place that is even an envy to the young white artist. True, he has been working and winning his way in Europe for several years now but back of it all we must not lose sight of the fact that he is a Negro, American-born and reared. [Alexander] Smith has a gift—a distinctive gift—as well as the stamina that must go hand in hand with genius. But let us turn to the Negro artist who is still in the embryo, the Negro with a vision and a hope.

Few of us know that there is such a person as Elmer Stoner[6] who daily works at his easel, painting, dreaming, hoping. Just an ordinary person to all appearances Mr. Stoner has the soul of art in him. It is almost a bomb-shell to disclose the fact that there is a young Negro whose name is Charles Keene who toils away at his art with indefatigable desire to scale the heights. Augusta Savage[7] still plies her modeling tool with assiduous care and amazing precision. And in like manner I could name a score of art students in the New York colony alone who are daily applying their time and efforts to art. But let us come a little closer home.

How many people know that right here in our midst at Howard University are students who have the divine fire kindled in their bosoms? A precious thing is entrusted into the hands of those who have the privilege to give them instruction in the precepts of art. One must step lightly for this may be holy ground.

As a teacher of the art students at Howard University I can see much in the future of the Negro artist. Let all of us who sense the burden of the future hold out a helping hand to those who may not be in touch with the art movements of the time. Somewhere in the South or in out of the way places may be dreaming and hoping a Tanner or even a Michael Angelo. The Negro of ancient Africa has given us a heritage; it is for us who are living and learning in this day and time to guard and cherish the future of the Negro in art.

The American Negro Paints

Southern Workman 57.3 (1928): 111–12

From January 6 to 17 an art exhibit was held at the International House on Riverside Drive in New York City. This exhibition was of work in the fine arts by American Negro artists, hung under the auspices of the Harmon Foundation and the Commission on the Church and Race Relations of the Federal Council of Churches. In the catalogue listing the works shown there was this foreword:

PURPOSE

The Harmon Foundation[1] and the Commission on the Church and Race Relations of the Federal Council of the Churches of Christ in America have placed this exhibition before the public in the hope of accomplishing three things: Creating a wider interest in the work of the Negro artist as a contribution to American culture; stimulating him to aim for the highest standards of achievement, and encouraging the general public in the purchase of his work, with the eventual purpose in view of helping the American Negro to a sounder and more satisfactory economic position in art.

It is in the light of this foreword that I looked at this exhibition. Had it reached all the goals its promulgators set for it, there could be no doubt of its success, and the likes or dislikes of any one individual would be of little account. But let us see whether this exhibition of work by American Negro artists lived up to the sanguine hopes of its fosterers.

Did this particular exhibition create a wider interest in the work of the Negro artist as a contribution to American culture? Had this last phrase been left unsaid I might have bowed my head in cheerful acquiescence. Certainly this hanging of pictures did create quite a widespread interest in the work of the Negro artists, but it is extremely doubtful whether it can be viewed in the light of a contribution to American culture. I wonder if those people who go into ecstatic tantrums over the Negro's contribution to American culture realize what such a contribution should entail. Mind you, I refer only to the pictorial and sculptural arts. Cultural contributions can only be judged in the light of their artistic permanency. When the pictures here shown are some hundred years old I doubt that they will have any greater value than that of personal record. Regarding them in comparison with the spirituals, which are without question a contribution not only to the culture of America but to the culture of the world, these pictures fall away to nothingness when evaluated as cultural contributions. I doubt if a hundred years from today this showing of pictures by Negro artists will receive more than a passing word of comment from the tongues of even racial historians. It seems to me that they lack the essence of artistic permanency. On the other hand, there can be no cultural contribution unless something distinctive is given, something heightened and developed within the whole form that did not exist before the artist's hand took part in its molding. But where in this exhibition is there any such deftness of hand? Mrs. Laura Wheeler Waring takes the spotlight for having used the existing academic form to its greatest advantage. However, sheer technical facility alone does not make for racial contributions to a culture in the making.

The committee on admissions took a rather roundabout way of realizing their second criterion. Surely the Negro artist needs no greater stimulant to aim higher than to have viewed as a whole the work hung at this exhibit. Many of the pieces were not even of good academic technique. I was surprised to see many pictures in which the actual drawing was out of scale. Here again the work of Mrs. Waring served the committee in good stead. Her work along with that of Palmer C. Hayden,[2] winner of the 1926 Harmon Awards for Distinguished Achievement Among Negroes in Fine Arts, Sargent Johnson,[3] Aaron Douglas, and Hilyard Robinson[4] gave the other competitors an adequate standard of proficiency by which to judge the work that they will send to the committee in the future.

And in accordance with the final aim of the sponsors many of the pictures and pieces of sculpture placed on exhibition were sold. This was indeed a good thing. It is extremely encouraging that most of these purchases were made by Negroes. Too long has the Negro waited for the white man to do his buying for him. However, I must quibble with the point of making a sound economic position for the Negro artist the "eventual purpose" of this exhibit. Seldom have the paths of economic surety and artistic freedom run parallel. It seems that higher aim than economic soundness would be a true expression of a real art.

The Plight of the Negro Is Tragic

Better Times, 12 Mar. 1934, 27

To prove that the professional group in Harlem—the Negro doctor, dentist, nurse, teacher, writer, etc., has been harder hit than any other similar group throughout the city one would need comparative figures which do not exist. However, even without such figures, social investigators who are well informed on the subject are convinced this is true. The Negro professional man by the very uniqueness of the community in which he lives has always been subjected to more trying conditions than his white associates. The reasons for this are many and varied. Barriers of color that thwart advancement, the lack of finances for post-graduate and specialized training, and the poverty of his clientele that militates against the charging of fees commensurate with the cost of equipment are a few of the contributory causes.

The depression has, of course, aggravated the need of all people. This is doubly true in Harlem where the common saying is that the Negro is "the first to be fired and the last to be hired." The Negro professional man is inextricably woven into the fabric of his community. The Negro doctor, lawyer, teacher is more than just a professional worker in Harlem; he is usually a leader among his people; his vision must see their need and he must interpret these needs to his white associates.

Nevertheless, the Negro professional man now finds himself in the position of a hanger-on whose talents and mental equipment are but slowly rusting tools, whose faith in the efficacy of training has tarnished, and whose hope for the future is uncertain. In many instances, motivated by an outmoded pride, he endures actual physical suffering without applying for relief. Greater even than his physical suffering is the spiritual anguish that he is undergoing with remarkable fortitude.

The Negro teacher, long considered the favored child of his group, has been reputed to have felt the effects of the depression less than any other individual in the professional group. However, the situation bears analysis. Although the teacher's salary has been cut only seven and a half percent and but a small part of it has had to be donated for relief work, his or her obligations have increased out of all proportion to the income received. Relatives of teachers have been unable to get relief because of there being a teacher in the family. The burden of supporting entire families has accordingly fallen to the teacher. This is, of course, true in communities other than Harlem. However, the Negro teacher in Harlem is a peculiar victim of the high rentals. In fact the cost of living according to the standards expected of them has remained extremely high for teachers and other Negroes in the various professions. The problem of the unemployed teachers is even more acute. Out of 173 applicants for jobs registered at the 137th Street Branch of the Y.W.C.A. during December of 1933, 65 were teachers. Unemployed teachers registered at this same agency during the first two months of 1934 are approximately half the total of all applicants for jobs of any kind registered during the entire year of 1933. Fortunately many of the unemployed teachers have been assigned to C.W.A.[1] work during the last few months, but there still remain scores of well-trained Negro teachers who have had to resort to house-work; many others are on the lists of the Home Relief Bureau.

Even Churches Closing Doors

The plight of many private music teachers is most abject. Some of them are forced to give music lessons for as little as twenty-five cents as hour. Many are giving church concerts from which they realize little more than five dollars after weeks of preparation. The instance of the graduate from the Juilliard School of Music, who after applying for work at various agencies for months was forced to turn to house-work, is more nearly typical than an isolated instance.

The story of the ministers is that of other professional groups. Congregations make smaller contributions to the Sunday collections. Mortgages and rentals have used up most of this money so that the minister's salary has had to be cut, in some cases by fifty per cent. Many smaller churches have been forced to close, throwing the pastor out of work.

Even at St. Phillip's Episcopal Church,[2] Harlem's wealthiest church, the yearly budget has been reduced from $50,000 to $15,000, and the church's large property holdings have been assigned for the next ten years for payment of taxes and interest on mortgages. This is significant in view of the fact that the membership of this church is composed of Harlem's upper classes including many of the professional group.

Of a dozen drugstores, owned by Negroes, only four now remain. Two druggists are now employed as janitors and one of Harlem's most prominent pharmacists and former drugstore owners is now an elevator man.

For a long time dentists and physicians have been considered Harlem's most successful professional men. Here too unemployment has brought havoc. Of thirty-four dentists on the clinical staff of one hospital in Harlem more than half are themselves in dire need, in the opinion of one close to all of them. One dentist of several years' practice in Harlem has been evicted from his office and practically all dental offices that in other years have been crowded are now strangely empty.

Few of the 150 physicians in Harlem are covering their expenses, in the opinion of one of their outstanding leaders well known to public health and welfare agencies. Even the most successful physicians in Harlem have seen a decrease in income of more than fifty per cent. At least ten per cent of the doctors of Harlem have entirely given up their practices and returned to the South or the West Indies. Negro physicians who have for years planned for their children to go to colleges of the highest type, find themselves unable to send them even to colleges of lower rating or, in many cases, to any college at all. A surgeon whose professional connections afford an intimate acquaintance with most Negro physicians estimates that twenty per cent of the physicians in Harlem are absolutely destitute.

One Bright Spot

The one bright spot in the otherwise depressing picture is the situation of the nurse. There is less unemployment among nurses than in any other professional field in Harlem.

o   o   o

I Go to Camp
Opportunity, Aug. 1934, 241–43

> *Here is one of the answers to child delinquency in New York. Miss Bennett is employed by the Department of Public Information and Education of the Welfare Council.*
> —THE EDITOR

A blistering day in July would hardly seem a good time to relive my two precious June days spent at Camp Normana in Interstate Park. It is proverbial that the fever-ridden patient thinks maddeningly of cool running streams and sequestered spots, dark with leafy shade. In like manner I wipe away the quickly recurring perspiration and live again my brief stay at camp.

The city was drenched with rain when we left for camp. Going to camp in the rain! It seemed utterly ridiculous but I knew anybody could go to camp in the sunshine. To see what happened at camp on a rainy day seemed more important than anything I might see on a day conducive to outdoor life. Even the mist-draped Hudson made a fitting drop for the dripping country-side.

"Let's take the back road into camp . . . it's rough but I love it so," said Miss Grace Gosselin.

We took the back road, deep-rutted and overhung with trees. Four miles of country road wound through the mountains studded with rain-sweet laurel. My experience with laurel had been limited to florists' windows and measly plants that ambitious landscape gardeners have sought to make germane to suburban homes. I was totally unprepared for the luscious pink blossoms that grew in such profusion on the mountain-side.

My going to camp was not occasioned by the need of rest or a search for pleasure. I went to observe a very humane venture that has been successfully at work for four years.

Miss Grace Gosselin, who had conducted Camp Normana for three years under the auspices of the Crotona Community Club, suddenly realized that it was a shame not to have so lovely a spot as this camp in use during June. It was at a luncheon of social workers that she first voiced this thought. Near her was seated Robert J. Elzy, executive secretary for the Brooklyn Urban League. As though by inspiration, she turned to him and asked, "Would you like to use Camp Normana during the month of June?" His affirmative answer was immediately followed by the laying of plans that have been in operation for the past four years.

Each June during this period the Brooklyn Urban League has sent a group of Negro mothers and their children, who are not of school age, to Camp Normana for a two weeks' vacation. The group is supervised by Miss Carolyn Dublin, social worker on the regular staff of the Brooklyn Urban League. Miss Helen Ray Walker, executive secretary of the Crotona Community Club, has charge of the camp during June and for the rest of the summer. Until this year as many as 110 mothers and children have visited the camp in two groups, each group staying two weeks. Only one group could go this year—20 mothers and 44 children.

This June camp is supported by a private contribution and by funds raised by the Brooklyn Urban League. It has usually taken approximately $1,000 to finance it. This year it was impossible to raise even so small a sum. This lack of funds, together with the fact that many of the women who attended camp for the past three years were employed on the CWS[1] Houseworkers Project, made this year's attendance smaller than that of any of the previous years.

The majority of mothers who go to Camp Normana are women from homes that have felt the depression keenly. The greater number of them are on Home Relief. Even those whose husbands have steady work are not able to afford this type of vacation, if they had to pay for it. The women are of a high grade of intelligence, many of them having completed a normal school[2] course prior to their marriage. A number at camp this year have been coming to camp every year since the opportunity was afforded them.

For two weeks these women have regular, balanced meals, supervised rest and play. Both they and their children thrive upon the daily routine of fresh air and pure food. Nerves are relaxed and for the time being the worries of meagre home lives are forgotten. Although the June camp was not started as a relief measure for depression-stricken mothers, this project has yet served to carry these Negro women through the past four harrowing years.

So important a part of their lives has this camp experience become to many of the mothers who have been going to camp every year that they have banded themselves together as a mothers' club. This club meets weekly at the Snyder Avenue Boy's Club, conducted by the Brooklyn Urban League. These weekly meetings are planned and supervised by the same Miss Dublin who works with the group while they are at camp.

For the most part these mothers are young women who have married early and who have had many children. One of them is only twenty-four years old and has had twelve children—one set of triplets, four sets of twins and one single child. Since the project began she has been coming to camp, bringing her children, only four of whom are living, and entering into the life of the camp with a joyous fervor that is unbelievable. Another of them who has also been coming to camp for four years is twenty-two years old and has nine children. Despite the fact that their lives have been set in a pattern far beyond their years, these women seem to revel in the child-like carefreeness that this camp experience brings them.

. . .

A day's rain had meant that the children and mothers had stayed indoors all day. The large recreation hall fairly rocked with the sound of children at play. Strangely enough the mothers displayed none of the nervous strain that a long rainy day in small crowded rooms would have brought. The children were put to bed early that night. As Miss Walker explained, the mothers were a bit subdued from a day indoors with the children scurrying about so that they sat quietly before the fire in the recreation hall. Some few of them played cards and ping-pong. Walled in by the rain that dripped slowly from the trees after the day's steady downpour, they seemed caught in a world that stood still. This first night gave a clear sense of what their brief camp vacation meant to them—a rare respite in which they recaptured the escaped happiness of childhood.

There was swimming in Lake Tiorata[3] before breakfast the next morning. The sunshine shone with such brilliance as to make one forget the rain of the day before. In the same manner the exuberance of the children and mothers bubbled forth. Breakfast was scarcely over before the children were at play.

Here we go loopty-loo-loo,
Here we go loopty la-a,
Here we go loopty-loo-loo—
All on a Saturday night.

The voices of little children in the woods! Their wavering treble had an elfin quality that seemed to fit the leafy setting. For a half hour they played ring games with Miss Williams, Miss Dublin's assistant. Then they went for a short hike with Miss Williams.

While they were gone, Miss Dublin held sewing class for the mothers. Such changes of occupation as this are supervised but you would never suspect it, if you could see the mothers like so many school girls giggling and chatting at their work. One look told the story that all was well here. It was a fine time to slip away and see Melvin.

Melvin is a little boy who wears a spinal cast and has been coming to this June camp for the past four years. His tiny, pain-ridden face lit up when asked how he liked coming to camp.

"I love to listen to the trees and the birds . . . when I'm here I don't mind being sick in bed," he said.

That afternoon the mothers went on a ten mile hike up the mountain to the fire tower. You would not have known Miss Dublin was a supervisor so much a part of the group was she. Although worn out when they returned to camp, they eagerly joined in the preparations for dinner.

A separate eulogy would be necessary to tell about the food at Camp Normana. "Chef" has been cooking for this camp for the past seven years. He is that rare combination of cook who can arrange economical meals for a large number of people and yet retain a home-cooking quality in the dishes he evolves. The mothers and children eat as much as they can hold— there are no set rations. The quantities of milk consumed by the children is unlimited. It is little wonder that Miss Walker points with pride to the fact that one mother gained eleven pounds during a ten days' stay at camp.

That night when the children were in bed the mothers held a frolic that would put to shame the gaiety of a debutante's ball. Pounds of marshmallows were toasted and eaten from sticky fingers. One of the number played the piano while the rest danced everything from a waltz to a carioca. And the games they played! There never was such merriment over "The Walls of Jericho"! [sic] "Follow the Leader," "Blind Man's Bluff," and games they must have originated themselves.

A long dreamless night and we were again on our way to the city. This time though dazzling sunshine laying warm hands on verdant hills. So rare had been my two days at camp that I could not even thrill at the fleet lying at anchor in the Hudson.

o   o   o

The Harlem Artists Guild

Art Front, May 1937, 20

With the assumption of its duties as part of the national steering committee of the Federation of Artists' Unions, the Harlem Artists Guild definitely comes of age. Organized originally with the intent of guarding the cultural, social and economic integrity of the Negro artist, the Guild within two years has arrived at the point in its development where it sees itself in relation to all artists, black and white. From such a point in its organizational development the Guild does well to pause in retrospective evaluation of its accomplishments up to the present time.

Following an exhibition of work by Negro artists, sponsored by the College Art Association and the W.P.A. in March, 1935, the Harlem Artists Guild was organized with less than a dozen members who saw the need for an organization that would have as its aim the welfare of Negro artists. Its present membership of approximately ninety artists has the same aims augmented by the growing understanding that the fate of Negro artists is identified with that of all other artists. The Guild plans to become more active in the organizational work of the New York Artists' Union, the Coordination Committee and the American Artists' Congress. While concerned primarily with problems peculiar to Negro artists by virtue of their bond of color and persecution, the Guild membership has been invigorated and heartened by the support its small number receives from the thousands of artists, banded together for their mutual welfare.

Part of the original program of the Guild was a plan for a Harlem Community Art Center. The Federal Art program in Harlem is now housed in the West 123rd Street Music-Art Center preparatory to moving into a large place devoted solely to art. The opening of the Mayor's proposed art center will go far toward materializing the program put forward by the Harlem Artists Guild. While supporting the need for an art center and critical of faulty attempts in this direction, the Guild is ready to lend its assistance to both ventures. The opening exhibition of the present Music-Art Center combined work done by the artists and children working under the guidance of the W.P.A., and paintings and sculptures by members of the Harlem Artists Guild. Attendance in the life-class at the W.P.A. center is part of the indoor program of the Guild. Through conference with the Committee of One Hundred, a municipal body headed by Mrs. Breckinridge,[1] and consultation with members of the Board of Education under whose aegis the proposed art center is to be set up, the Guild is keeping a watchful eye on the directions its organization is taking.

Employment of Negro artists has always been one of the Guild's major problems. When the Guild was organized, there were only a half dozen Negro artists employed on the W.P.A. project. This number has been materially increased. Through the efforts of the Guild, Negro artists are now employed in the teaching, mural, easel and index of design departments of the Federal Art Project. Before the formation of the Guild there was no Negro supervisor on the W.P.A. Projects; now in the Federal Art Project there are three Negro supervisors. Delegations from the Guild meet with the Administration of the Project and with organizations dealing with the problems of employment and quality of work among artists. In this connection the Guild hopes eventually to compile a roster of Negro artists from all over the country, their status—whether employed or unemployed—and their qualifications.

The cultural program of the Guild is steadily expanding. Lectures, symposia, and debates on technical subjects of interest to artists are arranged monthly for Guild members and associates. Sessions devoted to music, literature and other cultural subjects are offered to the general public once a month. Exhibitions of painting and sculpture have been shown in Harlem community centers and schools. An exhibition of work by the Harlem Artists Guild is being prepared for the American Artists' School. Through sketch classes, museum tours and lectures for the benefit of its membership and the community the Harlem Artists Guild seeks to create a cultural program that will ultimately place the Negro artist in a position of importance in the society of which he is a part.

The Guild sets out to combat those forces that keep the Negro artist from his place in the sun, to strengthen and aid those forces that militate for his good. The Guild stands shoulder to shoulder with artists and organizations fighting on a united front for the freedom and integrity of all artists regardless of race or color. It has given no quarter to ignorance and prejudice; no ground to malice and ill-intent. What will the Guild do? It will continue its fight for the Negro artist's legitimate place as a worthwhile force in the society of which he is a part.

Unpublished Works

Introduction

In addition to the aforementioned published poems by Bennett, our discovery of over fifty unpublished poems reveals another side to her artistry.[1] Her unpublished poetry shows a highly political and socially active author who was seeking change in and around Harlem in the midst of the Great Depression. This is reflective of a number of people, both African American and white, who turned leftward during the hard times in the 1930s. The unpublished poems presented in this anthology generally fall into two types: short poems about nature or loneliness, and poems of a more political nature. The first type is similar to her published work of the 1920s. "Two Poems," written while Bennett was in Paris in 1925, is a good example. The free verse poems are dominated by words such as "twilight," "gray," "shadowy," and "dusk," indicative of her early impressions of Paris. She writes, for example, in a letter to Countee Cullen on August 28, 1925, of feelings of "extreme loneliness and intense home-sickness." Around the same time (July 26, 1925) Bennett wrote in her journal that she was overwhelmed by "a homesickness more poignant and aching than anything." The poems' mood matches Bennett's despondency. In the first poem, "twilight" descends almost imperceptibly and provides "tenderness" from the speaker's "day-thoughts." In the second poem, "twilight-time" brings comfort not from the day, but from "night," which comes "With soothing weariness." Twilight brings with it "thoughts of home," which come "Like little, old, forgotten friends" to provide succor "Through the dusk / Of my loneliness." Another poem by Bennett, the undated, untitled Italian sonnet beginning "Across a room when other ones are there," is a more concrete manifestation of the speaker's loneliness. When the speaker is in a crowded room with her lover, they share a bond that unites them. They are able to tune out the people and noise about them and enter a "zone / Of singleness that we together share." However, when the two of them are alone, there is an "aching fog" that seems to separate them as they are unable to share their feelings with each other. Thus, ironically, the speaker is unable "To feel you half as close as with a crowd!" "Train Monotony" (1928) also fits this glum mood as the speaker states, "My days are like these fields, / Bleak stretches / With now and then / Some homely thing." The empty landscape serves "as a simile for the speaker's quotidian life" (Honey 98). In all four poems Bennett's loneliness is overwhelming. They reflect an inner turmoil and a sense of despair that belies the generally vivacious, highly animated personality others often saw in her quick smile and beguiling demeanor, which caused many to be drawn to her.

Bennett's later poems often take a less lyrical, more socially conscious tone than does her earlier work. As Brian Dolinar notes, "Bennett increasingly identified with the masses struggling to survive" (46). Since returning to the New York area in the early 1930s, when these poems were written, Bennett worked for several progressive—or as the House Un-American Activities Committee would later charge, Communist—organizations. These included the Federal Writers Project, the Harlem Art Center, the Harlem Community Art Center (which she directed for several years), and the George Washington Carver School (which she also directed). Many of Bennett's poems from the 1930s reflect her increasing interest in social justice issues.

After having lived in the South and experiencing overt racism, she could write with firsthand experience of life for African Americans there. In "Sweat" (1938) Bennett discusses the labor completed by African Americans "In the deep South." She goes back to the times of slavery, through the sharecropping years, as African Americans toiled "Beneath pitiless suns / Of cotton fields, / In orange groves, / Under tobacco sheds." Yet somehow all the sweat from these jobs has "baptized" the laborers and "Made [them] clean and sweet again."

"The Hungry Ones" (1938), written in free verse, speaks of all the poor, struggling people who must deal with finding enough food to eat on a daily basis. Written in five stanzas, the first four stanzas each end with a question, leaving the reader with disquieting, unanswered queries about the fate of all these desperately hungry people. For example, "Who are all the hungry?" at the end of the first stanza and "Are they all the hungry?" repeated at the end of the second, third, and fourth stanzas, reinforce the urgency of the situation. The final stanza gives a fearful answer. They will rise in anger and strike their hands "bleeding on the doors / Of those who feast incognizant who all the hungry are."

"Wise Guys" (1938), in contrast to the rural paean "Sweat," is a long urban tale. In it Bennett celebrates the many poor people, often marginalized as racial minorities or immigrants, who are all trickster figures in one form or another and do what they need to in order to survive. Whether they are Irish, Jewish, African American, or Italian, they are all Americans in the speaker's eyes, even if "The good citizens" may call them "public enemies." In the true spirit of American capitalism, they do on a much smaller (and more sympathetic) scale "what guys in Wall Street and Park Avenue / Do every day and get fat jobs for."

Bennett's vision for a united nation was also evident in her poem "I Build America" (1938), which could almost be seen as a companion piece to Langston Hughes's "Let America Be America Again" (1935). In it Bennett brings together everyone, from all walks of life, who have toiled away "Building America."

Bennett also expresses a concern for global affairs in "Threnody for Spain" (1939), written about the bloody civil war in Spain between the Fascist-backed general Francisco Franco, on the one hand, and the Communist faction, on the other. The poem was occasioned by the fall of Madrid to Franco's forces on March 27, 1938.

Bennett's at times politicized, socially conscious poetry reflects the period in which she lived and the frustrations many Americans, particularly African Americans, felt during the Depression. Bennett tried to publish many of these poems, but her "Communist activities," as dubbed by J. Edgar Hoover's FBI, which kept extensive records on her in the early 1940s, likely made it impossible for a publisher to consider her work. As William J. Maxwell writes in *F.B. Eyes: How J. Edgar Hoover's Ghostreaders Framed African American Literature*, even though Bennett "won acquittal [. . .] before a hearing at the WPA's New York Office," the "Bureau was a hanging judge, interpreting the hearing as reason to launch its own 'Internal Security' watch lasting until 1955" (88). In a note left in her papers, Bennett indicated that she published some poems in the left-leaning *New Masses*; however nothing under her name is listed in Theodore F. Watts's *Indexes to the* New Masses, *1926–33, 1934–35, 1936* and Bennett denied at the WPA hearing that she "had ever wrote under a pen name" (qtd. in Maxwell 88).

Two Poems

Paris, 1925

1.

Twilight is like a gray mantle
That drops itself stealthily
About the corners of my heart,
Covering my day-thoughts
With a tenderness.

2.

I shall always think of home
At twilight-time . . .
Just before night comes
With soothing weariness,
The thoughts of home
Will come
Like little, old, forgotten friends
To sit and chat a while
And nod their shadowy heads
Through the dusk
Of my loneliness.

o   o   o

Thin Laughter

1928

I heard thin laughter
Among ice-covered trees
In late December.
Thin, too, was the laughter
Whispering
Through the forest
When the last autumn leaf
Fell . . .

The moon wore a sinister smile
That August night
When we said <u>Good-bye,</u>
As thin laughter
Crept into my heart
And curled painfully
About my lips.

o   o   o

Train Monotony

1928

My days are like these fields,
Bleak stretches
With now and then
Some homely thing—
Houses or trees
Or tiny crooked paths
Where leaden feet have trod . . .
Drab stretches of canvas,
Taut between the pegs
Of towns or cities,
So my days . . .
Barren tracks
Between the mounds
Of some joy or sadness.[1]

o   o   o

Dirge for a Free Spirit

Hempstead, 1933

The minister crossed himself and said
That Death's dark angel hovered round your bed.

I saw your lips curled in a smile
Half scornful and I knew the while
They prayed your soul into a Paradise
You lay there mocking all their silly lies.
I knew that on some far and rain-drenched hill
Your lidded eyes would drink their fill
Of all the sweet and earthly things;
That birds for you sing sweeter songs than ever angel sings.
With arms flung wide in undecorous glee,
You'd clasp your dear dead body to a tree,
And digging deep into the earth
Your body shake in such unconsecrated mirth.

They laid you out in saintly white,
Surrounded you with candle light,
And knelt beside your flowered bier
Shedding for you tear on pious tear,
While all the time I knew
Heaven was no place for you.
They prayed for you and laid you in the ground -
I heard your laughter, such a wicked sound!—
Go gaily on the breeze
And tangle in and out the trees.
How should they know? Why should I tell
That you were happy now in hell?

o   o   o

Fulfillment

1935

To be with you is to know peace again
And the deep understanding of things.
The height of sky and depth of sea
Are become simple and plain.
The essence of time is contained

In the smallest moment and caught
In the imperceptible shift of sand and winds.
With you I am fulfilled
And made alive to all the pulsing things of earth.
No quickest wind nor swiftly rising tide
Can shake the deep peace of my understanding;
Nor quickened moment disturb the height and depth
Of my fulfillment.

o   o   o

[Give me your hand, beloved]

1935

Give me your hand, beloved,
That I may walk safely
Through the broken stubble
Of the long forgotten years.
Clasp my hand tighter
As my breath catches
At the sight of a broken flower
Or a fallen bird.
Guide my feet gently
Around the edge of bog or cliff,
Lay cooling hands
Across my eyes
That I may not be blinded
By the bright mirage
of <u>Forever.</u>

I Build America

November 30, 1938

I build America—
Mortared brick on brick,
And in with each I lay
The heart of all my brothers,
Dead from coast to other sea.
Mixed with gravel and cement
And sand, I turn the powdered bones
Of all the dead
Who lie from Canada
To Mexico's warm Gulf.
I am the dead,
Building America.

I died in a smelting furnace
White-hot and shining molten, I,
To make a bridge or singing rail;
My body flew winging
Through the walls of that great dam
That holds a waterway in steady check;
I am the top-soil,
Strewn over storm-tried Florida,
Where I, a thousand strong,
Lay piled against a mourning day;
It is my last breath
Soughing[1] through that burning coal,
Mined where the shaft fell.
That riddled thing,
Lowered by weeping Negroes
From a lynching tree,
Was me . . .
That dangling scalp,
Hanging from a Redskin's belt
Was mine . . .
And that slim, red body,

Laid high on a funeral pyre,
Had a bullet through my heart.
The red men, the black, the white,
Lying end to end
Beneath cities and towns,
In river-beds,
And under docks,
Whose dust is mingled yet
With farm and field
And growing grain for food or cloth,
Are one with me.
I died a thousand deaths,
A million strong,
In a thousand different places—
Pioneering, on battle-fronts,
In strikes, at the hand of brother citizens,
By lynch-ropes and with police clubs.
I died,
Building America.

And so . . .
I, the dead, build America.
My fleshless fingers
Build American cities,
Stretch bridges and pile up towns.
My unmuscled arms
Swing hammers and dig subways.
My sightless eyes
Survey the plains and chart railways.
All the cities and subways and trains
And bridges and people
Are my bones,
Covered with brick and cement,
With steel and rock and flesh.
From the empty space
Between my gaping ribs
I, knowing death

And understanding how life is,
Breathe a living song
Into the nation that I build.

I build America . . .
I, underneath the ground,
And rumbling through the air,
At work at machines,
Guiding roaring motors,
And teaching unborn children—
I am the dead,
Building America.[2]

o   o   o

Sweat
December 1, 1938

Bathed in an ocean of sweat,
All the black men stand, whose bodies
Laboring through countless noons
And nights,
Have been purged and made clean
By the odor and strength
Of sweat.

In the deep South
The black man's suckled food
Was mingled with his mother's sweat
Making him strong.
His wet back grew broad
Beneath pitiless suns
Of cotton fields,
In orange groves,
Under tobacco sheds,
And in the sticky heat

Of turpentine forests.
Songs grew acrid
On his lips,
As sweat rolled off his forehead
While heaving sacks
In a stevedore gang.
His melody grew sad
In his heart,
As sweat blinded his eyes
Peering through the gloom
Of cypress trees, rooted deep
Soft, oozing mud[,]
He sang a spiritual,
God-inspired and frenzied sweet,
And his sweat flowed.
The blood in him is mixed
With the sweat of black women,
Leaning over wash-tubs
And brightly polished stoves;
Mixed with the cold moisture
On the brow
Of men fettered to a chain-gang;
With the agonized sweat
From racked bodies
Bearing unwanted children;
With the chilled dew
On the face which met death
Upon a hill of pain
Beneath a charred and broken bough.
In his blood sweat flowed
Strongly,
Salting his wounds,
Saddening his songs,
Lengthening nights and days.
Swamps, fields, prisons,
Dingy back rooms,
Mines, boiler rooms, toilets,

Dining-cars, and kitchens and [P]ullman trains
Have reeked with the sweat
Of his black body.
His sweat has fallen on living things,
Making them rich and strong,
And on hopeful things,
Turning them bitter and sometimes dead.
His songs are tuned in sweat;
His dances measured by its trickle;
His story burned in words of sweat.
The life and death and little deeds
Of black men
Are nurtured and tended
And made to live and flow
By waters from their sweat.

In an ocean of sweat
The black man is baptized,
Made clean and sweet again.
Labor and pain and love
And joy and fear and hope
Have flung the black man high
On a swelling wave of sweat.

o   o   o

Wise Guys
December 2–3, 1938

We guys, gangsters,
The newspapers say—
We got a line on America . . .
We're smarted up, see.
Seems to us it's a slicker line
For us to get them
Before they get us.

You see, we wouldn't have no chance
Living straight and doin' right—
This country is a set-up
For the fall guy,
For the dummies that go in
For flag-raisin' and all that stuff.
We know . . .
We seen a lot in our day.
Our folks been livin' straight before us
And they never got nothin' for it.
That's a sucker's game—
We're wised up, see!

Take Guimpty . . .
All cracked up by a truck,
When he was a kid—
A truck owned by some big-shot firm.
The board of directors
Slipped his ma a couple of centuries,[1]
God knows she needed 'em,
And then forgot about him, see.
Well, after he got off the ward,
He got pushed around at the clinic
For a couple of months
And ends up with one hoof shorter 'n the other—
That's how he got his name,
Guimpty.
What chance did he have then?
His ma doin' day's work;
His pa dead;
His sister slingin' hash.
There wasn't no dough for doctors or nothin'.
What chance did he have
With him quittin' school
Cause kids poked fun at his guimpty leg
And not being able to get a job
Being cripple, you know?

But he got wise, the little mick[2] . . .
He runs a con joint
Over on the avenue.
What a guy!
The dicks[3] can't get a thing on him
With that limp
And them sad eyes
He keeps them all guessing—
He's a smart guy, Guimpty!

Now look at Izzie . . .
Him looking like the map of Palestine
In the face.
What chance did he have, being a Jew?
He'd either have to sit around,
Noddin' over a book
With one of them Jew caps on,
Or sell clothes
Or get a push-cart over on Delancey Street,[4]
If he wasn't so smart.
Why, he won all the prizes,
When he was in school.
He coulda been a doctor
Or lawyer or something,
Picking up a penny here
Or a penny there
And then maybe being framed
By some dame in trouble
Or some slick guy
Trying to turn a hot trick.
None of that for Izzie—
He's in the real mazooma[5] now.
Why, that little kike[6]
Is the best pick-up man
In this man's town.
They say he gave Dutchie
The dope on handlin' numbers—

Izzie said he couldn't be bothered
With chicken-feed!
Well, he's a wise guy
And packin' some real gold.
No on-the-level rackets for him,
Not Izzie!

And Shag Boston
Up in Harlem . . .
He ain't no dummy neither—
He's a smart black man.
Knows what he's doin' all right!
Came from down South . . .
Says a nigger never gets a break
In these United States.
Says his brother was strung up
By a mob
In Georgia
'Bout some white floozie[7]
He hadn't even seen or touched.
'Course, I don't hold with them
Mixin' with our women—
That's out—
But lynching—that's bad.
Shag's got something besides wind
In his nut.
He's got all them rug-cutters[8]
And pimps
And snow-birds[9]
And hot men
Toeing the mark in Harlem.
Said he wasn't fixin' to be no boot-black
Or porter or glory-shooter.
He ain't no guy
For piddlin' around,
Making a dime or nickel.
Money talks in America, Shag says,

And black money talks same as white money.
Believe me, he's got plenty of what it takes.
He's smart, Shag is!

And me, take me . . .
I ain't dumb neither.
I'm a wop,[10] see,
And cause my ole man
Ran a fruit stand
Till he got pneumonia and died
Wasn't no reason why I should.
Didn't take me long
To find out a quick dime
Beats a lot of hungry organ grinding
And spaghetti eatin'.
Then the war came—
I got a chance to see a lot of dyin' . . .
A lot of good, honest guys
Took the rap.
I was one of the best trigger men
On the East Side,
When I came back,
But I got wise to that, too.
They call me big-shot now.
Somebody else does my bumping off.
I'm worth plenty of green
And I know my way around, see.
I didn't make my pile
Playing marbles neither.
It didn't take schoolin'
To learn me that the guy that draws first
Gets the dough.
That's the way things run in America
And I catch on quick.
I run a benevolent association,
Control the fences, too.
I ain't no push-over, not me!

There's lots a other guys
I could tell about . . .
Smart guys that grew up right here
In America
And learned to read and write
And sell papers and shine shoes
And go hungry and cold in the winter.
You get smart being poor . . .
Guys get tired of being on the short end
Of everything.
They get wised up to the meaning
Of dog eat dog.
There's guys that never thought of
Stealing or doing nothing wrong,
That learned what was what
The hard way.
Frank and Touch and Ed and Johnny—
These guys got framed
And sent up to the Big House
For just being poor and looking suspicious
And not having no dough for lawyers.
They got a lot of fancy names
For guys like us—
Counterfeiters and procurers
Pickpockets and dope peddlers and jewel lifters.
When you go around
Waiting for a bullet
To rip your guts open any day
You get so you don't care
What people think or call you . . .
Guys like us are underdogs
And we know, if we wanna live,
We got to stay smart, see!

We guys, public enemies,
The good citizens call us—
We know what goes on here.

We're Americans, too, ain't we?
Don't take a Houdini to know
That less you're on the inside
Going straight don't mean nothing.
Seein' folks get pushed around and staying poor
Makes us mad . . .
We're smart enough to see
That what we do ain't no different
From what guys in Wall Street and Park Avenue
Do every day and get fat jobs for.
We string along and get ours
And pay income tax and vote like them
We do the dirty work but we hold our guts
Against getting shot and taking the rap.
We're smart but not enough
To understand the difference.

o   o   o

The Hungry Ones

December 4–5, 1938

The hungry ones go slowly forward,
Weaving, a long and sinuous line,
Through rich fields of grain
Past great barns stored with food,
Granaries, packing-houses, refrigerators,
Past all of these the hungry go.
Flanked by plenty, they go starving,
Dragging weary feet from one breadline to the next,
And ever on the fruitless tramp,
Holding their coats and stretching out their hands,
Asking always the same piteous question:
Who are all the hungry?

Children, pale and pinched,
Walk in pathetic files
Before shining windows,
Shielding operations in large bakeries,
Watching loaves of bread wheeled by
And loaded into fine, shiny trucks.
Thousands and thousands of loaves of bread,
Giving off warm, sweet odors
That pervade the air,
Filling the nostrils of children filing by.
These pale children—
Are they all the hungry?

Men, irresolute and desolate,
Crouch close to buildings,
Yearning toward the small opening
Through which will come the bowl of soup,
Symbol of hungry days on days
And manly pride destroyed.
Bowls and bowls of tepid soup,
Sending a thin stream of warmth
Through veins but all stopped off
With rabid courage for each tomorrow.
These desolate men—
Are they all the hungry?

Women, crazed and desperate,
Go fearfully to market and store,
Clutching small coins or holding nothing
In hands eager for kneading bread
Or touching vegetables and good meat
To make their men and children strong.
Thinner and thinner the women grow,
Planning, and rocking, and biting their nails,
They hold their frantic babies
To teats inadequate of warmth or strength.
These desperate women—
Are they all the hungry?

More than these the hungry slowly go,
An awful, swelling desperate world
Of women and men and children,
Pathetic, desolate, irresolute and crazed,
Those hands are always stretching forth
Toward some warm, steaming thing
To stay the gnawing fire their bodies hold
And give them strength for one more morrow.
And when tomorrow comes
These poor, irresolute and hungry ones
Shall rise their hands and strike them bleeding on the doors
Of those who feast incognizant [of] who all the hungry are.

o   o   o

Threnody for Spain
1939

<u>Teruel and Barcelona,</u>
<u>Guernica and Tarragona,</u>
<u>And the beautiful Madrid!</u>

The lovely names of Spain are hushed today—
Their music, whispering with a muted tone,
Caresses softly mounds of restless clay
Where urgent seeds of liberty were sown.

While silver-clear above the quiet plain
There cuts the voice of all the loyal dead
In challenge to the ones whose living pain
Must forge again the sword for which they bled.

As counterpart to what the dead men say,
There sweeps the flagrant tyrant's martial tread—
Immune to brother blood which they betray,
They lay a petty price on freedom's head.

Cordoba and fair Granada,
Oviedo and Lerida,
And the fabulous Toledo!

The beauteous names lie blood-soaked on the way
The alien hordes have forced their cruel gain,
But plaintively, beneath the loud affray,
A song is weaving like an argent[1] vein.

From out the bosom of the earth there rings
A keening melody, both dread and sweet.
From every tortured Spanish throat it wings
And journeys fast along each shell-torn street.

Its clarion call affronts the silent air—
The note of courage from the unborn years—
And bugles forth a tune to thwart despair
In hearts of men who grieving shed no tears.

Oh, beat the solemn drums for fair Madrid,
And sound a dirge for those who lie at Teruel!
Across the Ebro fling a muffled chant,
And click a mournful measure with the castanets
For Oviedo and for Barcelona,
And tread a stately dance for all the lovely Spanish towns . . .

The lovely names shall not forgotten lie,
So long as flowers bloom in future Springs,
And every newborn blade of grass shall cry
The meaning of your bitter sufferings.

The noble valor of your stainless cause
Shall consecrate the nations of the earth,
And men from still unseeded wombs shall pause
In glorious tribute to its timeless worth.

And from your soil and from the bones beneath,
For those who quest anew a Golden Fleece,
A sword shall rise, undaunted from its sheath,
To cleave a path for universal peace![2]

[Across a room when other ones are there]
n.d.

Across a room when other ones are there
I feel your hand reach out and grasp my own.
As close to me as though we were alone,
Your fingers wander gently through my hair
And twine about my heart, though unaware
The people's voices round about us drone
Nor can they ever cross into the zone
Of singleness that we together share.

Secluded in a room with no one near
We say our words unhampered and aloud,
And listening I seek some accent clear
To cut the aching fog that seems to shroud
The thoughts your mouth would tell my willing ear—
To feel you half as close as with a crowd!

o   o   o

[Rapacious women who sit on steps at night]
n.d.

Rapacious women who sit on steps at night
And beckon to men whose will it is to pass
Are part of Harlem,
Part of Harlem's fetid life.
The scrawny cats with bellies low
That creep along the gutters after rats,
Claw-footed, scurrying toward the city parks,
Are like the hungry Harlem children
With fingers scratching garbage out of cans.
The rats like men with furtive eyes
Seek cover in the leveling dark.
A part of Harlem, too, are those who stand,

Eyes worried, on a waiting line that asks relief
And, wounded, begs a crust to eat, a pallet on the floor.

Who looks at Harlem with a lecher's glance
And sees the wide-spread grin and hears its beat
Must pull his belt against the chance
That he might meet the deadly scavenger that stalks the street.

o   o   o

[So this is how it is]
n.d.

So this is how it is
Remembering a love that never was.

Thinking again how your hand
Rested lightly,
Almost with faint disdain
Upon a chair
In a room I never saw,
I licked my tongue
Across my bruised mouth
Which your lips had never touched.
The page turned down—
Had you stopped there?
Did your impatience with a printed word
Lay mutilation on the tranquil page?
That sound that suddenly rushed by
Was just a ghostly whisper
From your silent, pulsing throat,
And I hold warm
Within my aching palm
A something which I cannot grasp.

I now remember . . .
How my heart had ached before
Squeezed thin of pain
And saddened by a sweet forgetting
Of a love I never knew.

UNFINISHED NOVEL

Introduction

It is difficult to know exactly when Bennett was working on her unfinished novel *The Call*, but it was probably between 1928 and 1932. While there are only scraps of chapter 1 extant, Bennett does provide a brief outline of the spiritual journal the narrator, Minerva Edmunds/Edwards[1] (fittingly, the name evokes the Roman goddess of wisdom and the arts), would take from her small Southern home town to the big city. There, she becomes a spiritualist and meets a singer. Eventually, he drains her of money and leaves her to have affairs with white women. Though fragmental, the piece does provide a tantalizing taste of Bennett trying her hand at writing longer fiction, one of the only such examples we have from her. We also see her attempting, with some deftness, to use Southern black vernacular. In addition, she demonstrates her poetic and painterly skill in several descriptions, for example when she states that "one sable arm [of Minerva] was festooned with bracelets of soapsuds," or that "the sun cut in pitiless slashes of heat through the roof of the wash-shed." She describes the "twanging" of the screen door, and gives the scent of a woman who "emitted the mingled odor of cinnamon, shoe polish and perspiration" to provide a vivid scene. Most important, we perceive her ability to capture the homely lifestyle and the warmth that exists within the family. Even in these short selections Bennett has established Minerva as a strong, vibrant character, one who deeply loves her father and is willing to face the scorn of the gossipy community in order to mourn his death in her own unconventional manner.

Chapter Outline for the Unfinished Novel *The Call*
n.d.

Outline for a novel as per Rada and I.[1]

Chapter One: Introducing Miss Edmunds in her home town in the South at the age of twenty. She receives a <u>call</u> to go to the city.

Chapter Two: She comes to the city—gets work in private family who upon death of the father split up and go traveling in several directions.

Chapter Three: Gets work in laundry and her reputation as a medium grows.

Chapter Four: Establishes herself as spiritualist.

Chapter Five: Success. Weave street singer in slightly through letter from home telling of strolling singer.

Chapter Six: Introducing the singer as a magnetic person. He hears a call to go to the city, leaves wife and child.

Chapter Seven: Meeting.

Chapter Eight: She supports him. Their simple happiness. Schooling etc.

Chapter Nine: He becomes a drain because of his intellectual friends.

Chapter Ten: She becomes a faker and he is taken up by the Van Vechten type of person.

Chapter Eleven: She loses hold of the confidence of her clientele and in vain efforts to get hold of the call cannot get in touch with the spirit.

Chapter Twelve: He meets more white women . . . she sees change in him. He leaves her and goes to Europe.

Chapter Thirteen: Concert—at which uninvited she attends, shabby, ticket bought with last penny, hears him . . . repetition of street incident . . . polite applause until he sings classics . . . other woman . . . show contrast her and them . . . last call . . . She is drawn to go back stage but does not go because she feels out of place. She goes out.

End.

Name of the book: The Call.[2]

o   o   o

Excerpts from *The Call*

c. 1928–1932

Chapter One

I

The sun cut in pitiless slashes of heat through the roof of the wash-shed, laying stripes of light on Minerva Edwards' back as it bent backward and forward over the wash-tub. The steady rubbing across the wash-board seemed unstudied and without purpose in its monotony until she half-straightened herself at the bench and the pattern of her black hands upon the hard white twist of a garment showed that one more piece had passed the first stages of its cleansing. She scarcely turned her head as she dropped each piece of clothing into the large basket a few feet to her side. Occasionally [she] stopped to wipe the perspiration from her forehead with the corner of her apron. The length of time and the ardor of her work could only be measured by the increasing frequency with which she wiped her forehead or the increase in the patch of dark dampness that showed between her shoulder blades on the blue dress she was wearing.

"You, Min-er-ervah!"

It was the call of her mother, rending the sunlit monotony that had made the pile of snowy garments that now reached the edge of the large basket. She stopped, leaning one dripping hand on the wash-board as she caught her breath before answering.

"Min-er-ervah! You'd better come in de house and get yo'self somep'n to eat."

"Aw right, ma."

She turned back to the wash-board and rubbed out two more pieces. She ran her hand in a circle around the water in the tub and caught up two handkerchiefs which she rubbed between her knuckles. Once more she reached down into the water to make sure she had washed everything. One sable arm was festooned with bracelets of soapsuds as she raised the wash-board from the water and rested it against the side of the shed. She picked up a large white rag from the bench beside the tub and spread it neatly across the clothes in the basket. Her preparations for leaving the wash-shed were unhurried; there was about her every movement an undulating calm almost of detachment. As she stepped through the door of the shed, a lizard that had been sunning itself in the path scuttled away into the grass.

As she walked across the long yard to the house she looked as a Millet peasant[1] might look on a canvas darkened with age. Minerva had just turned twenty years but there was a womanly serenity about her that did not seem in keeping with her youth. The black satin of her skin was tightly drawn over large bones and strong muscles. Her blue cotton working dress was held to her rounded figure by a black and white checked apron. The hot Florida sand did not seem to burn her bare feet. The black wool of her hair was neatly wrapped with white cord and lay close to her head in an intricate pattern of criss-crosses. Her features were full but her eyes robbed them of their sensuality. They were the eyes of an old sea captain, clear and far-seeing. Her eyes did not seem trained to the ordinary things about her but gave the impression of looking through and beyond what other eyes saw. She turned from the path to walk down a row of the bush-beans that grew on one side of the yard. Stooping she picked one or two grub worms from the ground near the beans. She crushed them with a stick and rose with a sigh. She stopped several times on the way to the house; once to pick up a clothes-pin; once to pick up one or two pieces of paper that had blown into the yard from the road beyond the front of the house. She stopped in a strange moment of awareness on the step leading to the back-door of the house, then with a curious baffled feeling opened the twanging screen door and stepped into the kitchen.

Her mother turned from the small coal-stove where she was stirring grits.

"You mos' nearly done wid du washin', Minerva?"

"Yes'm. I got Mis' Crowley's clo'se through du first rubbin' and I reckon Missus Yale's clo'se is mos nigh hard enough fo' sprinklin' by now. I ain' been down du yard to feel 'em yet. Mis' Mairy ain' brought hern yet, have she?"

"No, you know how dem folks is—dey done even get up till most nigh noon an' Mis' Mary allus brings de clo'se husself."

For the time being there seemed nothing more about which to talk. Minerva, holding the screen-door open with one hand and fanning her apron with the other, attempted to rid the room of flies while her mother put a plate of fried salt pork and a bowl of hominy grits on the table. She broke off two pieces of corn-bread from the golden circle in the frying-pan and put a lid over the remainder so that it would keep warm. They sat down. Both hands were bowed reverently as the mother made this prayer:

"Lawd, make us thankful fo' de food we's 'bout to receive and fo' all udder blessin's fo' Jesus' sake. Amen."

Minerva murmured and answer[ed] "Amen."

"It do look like yo' paw don' git no better."

"Po paw. How's de misery roun' his heart dis mawnin'?"

"Jes de same. Look like he kinda choke up in de night. He ain' slep' a wink tell jes 'fore [until just before] you went out dis mawnin to start de washin'. He's still sleepin'. Ef he keeps on sleepin' I reckon aw'll be able to hep you wid hang'n out de clo'se."

"Dat's all right. I'll be able to manage. Miss Crowley's clo'se is so clean I don' reckon dey need no boilin' this week. I'll fetch Missus Yale's clo'se fron off du line and you kin damp um down fo' me an' den you won' have tu leave du house. Ahm goin' tu try to git her big pieces ironed off dis evenin'."

"Do look like it's a shame you cain' go to Tavares wid Sally an' them dis evenin' for to hear de singer deys goin' to have at Shiloh. Maybe you jes' oughta leave de clo'se an go anyhow."

"No'm I wouldn feel right leavin' you here by yoursef with paw so poorly. A change is lible to come any minute and I'd wanta be here, if it did."

"Minerva you sho' is a good chile. De Lawd's gonna bless you fo' lookin' out fo' your paw and me dis a way."

She reached over and laid her horny hand on Minerva's arm. There was an embarrassed silence between them for a moment as though this tenderness were out of place between them whose lives were filled with such everyday things. Minerva squeezed together a piece of bread and holding it in all her fingers mopped up the last of the bacon grease that was left on her plate. She picked up her plate and knife and fork and carried it over to the dish-pan that was on a large packing-box that served as a table. Lifting the newspaper from the bucket near-by, she dipped up some water which she drank in one long draught. She laid the dipper on the table and wiped her mouth on the corner of her apron.

"I'll be goin' back to du clo'se now, ma."

"Aw right Minerva."

THE FUNERAL

The heat snuggled oppressively around the ragged shanties of Egypt. Life seemed slowed down to an expectant quiet as noon blazed its way across the sky. No children at play disturbed the blanket of silence that hung over the hot sandy place. Birds were still; no people were astir.

Sister Mary Anderson sat fanning the flies from over the dead body of Pa Edwards as he lay in state in the tiny front room of the Edwards home. It wasn't respectful for the living to let flies disturb the sleep of the dead. Sweat trickled down the side of her face from her greasy hair. She stopped now and then to mop her forehead and to wipe the sweat from the many creases of her neck. In the kitchen Minerva and Sister Lucy Green were busy preparing food that was to be served later on the tables that were laid in the back-yard just beyond the wash-shed. As Sister Green turned about the kitchen she kept wondering at the calmness of Minerva. It didn't seem right for a person to be so quiet when her own pa lay dead in the front room. One of the other sisters of the church had volunteered to help with the cooking but Minerva had said that she would do it. Sister Green went about her work absent-mindedly as she kept thinking that it just wasn't natural for Minerva to work with such a will. She ought to have been in the bed-room where Pa Edwards had died with her ma whose moans could be heard by the workers in the kitchen. Twice Minerva had left the kitchen to go into the front room where she had stood quietly beside her father's coffin. Each time she went to the coffin Sister Anderson had straightened herself expectantly, hoping that at last Minerva would break into the loud mourning that was characteristic of colored people at the time of death. When Minerva simply smiled tenderly down at her father, Sister Anderson settled disgustedly back to her fanning. After her second trip to the front room, Minerva remarked upon reentering the kitchen:

"Sis' Green, he do look beautiful laying in there. Jes lak he was sleepin'."

Sister Green omitted a sound perilously new to a snort and stirred the corn-bread she was mixing more vigorously. Minerva looked about quietly to make sure everything was about ready for the funeral feast then turned to prepare herself for the funeral.

"You goin' tu git ready now, Minerva?"

"Yes'm, Mis' Green."

"I holler cross de back fence fo' Mary Jones to hurry up wid de black dress she's pressin' out fo' you to wear. She ain' wore it since her Ma died come three years."

Minerva hesitated for a moment.

"You needn't bother Mis' Green. Thank you jes the same but I ain' goin' to wear no black dress."

"Ain' gonna wear no black dress?"

She leaned against the table for a moment, dumbfounded by such heresy.

"No'm, I ain' goin' to wear no black dress. Yestiddy I done washed out my white usher dress fo' to wear. Pa allus liked me to dress in white."

"Gal, you cain' do dat. Evybody what has someun die wears black. Do look lak outa respect fo' de dead you would put on black."

She fought hard to keep back the other thoughts that were seething in her brain. Minerva turned quickly around. Anger flashed beneath the faraway film in her eyes.

"Dont yawl go talkin' 'bout respect fo' de dead. Dat's my business what I wears to my own pa's funeral. I done been a good daughter to him and Ah cain' have no mo' respect fo' him dan dat. When he gits to Heaven tonight he ain' gonna be worrying his head bout whether ah's wearin' white o' black. Yawl cain' tell me bout how to respect my own pa."

The look in Minerva's eyes and the sharpness of her words made Sister Green turn again to the stirring of the bread she was making with a troubled,

"Laws a mercy."

Minerva turned sharply on her heel and walked quickly through the front room to her bed-room beyond. Sister Anderson watched her until the door was shut then rose from her seat beside the coffin and hurried to the kitchen door.

"Ain' dat awful, Sis' Green. Ah ain' never heared o' nobody goin' to dere own pa's funeral widout wearin' black."

"Ummh, chile, don' say nothin'. That Minerva allus were a funny gal walkin' roun' lak a ha'nt.[2] She ain' never let out nary a cry since her pa died. It ain' natchul."

A bustle at the front door made them both turn from their whispering. Mary Jones was entering with a small child following her, carrying a large parcel wrapped in newspaper. She was a large woman with skin so black that there wasn't even a shine to it. Her large bosom was strained into a black silk waist trimmed with ruffles of black lace. She wore a heavy black skirt of woolen material. On her head she wore a black hat of stiff straw that smelled faintly of shoe polish. Her large hand clasped tightly the handle of a purple silk umbrella. As she billowed into the room she emitted the mingled odor of cinnamon, shoe polish and perspiration. Her face was wreathed in a broad smile that betokened joy at setting out for a festival.

"Lawsy, yawl done lef' the dead to be et up by de flies."

The conference at the kitchen door broke up in a flurry. Sister Anderson scurried to the side of the coffin where she began fanning rapidly. Sister Green began to turn the batter into the waiting pan. Mary Jones stood in the middle of the front room just as a star might as she awaited the applause to die down after her entrance on the stage.

"I done brought de black dress fo' Minervie and de veil I wore when Caleb died fo' Mis' Edwards. Come here, Jenny, gimme dat pa'cel."

Sister Green came back to the kitchen door.

"You done waste yo' time. Minerva ain' gonna where no black dress."

"Ain' gonna where no black dress?"

Sister Anderson stopped fanning.

"No she shore ain'. She done tol' Sis' Green where tu git off when she tried tu tell [her] dat it want respectful not to dress in black at her pa's funeral."

Soon the three women were together at the kitchen door whispering and gesticulating in the heat of their discussion. Flies swarmed, unheeded, about the dead man. Jenny stood, one bare foot upon the other, tracing circles on the side of the coffin with a grimy finger moistened with saliva. In her bedroom Minerva lay across the bed with her face buried in her pillow, her body shaken by great, dry sobs. In the next room her mother rocked to and fro with her arms tightly crossed over her bosom, moaning loudly.

Outside the heat still hung like a thick cloak about the worn shoulders of the tiny shacks.

FIRST VISITATION

The mocking bird suspended its song on one solitary minor note. The night air seemed to drip with an eerie silence. The moonlight was torn by the ghostly fingers of Spanish moss that hung from dead Florida pines. A something rushed through the stillness that surrounded Minerva as she sat fanning herself on the porch. The rocking-chair in which she was seated was in the shadows of the porch so that her face could not be seen. The chair creaked sharply as she sat stiffly upright, dropping her fan and clutching the arms of the chair. She sat in the charged silence of fear for a moment or two. Slowly the chair gave a creaky sigh as her muscles relaxed themselves back into their former position. Her hands slowly released their grasp. She sat for five or ten minutes with her entire [body] being released into the pregnant stillness about her. A shudder shook her as she clutched nervously at her bosom. In a hushed voice she murmured,

"Lawd, have mercy."

The night sounds surged back filling the void of silence. The mocking bird flew to another bush and took up his song where he had left off. A cricket began to fiddle away at his chirping tune. A frog croaked in the swamp beyond the trees. Minerva arose suddenly and rushed into the house to her mother's bed-room. She hurriedly reached the side of the bed, arousing Ma Edwards from her first troubled doze.

"Ma, he done been here. He done talked to me . . ."

The hysteria in Minerva's voice jerked her mother roughly from her sleep. She sat bolt upright.

"Who done been here? What you holler'n so 'bout?"

"Paw—I done heared him . . . I done seen him."

"Hush, gal. It ain' fitt'n fo' you to talk lak dat when yo' paw ain' even cole in his grave. You mus' be crazy."

"No'm ah ain' crazy. I tell you I done seen him. He done talked to me."

Minerva was quieter now; her voice more insistent.

"Sho as I'se bawn to die I done seen him an' he done laid his hands on me."

"You mus' be sick—you ain' et nothin' today."

Minerva's quiet insistence had touched her incredulity. More quietly she said,

"But maybe you is done seen him. What he done say?"

"He done talk quiet lak he usted to when he was preachin' an' he said, 'Daughter, God done called you. You gots to go from here. De Lawd done choose you fo' his band.' 'Den he smiled at me an' put his han' on my shoulder an' Ma, I felt sweetern I did when I got religion."

"What he mean when he say, 'go from here'? Dis his own house what he build fo' us two wid his own hands."

"He don' mean dat. I'se sho he don' mean dat. Seem lak he was tellin' me to go clean away from dese parts."

"You ain' gonna leave yo' ma, is you honey?"

Fear made her speak tenderly.

"No, ma, he gonna fix it somehow so dat evything's gonna be all right. I fell it in ma soul. De ways gonna be showed to me."

Suddenly she felt tired as though she had been through some physical struggle. Fatigue seemed to drug her very thoughts.

"Ma, I'se tired. I'm goin' to bed."

"Aw right Minerva. You ain' got to wash in the mawnin' so you kin sleep till good sun-up."

"Yes'm. Goodnight, ma."

"Goodnight, chile."

The simple things of her life had reclaimed the one whom God had chosen for his band. She tied a white head cloth around her head. With a relieved, "ummmh," she took the shoes from her unaccustomed feet. She climbed into bed and pulled the covers tightly up to her chin for although it was summer the night was cool. The air was filled with the quiet symphony of night-sounds. Soon she fell asleep.

ESSAYS

Introduction

In addition to her poetry, many of Bennett's unpublished essays[1] are particularly illuminating about life in 1920s France, 1920s and 1930s Harlem, and 1930s Florida. Taken collectively, they present the outline of an autobiography (notes in her papers indicate this was her ultimate intention), and they often provide information about her life available nowhere else. The essay "My Father's Story" is the most significant source about Bennett's troubled childhood. It is also possibly her most personal piece, one that she says "may never be written . . . it never has been written because it is still, after many years, too close to me for printed words." The essay not only tells of her father's upbringing and his rise to prominence as a lawyer but also Bennett's own somewhat idyllic youth growing up on an Indian reservation. These halcyon days do not last, however, as her parents frequently quarrel, leading to their estrangement. Her mother took primary care of Gwen, while her father was granted visitation rights. One fateful day, though, when her father was supposed to take her on an excursion to Mount Vernon on George Washington's birthday, he absconded with her. The last childhood memory she has of her mother is "as she kissed me 'good-bye' for I never saw her until some sixteen years later."

These early years are also documented in the pieces "[Ward Place]" and "Lancaster, Pa." The former essay discusses her memories of her life in a poor area of Washington, DC, when she was only about five years old. Here, she has fond memories of dressing up in her favorite color of the time, red. It was "a sweet, remembered place," recalled Bennett, yet it was also tinged with sadness, embodied by the melancholy cry of a fruit vendor selling his wares. It is a sound, notes Bennett, that still brings a lump to her throat when she hears street vendors. In the essay, it is clear that Ward Place also had harsh memories for Bennett. It was where she was sexually molested by a young male babysitter and was also the site of her first realization of her parents' troubled marriage and of her father's philandering. The latter essay, "Lancaster, Pa.," details the early years after her father had abducted her and the family was living on the run. Her memories here are dominated by times spent living at the Elite Hotel, being entertained by vaudeville performers residing there, going to the movies and theater with a young friend, and eating candy that was so delicious, nothing she would eat after could compare. In a way, the candy encapsulates Bennett's childhood memories in this essay. They are recalled nostalgically, filtering out the unpleasantness of being uprooted abruptly, remembering instead only the happiness of being with her father.

Bennett's essays then move from her childhood to her early twenties, likely written between 1925 and 1927. "Let's Go: In Gay Paree!" concerns the year Bennett lived in Paris (between June 1925 and the summer of 1926). It is a lively, humorous discussion of African American dancers, including Louis Douglass and Josephine Baker. The Charleston, notes Bennett, had taken Paris by storm: "Every vaudeville house, every cabaret, every dinner club and every tea-dansante twirls to wild joy of the Negro's dance." Bennett conveys the excitement of seeing Baker perform the dance: "Her long shapely 'nigger legs' fly this way and that with a rhythm and beauty that is maddening. Her sleek black head turns this way and that as she twists her face into all sorts of ludicrous masks. With warmth and beauty she carries the rhythm of her race through a revue that is world famous." "25" (Bennett reached that age in 1927) perfectly captures the feeling of arriving at that somewhat charmed age. As she says, "There is something quite round and perfect" about it. It is often an "imperceptible" dividing line between periods of one's life. There is a confidence and experience that one did not have earlier, and also an optimism (and naïveté) about facing the future. It is this confidence that allowed her to fit in at such an early age with the writers and artists of the Harlem Renaissance.

"[Life as a Javanese]" sheds light on the troubled time after Bennett resigned her position at Howard University over her relationship with her future husband, Alfred Jackson. Desperate for money, Bennett turned to her art background, gaining employment making batiks. Despite having extensive training in this art form, Bennett was fearful of being rejected for the position because she was black. Consequently, she "passed" as Javanese in order to get the job. Though somewhat flippant in tone and with a "happy" ending, the essay has a more serious side, showing how blatant racism could cause an intelligent black person to try to pass for another race, even one that is nonwhite, and how easily the dominant race is often fooled by the disguise.

Much darker and even more powerful than "[Life as a Javanese]," the essays "[Ku Klux Klan Rides]" and "Last Night I Nearly Killed My Husband!" reflect Bennett's traumatic years in the South. "[Ku Klux Klan Rides]" discusses a frightening encounter between Bennett and Jackson with members of the group on March 30, 1929. The young married couple were paid a visit by "the ghostly cavalcade" after problems arose between the husband and some local white Floridians, particularly a pharmacist the narrator claims had said to one of her husband's patients, "We don't fill nigger prescriptions in this town." The narrator depicts a tense moment as the Klansmen slowly approached the couple's home: "There, some fifty yards away from the front of our house, came the ghostly cavalcade, driving in fearful, hooded silence up the one paved street in the Negro district of the town. [. . .] There was an eerie luminosity from the mingled low car-lights and the great, sheeted figures visible in the open automobiles being driven at a funeral pace." Here she uses inversion to slow their movement to a crawl, extending the sense of drama: "Almost they didn't move, so slowly they came." Minutes later the narrator notes, "Their white robes were grotesque as they come across the wide street to our front yard. There must have been a dozen hooded Klansman stepping onto the little rise of ground that served as a pavement before one entered our front yard. The first one had already started into our little dirt path. It was just about ten feet now to the front porch." With the Klan encroaching on their home the narrator recalls astonishment that the menacing band abandoned their initial desire to terrorize the couple as they became distracted upon seeing a rare tree growing on their property. Though the woman expresses with relief the Klan's decision not to terrorize them further that evening, she notes their brutality when she says, "The Klan had ridden about five miles beyond our house to the home of an 'uppity nigger' whom they had given a severe beating from which he had never fully recovered. From his house they had cut across short roads to Umatilla where they had tarred and feathered a well-to-do white man, a northerner, whom they had surprised in the bed of a much sought-after Negro prostitute whose name was Lily." The serendipity of Bennett's escape from the Klan illustrates the precariousness of life for African Americans in the South.

Bennett's other largely personal essay from this time period is the powerful "Last Night I Nearly Killed My Husband!" The semiautobiographical work is essentially a study of the slow, painful disintegration of the once seemingly idyllic union of Jackson and Bennett. Not only did the couple have to deal with the racial terrors of the South described in "[Ku Klux Klan Rides]," but they arrived in Florida at the most inopportune moment possible. In late 1928 and early 1929, there was a devastating infestation by the Mediterranean fruit fly that destroyed the citrus crop and, with it, the Florida economy. The couple decided to pack up stakes and move to Hempstead, Long Island, a relatively inexpensive, largely white, middle-class suburb of New York City. Unfortunately, the financial trouble the couple was trying to escape in Florida was compounded in New York when Wall Street collapsed in October 1929, leading to the Great Depression. The small savings the couple had amassed was soon depleted. The medical practice was destroyed. Not surprisingly, constant fights between the couple ensued, and the doctor in the essay turned to alcohol and another woman for relief. To make money, he performed illegal abortions. Trying to save their marriage and themselves, the wife takes a job with a publishing house; however, to get the job, she has to claim she is single, as the work requires a great deal of late hours. This brief lull of happiness lasts for about six months, until she is asked by her job to take an apartment in Manhattan. She does so, but continues to commute to Long Island, which is a contributing factor in the disintegration of her marriage: "It wasn't long before my life was one round of parties, dinners and night clubs." Still in love with her husband, but feeling overwhelmed, she contemplates suicide or killing her husband. It is only due to her realization that "killing myself would not solve his problems; killing him would only add to my sorrow," that she rejects the idea. Handwritten notes by Bennett for the story, on the manuscript in her papers, indicate that she planned an eventual "happy ending." However, unfortunately, in actuality, as in the extant story, there was no such ending.

The final essay we include, an untitled piece we label "[Harlem Reflection]," captures the surprise and frustration many African Americans felt during the Depression years, particularly after the heady days of the Harlem Renaissance. Like many of her other essays, Bennett chooses to remember an earlier time in the best possible light. In her essay she details how much Harlem has changed since the 1920s. Contrasting 1920s Harlem with the Harlem she found in 1935, Bennett's description is so vivid and personal that readers can visualize those drastically different decades. Bennett writes, "When I left Harlem in the late Twenties it was still characterized by the remnants of that period known as the Negro Renaissance, in which writers, artists and musicians frequented the night clubs and restaurants of the district and engaged in a more or less literary interchange among themselves. [. . .] In those far days there was still a certain debonair carefreeness to Harlem." Bennett notes that while there existed at the time "selfish gaiety the work-a-day life of Harlem, and close beneath the veneer of Harlem's reputed night life and emotional freedom lay that strata of life in which poverty and deprivation are boon companions with every family. But just the same, one still could walk from 7th Avenue and 135th Street North and be caught and swept along by what many white writers termed during their period of discovering Harlem as primitive abandonment." Fast-forward to 1935, however, and Bennett was perplexed by what she found: "I cannot begin to describe the shock I received. I had been in the South and seen their poverty and privation among Negroes and had steeled myself against it with the feeling that if I could only return to Harlem, there again I would find warmth and laughter. Harlem itself seemed shaken in the same type of shock that I was experiencing." In a state of disbelief, says Bennett, "dazed, I went to some of the old haunts where they still existed. I found no gathered group of intellectuals but rather the angry mutterings of Negroes who had come to seek the reason why. [. . .] I felt like some drunken soul [missing word] from place to place through the streets, into churches, community houses, schools, not only to find everyone busily seeking, seeking some solution for this tragedy that had descended upon them. I stayed indoors, I didn't want to see it, I didn't want to believe it. Where was Harlem?" Given Bennett's key role as a central figure of the Harlem Renaissance, her first-hand account of what she and the rest of the community are experiencing, and how sharply it differed from the Renaissance period, this article will be of great interest to readers of the anthology.

My Father's Story
n.d.

This story may never be written . . . it never has been written because it is still, after many years, too close to me for printed words. So that if in the telling of it you find me going off on emotional tangents be lenient for I cannot tell this story without telling it with all my heart and in that heart there are still places that have not healed with time.

I can easily imagine I see my father as a child—a sturdy little brown boy with his dusky hair tightly curled upon his little upright head as he looked with clear, innocent eyes at his mother as she told him at her knee the miraculous tales of slavery that her mother had told her and as she told him the stories from the bible that children so love. Even then his sensitive mouth, which never as thick as are most colored people's, must have drooped a little in childish sympathy for some forgotten black sufferer. Then again I can imagine I hear his limped clear laughter as his father came home from the white barber-shop he ran on the main street of that tiny Texas town. For that was his childhood as the youngest of a family of eight boys, eight boys in a family that worked hard but ate well in a little southern town . . . a childhood simple and sweet unmarred by the tragedies that were to follow his hectored days.

Then again I can see him as he stood a young man just entering college with eyes glowing for having reached this goal. He must have been living again his mother's old story of David and Goliath as he thought back over the endless rows of cotton he had picked and the potatoes he had hoed to get to this place. But there he was starting on his chosen path, the youngest and smartest of the boys who must be given his chance because his quick brain would become dulled having to do hard labor. So he started toward the great world that was to receive him, honor him and then kill him.

Prairie View College[1] never turned out a more brilliant student nor a smoother orator. Younger than most of the members of his class I have heard tell of how he stood on the platform time after time and held both students and faculty spellbound by his easy flow of words. A prominent white educator from the north was present delivering his valedictory address and when it was finished the educator turned to his neighbor one of the local potentates and murmured fervently . . . "That boy will go far."

It was an easy matter for the school board in a neighboring town to waive the matter of age and have as the "professor" this brilliant young man. In like manner was it easy for my father to see and win as his own the warm, beautiful woman who was later to be my mother. She was clever and entertaining and as a teacher in his staff of coworkers she was head and shoulders above the ordinary run of southern colored girls he had met. The color of ivory was her skin and her hair [was] straight and black like her grandmother's, a thorough-bred Indian. With the same ease that was characteristic of everything that my father did this young couple soon obtained positions as teachers in a government reservation for Indians in Nevada. Only two years had passed since they met but they carried with them the small bundle of brownness that now writes their story. It must have been a beautiful ride across those lonesome prairies for that young couple as they set out to conquer the world.

Those must have been marvelous days for them . . . close to the pulsing warmth of primitive peoples. Even I can remember from some where in the dim recesses of my baby subconscious mind the nights when the Indians reached back into their past and donned their war paint and danced the dances of the tribes. Nothing but beauty had touched their lives and mine in those far days.

Time flew swiftly from that time until I remember myself in a red dress with hair neatly curled and topped by an enormous bow of red ribbon walking to and fro on a small back street in Washington, D.C., waiting for Dad to come home from the office where he was a government clerk. The story of how he struggled and studied and equipped himself to be one of the fastest stenographers and clerks in the government service had been lived with the same ease that most things came to my dad. With the same persistent brilliance he started about his studying for the law at night in the local Negro Law School. Three years passed swiftly and found him passing the district board with ease and distinction. But these years of steady application had done something to the little clear-eyed boy who had listened so eagerly to the story of David and Goliath.

His eyes were no longer used to the long stretches of prairie and the great expanses of sky . . . his vision had narrowed down to the measure of city streets. And in the same manner his bright spirit had been toughened with the endless struggle to get ahead. I dont know what had happened to him but some thing hard began to creep into his nature. On the other hand my mother had spent the years in between caring for her baby and watching a new being develop and mature. I suppose that in some manner her own bright mind had been narrowed down to the small duties of home. Through the years of struggle she had not had time to keep pace with her brilliant husband, so concerned was she with making ends meet. A coldness sprang up between them. It was only natural that with the ease that he did everything my father should turn to the brilliant woman whom we shall call Genevieve with whom he had matched wits nightly at the law school.

I remember so well as a small but precocious child hearing the endless quarrels between my parents both of whom I loved with a passion which [was] more than the love of a child for its makers. Those years of struggle had made me more than a baby; I had been my mother's sole companion and confidante. Those were frightful years with my father's trying to establish himself as a lawyer and my mother's daily feeling more and more his lack of gentleness and attention. My baby heart ached with the horror of what was happening between them. It was such a far cry from those soft Indian nights on the prairies.

My mother's struggle began then. She tried many ways of getting employment opening first one form of business then another. Finally she went to work in a prominent private school for wealthy girls and took me with her. We were happy there, she and I. All the girls liked her and the school employed a large staff of workers so that her work was easy. I was going to the public schools and already beginning to show signs of being the bright child that should have come of such a union. Every Sunday my mother dressed in the pretty clothes she had sewed so beautifully at nights after her work was over and sent me with a young girl who was a friend of hers to visit my father. Oh, those were happy, long-to-be-remembered days. I must have had a good deal of my father in me for I too liked the escape from the solid domesticity that surrounded my life with my mother. With her I had already begun to feel that I was not quite up to the standard of some of the other little colored girls with whom I went to school . . . some of the daughters of doctors and professional men had upon occasion taunted me about not being able to give parties at my house because I lived with white folks. I remember well having come home crying to my mother with the stories of these painful thrusts. The following week was my birthday and my mother gave a party for me in the large beautiful back-yard that belonged to the finishing school. The party was in full sway and we children were exuberant because of the ice-cream donated by the directress [of] the school and the many presents and favors which the girls of the school had given to make the party a success. I was entertaining in a way that none of the families of the other children could afford and but few parents had refused to let their children come to my party. The gaiety was at its height when one of the wealthy neighbors called asking the directress to please have the noise stopped that we were making. I can just about imagine the name she used in speaking about us to the other white woman who was my mother's and my friend. As I look back on it now it must have been a pitiful thing to see my mother scurrying about, sending someone to the nearest druggist to buy ice-cream boxes, the small sized ones, filling them with the uneaten ice-cream, quickly slicing the birthday cake with no ceremonious blowing of candles and bundling off my guests before the childish happiness caused any trouble for the school. Let me say here that I never had another birthday party until I was eighteen years old. That was my life with my mother but not so on the Sundays and holidays that I visited dad. With him I was a person and he was somebody, a promising young lawyer. We did all the things that were fondest to my heart. He took me to dinner with families where I played with the children of the family with no shadow to cross the horizon; we went to the theatre, to restaurants for dinner, we went for long car rides and to all sorts of places of amusement, we laughed and played together. My father always seemed to be free from cares and worries; there was no job to which we had to hurry back; no pennies to be pinched for future necessities. I was indeed happy with him. As I look back on that time I think how pitiful it is that we cannot weigh values as children and also how my mother's heart must have ached as I jubilantly recounted our adventures to her at the close of these happy days with my dad.

These days something happened to my father, too. He found that I was getting to be a person whom he enjoyed; whose mind was developing; a daughter of whom he might someday be proud. Something of the old gentleness had been touched and he found himself fed up with his freedom and wishing that he too might have a part in the fashioning of my life. And so it was that he hit upon a plan to have me all for myself. I had always longed to go to Mount Vernon the home of our great George Washington. It was easy for me to tell dad the things I wanted to do and

I, who had heard of Mount Vernon in school was constantly prating about going there. As George Washington's birthday drew nearer he and I began to lay our plans. My mother was party to our excursion too. She had made me a pretty new dress and bought me new shoes for the occasion. I often have wondered in later years whether it was a mother's intuition that made tears come to her eyes as she kissed me "good-bye" for I never saw her until some sixteen years later.

o o o

[Ward Place]
1941

How can one reach back into the memories of childhood?[1] It is easy enough to recall some definite incident—some special thing that happened, some person or place. But to reach back into the sweet, far-off sounds or smells. How to achieve the memory of something that is now nothing more than an atmospheric memory—an unimportant nostalgia.

A street, no doubt ugly, but all the same the first street whose name I knew and a street which I have always remembered. Ward Place, Washington, D.C. Later, as a grown woman living again in Washington, I asked a friend what and where was Ward Place. Although the person could not tell me where Ward Place was, I gathered that it was somehow "across the tracks"—somehow not quite nice to have even asked about it. But for me it was a place compounded of many far off memories. Brick pavements it had and, as I can reconstruct it, small, I am sure unkempt, two-storied brick houses with one or two wooden steps before the front door, steps that I later came to know as "stoops."

My memory of the street has no beginning and end and there is no way to establish a beginning when I came to live there with my family nor an end when the family moved into another house. As I think back on that street, I seem to remember first my being dressed "for the afternoon" walking to and fro waiting for my father to come home from work. A small brown child, dressed in a red muslin dress with many fine ruffles at hem and neck, and wearing high-buttoned red shoes. As I remember it, I always wore white stockings in those days and so must have been wearing them on this first remembered walk. And my curls—even then it was something of a ritual to have my mother curl my hair freshly, using much water, for the afternoon. And always my hair topped with an enormous red ribbon. Red seemed to be the color I wore most in those days—days when I must have been about four and a half or five years old—at least red was the only color I seem to remember. Somewhere a little later on I remember putting up a howl for chocolate brown shoes with tassels and still later I remember developing into the stage of pinks. Well, anyway, Ward Place seems to fix itself in my memory with that particular afternoon on which I was dressed in red for the afternoon, walking to and fro waiting for Dad to come home from work. Nothing happened on that walk, nothing of that afternoon comes back to me except that around it seems to float the very essence of what Ward Place was to me and has always been—a sweet, remembered place—a street out of many streets on which I have walked, and always as I look back at "each chartered" street[2] I remember it with a nostalgic sadness—not just the nostalgia of things past and out of sight but as though all my life would be a succession of streets or remembered moments spent on some street.

Other memories of Ward Place jostle against one another and have always done so through the years. It was there that I first consciously heard a huckster's cry. A drowsy summer afternoon when my mother had made for me "a pallet on the floor"[3] for my afternoon nap. The fact that I always took an afternoon nap begins to establish in my mind the fact that I must have been quite young then too. I started school when I was just about five years old and remember very well that I did not start school from the Ward Place address. There I lay on my pallet, as children lay awake, being quiet and absorbing sights and smells that will go with them all their lives. I heard a huckster cry from his wagon, "Wa.a.a.—termellonnnn," with a sad rising inflection that comes back to me now in memory as one of the saddest sounds I have ever heard. Through the years, unimportant as it is, I always have been able to close my eyes and remember that sound, that particular afternoon, that particular sadness. The same lump always rises in my throat whenever I consciously hear a fruit vendor call out his wares. [. . .]

It was on Ward Place, too, that I first saw a penis. The twelve year old son of the family with which we lived showed me his. My mother and father had been out for the evening and had left me in this boy's charge.

When they came home I was crying because the boy had made me catch hold of his penis—never having seen anything like it, I was frightened and was in the act of being chased by the boy to do his bidding when my parents came home. I don't remember much else about it but the boy's fright at being caught, my father's stern remark that he would talk with his parents about the whole thing. I don't believe my parents said much more to me about the whole affair except that this boy was bad and that I was right to run from him. Nothing about sex and the difference between little boys and little girls was said, and it was not until many years later that I knew how such an occurrence might have conditioned my whole life.

Another memory arises from the time when we lived on Ward Place—the memory of the first quarrel I had witnessed and understood between my mother and father. I don't know how I came to know or understand that my father had what was called in those days, an affinity. And yet know it I did and well enough to inject myself into their bitter argument. I remember holding myself upright by the foot of the large wooden bed in which I had apparently been put to sleep and screaming at my father through the intensity of their quarrelling, "I hate that nasty Jeannette Carter." Perhaps my mother, overburdened with sorrow had talked either to me or in front of me. I shall never forget the look of half shame, half fright on my father's face. And that is all I remember about that quarrel.

Ward Place—what an incongruity of memories arise from my childhood days there! The memory of the street is the flawless memory of childhood and yet here already were the seeds of what my life was to be like. When I look back on my child hood I seem never to have been young. If there is a place from which to start remembering, it might easily be Ward Place in Washington, D.C., for from that point on life for me has never been without care.

o o o

Lancaster, Pa.
n.d.

I never knew how Dad chose the places to which we went in our long pilgrimage which never reached the shrine of Mount Vernon. We'd stay a year in one place and then suddenly with some engaging promise of newer, more exciting scenes he would announce that we were going to a new city. And in this way it came about that we went to Lancaster, Pa.

The Elite Hotel where we stayed has always been a source of wondrous memories for me. It was a great barnlike mansion of a house run as a Negro hotel by Aunt Frances, daughter of "Grandma Scott." One of the first things that impressed me about it was its name, the Elite Hotel, the meaning of which Dad was careful to explain to me. A real hotel! And an elite hotel at that! Imagine what these two ideas joined together would mean to a little colored girl who was nine years old! Over the fairly impressive doorway of the place there hung a great sign on which its name was lettered in blue. All night long this sign creaked back and forth on its iron rod, frightening the long minutes when, my mind filled with Grandma Scott's ghost stories, I could not go to sleep and punctuating my dreams. The four or five steps leading up to the doorway were of white marble. The fact that one of them moved about insecurely was explained by Grandma Scott by the fact that a ghost was keeping watch over a treasure buried under it. [. . .]

The people who lived in this hotel from time to time were no less extraordinary than the house itself. There was an intermittent stream of Negro vaudeville actors who travelled the regular circuits, occasionally hitting Lancaster. They were a motley group of second or third rate performers who always gave passes to members of the family. Odd snatches of memory come and go when I think of these vaudeville actors—memories that are difficult to catch and make intelligible. Of all those people I met I remember only a very beautiful, statuesque woman of a light cream color, with fine, uncurling hair piled high on her head in a wonderful pompadour who used to play the piano in the dining room and sing songs to me as I sat beside her. The songs I remember her singing were To You Beautiful Lady I Raise My Eyes,[1] Come Hero Mine from the Chocolate Soldier,[2] and Silver Bell,[3] an Indian song with the head of a beautiful Indian girl on the cover. With less clarity I remember a man and his small, brown wife who wore a bespangled oriental costume on the stage and in whose act an ordinary white reed clothes basket figured in a way I do not now remember. All I remember of a male quartette is that they practiced "Mr. Jefferson Lawd Play that Barber Shop Chord" interminably in the dining room.

In fact, the theater in one way or another began to be a part of my life in an active way in Lancaster. Frankie Scott, a nephew whose family lived across town in the colored section, went with me often to the the-ater—sometimes we would go as often as twice a week more often than not making use of the passes given us by the performers. As I remember it there was a moving picture house and an Opera house where drama and vaude-ville played interchangeably. Frankie was a stern, over-religious boy several years older than me. He always treated me as though I were a silly little girl and yet even then I could sense a repressed pleasure which he seemed to take in going to the theater and to church with me. Once we went to a movie entitled "Written in Blood."[4] It was a tale of a man who through the vicissitudes of fate and the machinations of his enemies in the grand style had been confined in exile to a turret of a wonderful castle that I have always remembered. Somehow a dove appeared at the grating of his prison room. He tore a piece of his shirt, slashed his arm, and wrote in his own blood a message that effected his release. It must have been a mighty dumb movie as I look back on it, but even at nine years of age I had begun to be a romantic girl. As we left the movie theater I sighed to Frankie, "Written in blood—isn't that wonderful?" He answered curtly, "Girls are so silly. What's wonderful about it? The only thing I liked about it was the fight-ing." Frankie was going to be an evangelical preacher when he grew up. In 1937 I met him at the National Negro Congress in Philadelphia and found him a moody longhaired young man with radical tendencies and wild eyes who said he had been so much in love with me when I lived in Lancaster. [. . .]

A small, light brown, well-dressed woman came to the Elite Hotel twice while I stayed there. Through the understanding that comes with the years I marvel when I remember that she was a travelling representative for the Martha Washington Candy Company.[5] Her coming brought delight to Frankie's and my hearts for always we had as much of the wonderful, rich Martha Washington candies as we could eat. I remember hearing her tell how she had started in the firm as a candy stirrer and had risen through being a chocolate coater, box packer and through other branches of the industry to be a representative—I imagine something of a salesman and demonstrator—for the company. Whenever I read articles or books about Negroes who surmount the barriers of color in the industrial or educa-tional world, I often think of her and wish I had remembered her name. Always I have thought of her as a pioneer. I have never forgotten the story she told of how, when she was first employed with the company, she was told to eat as much candy as she wished. Martha Washington Candy is so rich and wonderful that it seemed a wonderful thing to be able to eat all of it she wanted. As the company had expected, she ate so much of the candy that she had to go home sick at her stomach. After that she not only did not eat any more of the candy but eventually developed an actual distaste for candy of all kinds. As for us children at the Elite Hotel, the Martha Washington candies were like ambrosia. Through the years the memory of that candy has been able to stir my taste buds as no actual candy ever has since.

o   o   o

Let's Go: In Gay Paree!
n.d.

Authentically the advent of the Charleston into Europe is due to one or two unimportant turns done by second rate vaudeville actresses in the music-halls of the old world. However, the extent of the fad thus created may be measured solely by the length of the column devoted thereto in the European editions of American papers:—Tille So-and So introduces the Charleston; or Mollie O-what-Not brings new rhythms to the old World, etc. Even Paris, the New York of Europe, passed through these preliminary stages undisturbed and unmoved. Doubtless, these surface ripplings of chorus and ballet dancing in Paris that had come down as a pre-war heritage did much to prepare the way for the present-day madness that has swept away some of the former gaiety to give place to a more hectic and strenuous pursuit of pleasure. Oh, yes, the Charleston had been introduced in Paris but it never took a foothold here until October of 1925.

On the night of October second, <u>Le Revue Negre</u>[1] held its premier at the Champs-Elysee Music Hall with Louis Douglass[2] and Josephine Baker as the co-stars. With this opening came the fury that has swept over the gayest city in the world. A gorgeous curtain by Covarrubias[3] depicting water-melon pickers, stricken in the midst of typical jazz gyrations, was well in keeping with the <u>tempo</u> of the piece itself. Saxophones sobs [*sic*] while a black drummer went mad over a pair of cymbals and two slender sticks. Eight dusky chorus girls shook "wicked hoofs" to the time of "Yes Sir that's My Baby,"[4] while brown shoulders swayed as only Negro jazz-singers can sway them. The cake-walk of plantation days lived again in the feet and souls of the seal-skin browns and "high yallas"[5] that pranced about and sang "Here They Come, Those Struttin' Babies."[6] Louis Douglass did soft-shoe dancing as Paris seldom sees it done while the altogether perfect "Jo" won all Paris with her adorable mimicry. And through all its wealth of color there pounded the mad rhythm of "Hey, Hey! Bump-ty-Bump! Hey, Hey!"

Press criticism plainly showed the consternation that had entered the rank of the critics. They had never known such madness; never dreamed such abandon. Some said the music was too loud; others praised it for its primitive wildness. One said this new thing was too frantic; another avowed that a new and wonderful outlet for natural desires and feelings had been born. This critic complained that American Negroes were not truly Negroes but "mulattos" or international hybrids while this reviewer claimed that only the primitive souls of Negroes could conceive such rhythm. Meanwhile the Champs-Elysee theatre was packed and jammed night after night with audiences whose applause was roof-splitting. While Bedlam debated whether to accept or reject the new Negro jazz with its crazy intricacies, the infectious rhythm of the Charleston creep [*sic*] into the soles of French feet . . . Hey, Hey! with a French accent became the word of the day.

The contagion of the Charleston in America was great enough but even that was tame in comparison with the avidity Paris showed to learn its Terpsichorean complexities. Every member of the Revue Negre cast became a Charleston teacher. Every dance academy in Paris became a Charleston center. Every dance-hall and supper club in Montmartre and other night districts advertised Charleston dancers as entertainers. One went to the Claridge[7] for tea and saw chicly arrayed Parisiennes doing the Charleston with their escorts. One saw the Charleston danced at Les Acacias . . . or the Ritz. The Coliseum reverberated with the same mad rhythm as store-clerks and stenographers had their night out. French bands played "Yes Sir That's My Baby" with the usual Charleston break . . . bumpty-bump, hey-hey!

Charleston Revues swept all former productions before them. The Dolly Sisters[8] were featured at the Casino de Paris as dancers of the Charleston. Mistinguette[9] [*sic*] still holds forth at the Moulin Rouge with the Jackson girl chorus that does the Charleston. Every vaudeville house, every cabaret, every dinner club and every tea-dansante[10] twirls to wild joy of the Negro's dance.

With the same catching insidiousness the Charleston found its way into Berlin and the rest of Germany when the Champs Elysee company played there for three months. When the troupe disbanded some of the number were inveigled into going to Russia with a new show; others returned to Paris. Here this member danced at this cabaret while the other danced there. Even as they find their way back across the ocean they leave their trace behind them. The American Negroes who have been furnishing Paris with its music since the war have been quick to learn the new dance that compatriots have brought to Europe. And so the dance goes on . . . Let's go, Charleston now!

And mirable dictu [*sic*],[11] Saturday night, April twenty-fourth, marks the final coronation of the Negro as a jazz dancer. Josephine Baker, the dusky star opened at the Follies Begeres as the premier of the program. Her sleek brown body sways through the maze of white ones as night after night makes her more and more certain in her position as the idol of Paris. The inimitable "Jo" does a Charleston dance like no one else in the world, white or black. Her long shapely "nigger legs" fly this way and that with a rhythm and beauty that is maddening. Her sleek black head turns this way and that as she twists her face into all sorts of ludicrous masks. With warmth and beauty she carries the rhythm of her race through a revue that is world famous . . . Let's go, Jo! Hey, Hey! Bumpty-bump!!

o   o   o

25
n.d.

There is something quite round and perfect about reaching the age of twenty-five . . . There is none of the feeble mystery that octogenarians would impress [on] us when they comb their ample beards and speak to us in solemn tones about "a quarter of a century." Nor yet is there the faintest overtone of those new life-tremors that came at sixteen. Neither mystery nor nerves have their part in the nose thumbing processes of twenty-five. One has put aside the last effervescent eagerness of twenty together with the cock-suredness of twenty-two. At twenty-five one has just put aside the last vestige of acrid cynicism that simmered in the blood at twenty-three or even as late as twenty-four. Round and perfect is the age of twenty-five . . . and somehow very golden!

Physically the change that comes between the twenty-fourth birthday and the twenty-fifth is very imperceptible. If one is a man, one's mustache, grown at twenty-three, has long lost its novelty as well as its tickle. The frown one affected when Dr. Wigeler passed the wrong sheepskin to a hopeful but bored twenty-two has survived through twenty-four only to have become a faint line between the eyes after a hearty laugh showing a bravery about one's "boyish side." If one is a woman, alack and alas one may have gained weight! Then again the asceticism of the late twenties may have set in early and aided in the conspiracy for maintaining the pencil form. One's lips have relegated to the dump-heap of twenty the pensive smile and have taken on much of the guilessness [*sic*] of sixteen. Man nor woman has grown many inches between these two dates. Why not even the all-knowing glands have taken cognizance of the transition.

Twenty-five is a culmination point. Trousers have gone their cycle from the tight, tubular effect of 1922 through the bell-leg of 1926 on back to a pseudo-normalcy. Skirts have passed through three hobble stages.[1] Washington has won the pennant twice[2] and Penn has roundly trounced Harvard.[3] A World War has swum on the fringes of our adolescent ken; perhaps an older brother enlisted and after sending home a battered helmet never returned.

Twenty-five meets with assurity [*sic*] the fact that Lindbergh has crossed the ocean alone[4] and the miracle of the orthophonic.[5]

o o o

[Life as a Javanese]
n.d.

Graduation exercises at Howard University were over and my resignation had taken effect immediately, since I was not scheduled to teach during the summer session. I was without funds once again. It was necessary for me to find work for the period that intervened between the closing of Howard University and the Fall when I would begin my study at the Barnes Foundation in Merion, Pa., where I was to receive a fellowship stipend covering expenses. During the summer of 1927 the Want Ad columns of the New York Times were still long and filled with items that hinted of golden opportunities ahead. This item appeared under the A's:

Artists wanted for better class Batik
studio. None but experienced need apply.
Wittman, 250 East 22nd Street. Good
salaries with chance for advancement.

Here was work that I could do; work that I would love doing. The basic rules of how to make a Batik had been learned in art school. Out of all the branches of art I had chosen Batik as mine. Research had shown me that by careful technique, intense study, and application an artist of today could transform this prehistoric art of the Javanese people into something beautiful in terms of our modern needs. Already I had made some notable advancement in this direction. Pieter Mujers' [*sic*] book[1] had opened my eyes to the possibilities of Batik for a present-day artist. I had seen the startling effects of——————'s Batik murals. From the learning of Batik in art school I had by now progressed to the place where I had had two one man shows of my own Batik designs the last of which had been composed of wall hangings using pictorial subjects combined with traditional or original design motifs. While I was studying in Paris I had managed to sell a half dozen wall hangings for several hundred dollars. Here, indeed, was work I could do.

Having decided that the advertisements had brought to my attention work that was pleasant, even exciting, that I was certain I could do, my mind began to wander back to the conditions that had surrounded my answering of advertisements in other years. In the summer following my sophomore year at college I had answered a newspaper ad calling for elementary school graduates to do envelope addressing for the Butterick Publishing Company. Knowing how much greater the supply of clerical workers always is than the demand, I had gone early. I was fifth in the line which, by nine oclock when the office opened, stretched around the corner. The crisp tones of the immaculate official clipped the hopes of the hundreds of girls that stood in line. "What a line! We only need three or four girls." And there I was fifth in the line! The method of employment was to have the applicants write down samples of their handwriting. It had been explained that when four girls were found whose handwriting was clear, attractive, and legible the rest of them would no longer need wait. The first two girls wrote clear, beautiful hands and were asked to wait. The writing of the third girl could scarcely be read—she was sent away. I was in again! The fourth girl was kept. It was my turn and I was happy since at that time I wrote a beautiful Spencerian[2] hand which I had patterned after my father's handwriting. As I put out my hand to take the pen, the official, who up to this time had not looked closely at any of the girls, noticing my brown hand, looked sharply into my brown face. Clearly so that all the girls in line heard him, he said, "We do not employ colored here."

Another time I had answered several advertisements for an artist to design greeting cards. Plus samples of my work I had gone from house to house armed with letters of recommendation from several art instructors in Teachers' College and Pratt Institute. In these places there had been very few applicants. My designs were good—the Christmas before I had earned over a hundred dollars selling my own designs for cards to friends and acquaintances. Always I received the same apologetic announcement that they were sorry but they didn't employ colored. A little older now, I attempted to argue the point with one employer. "I know it isn't fair," he said, "but I must follow the Company's rules."

These memories came into my mind as I contemplated the advertisement calling for Batik artists. The fact that I had had excellent experience, would, I knew, have nothing to do with my being employed unless I could think of some way to get past the barrier of my color. With a more discriminating astuteness I knew further that it was not just a problem of color. In the summer white people prided themselves on getting tanned to a darker hue than mine. Black East Indians were accepted [in] places where I could not set my foot. Spanish speaking people who lived in upper Manhattan were my color. I must use this knowledge that comes so easily into Negro experience. My color and the texture of my hair would have immediately indicated that I could "pass" for Spanish—in Mexico, Puerto Rico, and South America one could meet thousands of people who looked just like me. But there arose the problem of language. The faltering High School Spanish was not enough in a city where hundreds of Spaniards moved in and out [of] the business world. I could be French, a Martiniquan. But why would a Martiniquan be applying for a job as a Batik specialist in a New York shop when the world's best makers of Javanese Batik were in Paris? Javanese Batik . . . that was it! Why not be a Javanese? Certainly the chances of a real, live Javanese walking into the Wittman Studios were negligible. Javanese was not taught in our schools. Javanese were brown people and furthermore they were the originators of the art in which I was professing to be expert. I would be a Javanese!

The preparations for my deception were simple. A part in the middle of my hair with it shining close to my head and tucked in a low knot at the nape of my neck was my usual headdress. Spanish-looking, my Negro friends said. If Spanish, then certainly exotic, foreign. I wore a flowered print dress that was filled with all the colors of the rainbow. Around my neck I hung all the beads that I could buy from the Five and Ten Cent Store or borrow from friends. In my ears I wore the heavy, handwrought silver ear-rings I had bought in Paris. They hung almost to my shoulders negating the telltale roundness of my face and the inexplicable upturn of my nose. Heavy lipstick and more rouge than I was accustomed to wear and I was a Javanese.

o o o

[Ku Klux Klan Rides]
n.d.

The Florida night had fallen with the peculiar black-out quality it had in the Negro section of the little town of Eustis. The darkness and the heavy scent of Crepe Myrtle[1] lay like a cover over all the houses and people. Things seemed snuffed out, like the vanished light—even remnants of song, as some housewife cleared away the supper things, were lost in the air suddenly. This night, as other nights so often seemed to me, had an unreality to it, too much of stillness. The dog's tense half-bark stiffened the nerves of our backs. We remembered what night it was.

On the night before my husband had come home excitedly telling of an announcement he had seen in the town Post Office. Hanging among the other regular Post Office notices a large printed poster had borne this message:

KU KLUX KLAN RIDES
      Tuesday, March 30th
         1929

Under this heading had followed some detail of the convocation, although the actual location of the meeting place and the direction of [the] march were not intelligible to the uninitiated who might read it. The whole notice was couched in the flowery, Biblical language so often used in the South by ministers and public officials when a call was made to Godliness, Chivalry, of Civic Pride.

My laugh had been more in relief than from amusement when my husband told of his abandoning his first impulse to take the poster down when no one was looking and bring it home. I had said, "You want to go on living, don't you?"

When our dog had barked the short, growling bark that accompanies an animal's uncanny knowledge of strangeness or danger, we knew why he had barked even before we had tipped to the side door from which we could look into the street beyond the yard. Simultaneous with our peeping out at the street we had given a choked command for the dog to "Be quiet!" As the sight, which had for so many years struck terror into the hearts of other Negroes, filled my eyes, my husband said with hoarse softness, "It's the Klan." How foolishly unnecessary his words seemed.

There, some fifty yards away from the front of our house, came the ghostly cavalcade, driving in fearful, hooded silence up the one paved street in the Negro district of the town. The night had never seemed so black before. Now there was an eerie luminosity from the mingled low car-lights and the great, sheeted figures visible in the open automobiles being driven at a funeral pace. My husband had seen the Klan ride on horses with padded hooves in Atlanta, Georgia, when he was a student at the university. I had never really believed it actually happened except in the far days following the Civil War, in distasteful moving pictures, and in books about the "Romantic South."

The mind darts in so many directions in a moment of intense fear! The week before there had been heated words between my husband and the druggist in Tavares, a neighboring town, when another drug had been substituted for one for which my husband's prescription had called. Just the day before one of his patients in Umatilla, another town nearby, had told how the pharmacist, after questioning him about the "new doctor," "We don't fill nigger prescriptions in this town." We had only been in Florida a few months; our car was new; we were well-dressed; I was a northern outsider. Maybe they were riding through this part of the town to frighten us! Else why hadn't they ridden through the other Negro section across town where the tougher element lived.

We went stealthily to the front door to look out from behind the curtain in the unlighted room. We could see the slowly approaching procession without detection here. As far as we could see down the street, as far as the place where Reverend Brunsin's trees cut off our view, the line of cars came slowly forward. You could scarcely hear their motors throttled at the low speed. Almost they didn't move, so slowly they came. Only a Negro who has watched such a procession come nearer can understand the prickled awareness with which one stands rooted to the spot that is somewhere in the eyes and deep in the heart.

When they were just about opposite the front door of our house, they came to a stop. You could not hear what they said as they turned to each other, making awkward movements in their ungainly drapery as they pointed in the direction of our house. Road lights were played directly upon the front of our house. The moment's indecision was over among them—they began to climb over the sides of their cars. How it was that we continued to stand peering through the curtain I do not understand. It is a mystery to me what stops the cry of fear rising in the throat at a time like this. Their white robes were grotesque as they come across the wide street to our front yard. There must have been a dozen hooded Klansman stepping onto the little rise of ground that served as a pavement before one entered our front yard. The first one had already started into our little dirt path. It was just about ten feet now to the front porch. The first Klansman turned making a gesturing motion with his clumsy sheeted arm to someone who had remained in the car. His great hood bobbed in assent. We could translate his unspoken words, "This is the place." Why didn't we move? Where would we have gone even had we been able to move?

Our fear changed imperceptibly to curiosity as something we could not understand kept these thirteen men, playing at goblins, from coming any nearer the house. They were in a circle, looking at something in our yard. Their movements were still awkward as they pointed and shifted about. Our hearts seemed to catch a new breath; the wideness in our eyes relaxed. We could see more clearly now that a few of them were beginning to go back to their cars.

Close to the entrance of our front yard, near the inn-post from which hung in rural indignity my husband's physician and surgeon sign, there stood a small tree, called the Cottonwood Rose.[2] It seems that this tree, rare even in its native setting, had been brought by the owner of our house from Georgia. Later I learned that it was the only Cottonwood Rose in Eustis or thereabouts. Now the Cottonwood Rose is a very unusual tree, about the size of a strong Maple of two or three years' growth. Its blossoms change color as they mature. The first showy blooms, half a foot in diameter, are like great white full blown roses. After about one day's flowering these blooms turn a deep, warm pink, shading to a rich red just before the petals begin to fall. Always when the Cottonwood Rose is in bloom there are at one time on its branches the three different colored blossoms— white, pink, and red. Unusual as the tree was, the Negroes in the town had grown used to it. We have since wondered what sort of man the Klansman had been who prompted this digression in the night's plans for the sole purpose—so far as we could discern—of showing his confreres a beautiful flowering tree.

In the exhausted let-down following our intense fright we were filled with wonderment at the strange ways of men. No logic that we could muster seemed to explain the strange thing we had seen that night. Nor did the events of that night seem less strange as we thought of them through the years that followed. All we ever learned about that night was the fact that the Klan had ridden about five miles beyond our house to the home of an "uppity nigger" whom they had given a severe beating from which he had never fully recovered. From his house they had cut across short roads to Umatilla where they had tarred and feathered a well-to-do white man, a northerner, whom they had surprised in the bed of a much sought-after Negro prostitute whose name was Lily.

Last Night I Nearly Killed My Husband!

n.d.

Over and over this thought jangled through my mind as I waited for my train. I seemed to stand on an island of silence in the bustling railroad station. People chattered as they rushed for their trains—they seemed so casual, so intent on happiness. Train noises converged with the sound of feet and eddied about me. Briarwood[1] was so remote from this metropolitan hurly-burly. I could almost close my eyes and see the gentle green of newly budded trees, smell the fresh, earthy country smells. And again I was jerked awake from my nostalgic reverie with the thought that last night I nearly killed my husband.

Fifteen minutes, ten minutes, five minutes—the time dragged along with sickening horror.

Right now the gun lay hidden under a bundle of clothes where I had concealed it so that it would be within easy reach. Only the fact that I had hidden it saved my pulling the trigger when I said,

"Before you can do this to me I'll kill you."

He was standing between me and the chair. Except for this flimsy circumstance I should be telling a different story. And now I was going to him with that sick feeling one has when visiting a dear one in the hospital. What would I do when I got home? What should I say? How could I snatch him back from the edge of the abyss that threatened him? I, who had nearly killed him perhaps only for the reason that I wished to kill myself.

The problems that confronted me seemed so insurmountable that I could see no other way out than killing myself. Driven to the consideration of killing myself I had maddened into almost killing him. And yet I knew that killing myself would not solve his problems; killing him would only add to my sorrow. Here he was a young physician at the end of seven years of hard work to build his practice caught in some spiritual turmoil from which he could find surcease only in drink. For the same seven years I had thought I was part of his life, sharing his burdens and shaping our future together. Now I was brought sharply up against the fact that something—I could not reason what—had driven him into the horror of drinking so heavily that both his career and our married life was threatened. What made him, a physician, turn into a virtual drunkard? Was he really caught in the toils [sic] of some unscrupulous woman? The events of the last few weeks would seem to point in that direction. Was he sick with worry because the need of money had made him resort to illegal practice in his profession? These questions kept time in my mind to the swift wheels of the train. More horrible than any certain knowledge that our life together was a failure was this maddening groping to find the causes that led up to the near tragedy of the night before.

The beginnings of our life together had been so bright with promise. Fresh from his internship after graduation from medical school with highest honors he had married me as I stood on the threshold of my own career. Together we would conquer the world—the bright hope of every young married couple.

We caught the tail-end of the "boom" in Florida where he started his practice of medicine. He made quick money for about eight months. This allowed us to enjoy moderate good living, keep a maid, have a laundress come in two days a week, dress well and deposit a neat sum of money in the bank. Towards the second year of our marriage the bottom fell out of things in Florida. The real estate boom had been deflated leaving the state in financial panic. We still kept the maid but there was no extra money to add to our moderate bank account.

Then came the Mediterranean Fruit Fly. Only people who lived in Florida during the last part of 1928 and early 1929 realize the part this lusty little beast played in what proved to be the forerunner of the holocaust which was to consume the nation's finance in less than a year. Those who had large worthless holdings in Florida real estate were attempting to turn their frozen assets into saleable vegetable and fruit crops. Vast sums of money were poured into advertising; Florida seemed on the way to another more lasting boom. The Mediterranean Fruit Fly cast the dissenting vote at all board meetings. Having destroyed vast acres of oranges, he began nibbling daintily at unsuspecting vegetables. The order went out to destroy all fruit and vegetable crops. There was no discrimination between large farms comprising wide acreage and the tiny truck gardens in which the poorer people raised their daily food.

More money was borrowed, there were runs on banks—the story of Florida's bank failures and financial collapse was front-page news all over the country. That a large bank closed with our modest thousand dollars in it was just a minor tragedy. My husband's practice was largely among the poorer people who made their living picking oranges and working in the packing houses. They not only had no money to pay their bills; the very food they needed for subsistence had been destroyed by state order. As yet Washington was not aware that thousands of people were on the verge of starvation. Relief had not become the nation's problem.

At the end of two years in Florida, with our last two hundred dollars, we pulled up stakes and came North to settle in Briarwood on Long Island . . .

The next three years were the story of any young physician in a small town whose ability gave promise that he would go far in his profession. True, we no longer could afford a maid and I found it necessary to do a large part of my own laundry work. The thought of continuing my career was pushed aside in the mad attempt to make ends meet. It required our combined efforts to give my husband his second start.

The reverberations from Wall Street on October twenty-seventh, 1929, had been felt around the world, but as yet Briarwood had not lost what relief commissioners were to call later "economic security." My husband and I again thought we were on the road to prosperity and happiness. We decided to borrow money and buy a home, a small place with a good bit of land on the outskirts of Briarwood in what would eventually be termed a restricted district. We seemed to be cashing in on the courage that had seen us through our lean years.

Like so many others we had miscalculated on what the future held. The black clouds of the depression were soon to envelope not only the extremely wealthy who could afford to gamble in Wall Street and the unskilled laborer who depended on the prosperity of big industry to make his living, but even that middle class whose position was usually most secure. The bank in which we had deposited our tiny savings had not opened after the Bank Holiday.[2] Most of my husband's patients lost their money in the same bank. Briarwood saw its first bread-line.

It soon became evident that unless something happened we would not be able to make the payments on the house and the money we had borrowed to buy it. Each night we went to bed sick with worry for what the new day would bring. That, at all costs, we must not lose our home became an obsession. It became increasingly difficult to keep up the front that is necessary for a professional man and his family in a small town.

Not even learned psychologists can give adequate reasons why two people who are in love turn on each other when outside influences cause worry. Yet every married woman knows that, as surely as the ill wind blows, she and her husband will begin to quarrel over little things that really do not matter. Our case was no different. None of his favorite foods tasted right to my husband. I laundered his shirts very badly in my attempt at economy. My ill-concealed worry made him accuse me of adding to his burdens by my not being cheerful. Although nothing between us was really wrong, at that time, a thousand causes for anger and recriminations arose daily.

I began to think again of my own career. Any kind of a job would help ease things at home and in so doing keep me sane. Money I might have spent for stockings was used for trips to New York in search of work. I couldn't go to our mutual friends for work—that seemed an indictment against my husband's ability to take care of me. I became identified with the rest of the unemployed workers who endlessly tramped the city streets in search of work. Heartsick and discouraged, I would return home only to be blamed for having spent the money in going to town.

These days of misunderstanding and estrangement did not lessen my love, nor my courage to go on. I knew that under all his testiness my husband still loved me. I must find a way to help him.

By some lucky province I found a job with a newly opened publishing house. They had known my name in the days before I had married. In applying for a job I had used my maiden name. One of the provisions for this job was that the person be a single woman. It seemed unimportant at that time for me to lie. No, I had never been married. It was explained that a person of my qualifications would be swiftly advanced to a position in which it would be necessary in editorial capacity to assist with the entertainment of visiting authors and publishers and it would be impossible to consider anyone who was tied down to a home and family. How easily we sell our happiness for a mess of pottage![3]

My husband's grudging congratulation should have been a foreboding of the unhappiness to come. We needed money so badly that I could not account for his coolness except as an added expression of worry or perhaps sadness because it was necessary for me to go to work.

For six months my small salary filled many gaps at home and we experienced no undue unpleasantness. The only change my working made in the home routine was that my husband had to eat his meals in a restaurant since it was impossible for me to prepare them. During this time I had been working hard and had just about learned the inner workings of my office. The office manager called my name one morning, as he said,

"We are very pleased with the work you have been doing. Yesterday the board decided to give you an assistant editorship."

I was so happy I could have cried, but I answered,

"Gee, that's grand. Thanks so much for telling me so soon."

"Of course, that will mean a raise in salary. Your raise was not decided upon in yesterday's meeting but it ought to almost double what you're getting now."

"I suppose there really is a Santa Claus after all."

"No, you've earned a raise. I suppose this is what the big boss had in mind when he took you on. I'll wager your experience beats that of most of the editors but they had to make you do chores until you got the hang of things."

It seemed as though the dawn of my bright star was balanced by descent in my husband's luck. There were weeks that he made less than half of what I was making. My only reaction to this was to be exceedingly happy that I was able to earn enough to make this change less keenly felt.

For several months my work varied little except for an occasional tea at which I represented the firm. I had been with them nearly a year when the president of the company sent word for me to come to his office. He was always pleasant to talk to—his greeting was cheerful. He lost no time in coming to his reason for sending for me.

"As you know, Fenton's last book went over with a bang. That and the next Grossmann translation will make it possible for us to stretch out a little. I dont have to tell you how important the social side of the publishing business is. That's the woman's part of the game. You're in line for a promotion. We've carried you along pretty fast but we're new and have to make long strides. You've gotten on to the knack of meeting people and doing the gracious part of this author-publisher business. What we would want you to do in your new position would be to step out a little, go to parties, meet the folks that are writing, find new talent for us. Sort of be in the 'know.' Be a kind of scout extraordinaire."

There was nothing for me to say as he paused for a moment. I knew he was feeling me out. With an unaccountable sinking feeling I waited for the catch—the conditions that made it necessary for him to indulge in so many preliminary compliments. He was smiling in a kindly way as he said,

"Now, if you lived in town."

Ah, that was it. I felt weak, ineffectual as I hastened to say,

"I've always found it cheaper to live in the suburbs."

"The Boyce Women's Club⁴ is pretty cheap, I understand. I dont see how you can commute and keep late hours and yet be up on your toes. This job we want you to do is tough."

I didn't know what to say. He didn't seem so kindly now. He knew what he wanted. If I was not prepared to do it, I was certain he'd find somebody to take my place who would. For the life of me I could find nothing to say. He returned to friendliness as he arose in dismissal.

"Take a little time and think it over. It isn't asking much and after all you're the person we want to do the job."

"You . . . you mean that I cant have the job unless I move in town?"

"Don't sound so woe-begone. Think it over and come in to see me early next week."

I talked it over at home—there seemed nothing to do but accept the promotion and get a New York address. I rented a cheap room in New York but continued to commute. That meant late trains and being dog tired in the mornings. It wasn't long before my life was one round of parties, dinners and night clubs.

o   o   o

[Harlem Reflection]
n.d.

In 1926, when beginning to write a column of literary and artistic chit-chat for Opportunity, a journal of Negro life, I chose my title for the column from William Rose Benet's poem on Harlem in which he said, "First issue of the Ebony Flute." Today, if I were conducting a similar column, and even as I say it I know that no such column would be proper and in keeping with the new Harlem, rather than sing Harlem on an ebony flute with its high and ecstatic tonality, I would feel that Harlem's song should be blared forth with trumpets, clarion calls and the marshal [sic] sound of many feet. So much has Harlem changed. When I left Harlem in the late 'Twenties it was still characterized by the remnants of that period known as the Negro Renaissance, in which writers, artists and musicians frequented the night clubs and restaurants of the district and engaged in a more or less literary interchange among themselves which was within the confines of their studios, transcribed into literary and artistic production that regarded the Negro from a more or less sentimental angle—one of the real liberating effects of the so-called Negro Renaissance with its "New Negro" was his ability to see partly in his people and his beginning freedom from the old stereotypes which made it possible for him to regard Harlem and its life in a light that was at least emotionally free.

In those far days there was still a certain debonair carefreeness to Harlem. True, there exists side by side with this selfish gaiety the work-a-day life of Harlem, and close beneath the veneer of Harlem's reputed night life and emotional freedom lay that strata of life in which poverty and deprivation are boon companions with every family. But just the same, one still could walk from 7th Avenue and 135th Street North and be caught and swept along by what many white writers termed during their period of discovering Harlem as primitive abandonment. By the same token one could still meet writers and artists who were interested solely in discovering a clue to their own personal effort in the artistic world. In those days, despite the underlying reason of real necessity, rent parties were given by the so-called literati with the same nonchalant gaiety one may toss off a cocktail. It was more or less smart to be poor and talented. Scattered all through the many streets of Harlem were those members of the Negro intelligentsia who were each concerned with writing some poem or composing some piece of music that would contribute individually to the sum total of America's artistic whole. Countee Cullen was translating a version of Ephigenia,[1] Aaron Douglas was afire with plans for painting the first murals[3] and Arna Bontemps had written a beautiful but sentimental novel about the far away days when Negro riders were the toast of the racetrack.[2] Harlem's hot spots were still necessary stopping places for sophisticated down-town New York.

The Krigwa players,[3] under the able direction and fired by the enthusiasm of Eugenia Andrews[4] was still the group engaged in discovering Negro talent for the drama and playing for the community solely a series of plays by Negro authors.[5] Laudable efforts, all of these, and certainly in their sum total adding to the individual glory of these Negro artists and to the general pride of race of all Negroes. At one and the same time these artistic efforts were assisting in bringing out a better understanding between Negroes and white people.

That was in the late 1920's. Except for short visits through the years I did not live in Harlem again until 1935, and what a change I found! Of course Harlem had taken its shattering blow along with the rest of the world in the depression that seemed to catapult all mankind into a veritable abyss of misery. In Harlem those examples of poverty that one had come to accept as a portion of Negroes who were forced to do menial labor had spread and tightened its grip upon the entire community. Heretofore, the young Negro man or woman had felt that if he or she could just make it through college and professional school his future was assured. The Negro doctor had only to live through a year or two of getting himself righted to reach what seemed to be a very assured future for himself and his family. What did I find in 1935?

It was during this year that it chanced my way to interview some forty odd professional men and women in Harlem for the Department of Education and Information of the Welfare Council of New York City. An article, based on the material I gathered, appeared in quite an emasculated form in "Better Times," their official organ.[6] What an anomaly—that I should write the story of Harlem during the depression years for a magazine whose name was better times! I had found that almost no physician in Harlem, almost no dentist or lawyer had escaped a closer contact with poverty than the ordinary middle class white person could ever imagine. One pharmacist, whose drugstore had occupied one of the most prominent corners in Harlem for some ten years, had been forced through the poverty of the community to lose his holdings one by one until in 1935 he was running an elevator in a down-town office building. This was a man who had graduated with honors some twenty years before from one of America's leading universities and had studied abroad on a scholarship for several years. His wife, a graduate of the Sorbonne in Paris, who had been accustomed to give French lessons to aspiring debutantes of Park Avenue for a price of $10.00 an hour, was forced in their dire emergency to work as a ladies' attendant for some of these same debutantes. One physician had become so undernourished through the poverty of this period that he had in his run-down condition contracted tuberculosis and because he was not able to go away to a sanatorium was practicing medicine with T.B. and living at the mercy of fellow physicians. Another physician had graduated with honors from America's leading Negro medical school but two years before the depression hit him. He could not make a living at his profession and was forced to go on relief and subsequently with the setting up of the C.W.A. and C.W.S.[7] to take a job as a teacher of chemistry in one of their classes at a salary of $20.00 odd a week. Lawyers, teachers, doctors, and professional people of all walks of life were hurtled together in a maelstrom of misery. I realize, of course, that this was true of all people, Negro and white, but the point I am making is that Harlem—laughter-loving Harlem, the playground of and pains [*sic*]—had now changed the character of its demeanor from that of a minstrel grin to that of a grimace of pain.

I cannot begin to describe the shock I received. I had been in the South and seen their poverty and privation among Negroes and had steeled myself against it with the feeling that if I could only return to Harlem, there again I would find warmth and laughter. Harlem itself seemed shaken in the same type of shock that I was experiencing. It had not quite squared its shoulders to meet the blow. Here and there there was [*sic*] still feeble attempts at living it through.

Dazed, I went to some of the old haunts where they still existed. I found no gathered group of intellectuals but rather the angry mutterings of Negroes who had come to seek the reason why. (Classes in dialectic materialism[8] being held by a group of doctors and professional people at the office of Ruben Young). In sheer desperation I went to the 135th Street Public Library which had been in the old days a haunt for Negro writers. I found them busily engaged in Adult Education work. At one of the first of their meetings that I attended Dr. Robeson, the eminent child psychologist was speaking on juvenile delinquency and her figures on Harlem were horrible to hear. Could this be the same library at which Langston Hughes, Countee Cullen and Eric Waldron [*sic*] had met with some of the rest of us to read and listen to Negro poets and writers and to join together. Langston Hughes in crying "Poem-p. 58—The Weary Blues.—Beautiful also are the souls of my people."[9]

I felt like some drunken soul [missing word] from place to place through the streets, into churches, community houses, schools, not only to find everyone busily seeking, seeking some solution for this tragedy that had descended upon them. I stayed indoors, I didn't want to see it, I didn't want to believe it. Where was Harlem?[10]

Introduction

Bennett's diaries[1] from various periods reveal the psyche of a female artist during diverse moments in her life, including her assessment of life for African Americans in France and her time with African American painter Norman Lewis. Bennett's diaries are important to readers because of their critique of life for an African American female encountering various difficulties in the United States and abroad, and her discussion about how to rise up in the face of such adversity. Bennett spent a great deal of time writing letters to friends and family when living both at home and abroad, but her diary allowed her an opportunity to write openly about more than she could in any letter.

The early excerpts from her diary in France were often occasioned by the dislocation of travel. Later entries, after she had become acclimated to Paris and begun to enter its rich social life, display her youthful exuberance upon visiting the City of Lights despite harboring a strong longing for home. Michel Fabre feels that her youth and loneliness are what makes Bennett's diary important: "Her loneliness rendered her particularly sensitive to the atmosphere of Paris and to its impingement on her sense of personal and national identity" (120). In the reflective entry from July 26, 1925, she describes the mixed feelings she has about the United States, understandable for the first time now that she is abroad. Bennett reveals how she has "a strange new patriotism" since she has been in France. "There are times," states Bennett, "I'd give half my remaining years to hear the 'Star Spangled Banner' played. And yet even as I feel that way I know that it has nothing to do with the same 'home' feeling I have when I see crowds of American white people jostling each other about the American Express." The point Bennett makes about race and the United States parallels her later point on August 2, 1925, about how white Americans treat African Americans in France. Bennett notes that on a recent visit to Bois de Boulogne she overhead white Americans critiquing herself and her male friend, Louis Jones, dancing: "They dance nicely, dont they? You know they have that native rhythm!" In Bennett's entry from August 8 she provides a more buoyant depiction of a night out clubbing with some of the celebrities she met while in Paris, perfectly reflecting the heady experience it must have been for the twenty-three-year-old woman. In addition to spending time with her friends, Bennett also honed her art by studying at the Académie Julian, the Académie Colorossie, the Ecole de Panthéon, and the Sorbonne (Govan, "After the Renaissance" 72). As Farrah J. Griffin and Cheryl J. Fish observe, Bennett's writings from Paris help encourage "a reevaluation of the geography of the movement that has to come to be associated with Harlem" (175).

Although not part of the diary proper (which ends with an entry from September 30, 1925), Bennett does provide a sort of coda with a loose piece dated April 29, 1926 (located on the second reel of her papers housed at the Schomburg Library). She remarks that the piece is a return to her "long neglected [Paris] diary," and was written shortly before her return to the United States. The entry is deeply personal, reflecting on her "distinct and definite experience" with Norman Rolff, whom she had met while studying art in Paris. In this entry, she gives a detailed description of how they met. That she chose to write of the relationship after not touching the diary for several months shows its importance to her. And the fact she ends the entry by saying she feels too "tired" to continue writing suggests the relationship is over and she does not desire to dwell on it any longer.

While Bennett ends the Paris diary with the termination of one relationship, her diary from the mid-1930s is dominated by her affair with the African American artist Norman Lewis.[2] This later diary, unlike the one composed by Bennett while in her early twenties and at the beginning of her career, depicts a portrait of a woman lacking confidence in herself, her relationships, and her ability to make ends meet in a Depression-ravaged Harlem. With her marriage to Alfred Jackson ending, Bennett began an approximately three-year relationship with the Harlem-born painter Lewis in 1936. Her diary (written between April 1936 and March 1937) is a vivid account of their troubled affair. The entry from April 8, 1936, is a poignant telling of what seems like a typical day with them, dominated by senseless arguments, harsh words, and mutual self-abasement. Even in bed, she describes the humiliating feeling of being "desired physically but not spiritually." This feeling of loneliness is reiterated in an entry dated April 9, 1936: "All thru this very rainy night I have felt a hopeless loneliness when a rainy night at home under the same roof with the man you love should be such a comfort." Finding no comfort, Bennett writes, "I shall emphatically shut this book and its emotions with it and go to bed with the hope that sleep will indeed 'knit up the raveled sleeve of care.'" With each entry Bennett's relationship with Lewis appears to deteriorate further, yet she does not appear ready to end the affair. An entry from May 7, 1936—which incidentally is around the time that Bennett's first husband Alfred Jackson, dies—concerns an affair Norm is having with a woman named Ernestine. The betrayal reminds her of similar mistreatment she had suffered under Jackson, and makes her wonder why she endures "such mental torture." While much in Bennett's and Lewis's relationship is unraveling, their passion for art remains. The entry from January 3, 1937, speaks of the efforts both Bennett and Lewis make to get their art work accepted. Despite the problems in their relationship, Bennett remains one of Lewis's most ardent supporters. From her diary entry it is clear that Bennett believes in the power of his art, writing that "he deserves success regardless of how unhappy his present actions make me." That entry is the last that indicates the couple is still living together.

The 1930s diary must have been very difficult for Bennett to write and, furthermore, to keep for so many years. Leonore Hofmann maintains that "writing about her painful relationship to Norm is a 'resistance to time' and an assertion of her self-worth" (70). The diary shows the depth of Bennett's spirit. Despite the pain of her relationship with Lewis, it allowed a personal growth in her. It demanded a brutal self-examination of who she was. When she emerged, she had a better understanding of herself and was better prepared to find a sense of peace in the final stage of her life.

Bennett kept a very brief diary of a vacation to Martha's Vineyard and Nantucket in 1958 with her second husband, the white social activist and teacher Richard (Dick) Crosscup, which provides readers a glimpse of this final stage of her life. Bennett's interracial marriage, still illegal in many states in the 1930s, is another sign of her willingness to cross barriers. The diary shows her at an ease with Crosscup that she had never experienced with Alfred Jackson or Norman Lewis. The entry that we have selected from June 19, 1958, describes a meeting with fellow Harlem Renaissance author Dorothy West. Their encounter, after many years apart, still speaks of an "intimacy" that exists between the two writers. Bennett speaks of being "filled with good feeling at having seen her again after so many years; a charming, bright sharply spoken person." Like Bennett's literary column "The Ebony Flute," which many thought was just filled with literary chitchat but really meant so much more to readers, Bennett notes in her diary, "When there is more time, I'd like to rethink the things about which she, Dick and I talked. On first thought, it seems to have been only chit chat, but underneath there seemed the [sic] have been something of importance exchanged between us." The entry is also marked by the openness and beauty of the landscape, in opposition to the normally claustrophobic and ugly backdrop in the 1930s diary. There is a calm that pervades the visit to New England. Bennett's light banter with Dick is far different from the often ponderous, quarrelsome conversations she had with Norman. Bennett's three diaries help trace the feelings and thoughts of a young, twentysomething girl living abroad, to a woman in her thirties struggling with her life and career, to one in her fifties reflecting on a life lived. Coupled with her other literary and artistic output, the diaries help readers understand the lows and highs an African American woman of Bennett's stature from the 1920s to 1950s.

France

June 26, [19]25

Could I mark this day I should put a black ring around it as one of the saddest days I have ever spent. I moved today to my new hotel . . . For two days now it has rained—the people tell me that this is typical Paris weather. A cold rain that eats into the very marrow of the bone . . . and I am alone and more homesick that I ever believed it possible to be. I had an engagement to meet "the Czechoslovakian professor" and to go with him to "The Exposition" but I couldn't find the address and the taxi man took me to the wrong Hotel Angleterre . . . and I missed Ann for lunch . . . and at the Foyer[1] they discourage my plans for studying art anywhere except at the New York School of Fine and Applied Art—which I think is silly! They talked to me as though I were a kid who had come here just to sort of dabble in art. And it rains . . . and I am cold and heartsick . . . and nearly starved . . . No umbrella, no coat except my suit-coat—no one . . . Paris!!! And at night in sheer desperation I go to the Cinema with a little French girl from the Foyer. It is long and tiresome although the pictures in themselves were not bad. She and I parted where Blvd. St-Michel and Rue de Vaugirard meet. I had miscalculated my distance and I had not counted on the winding of the street . . . It was dark and I became afraid and thought I was lost. All the horrible things that I had heard about Paris came to my mind and I was almost panic stricken. Frantically I asked each person I passed, "Ou la Rue D'Assas?" and they all gave me the same answer "la troiséme a gauche."[2] And when I got there it wasn't . . . I didn't realize that that was simply the turn. I was so frightened that I shall never forget it. I kept saying to myself "nothing can hurt me, can it Genie?"[3] . . . It was a simple child-like faith that nothing could hurt me while his love was about me . . . I finally got home safely . . . and Gene would like this story.

July 26, 1925

I have let many a day slip by without recording here my experiences, reactions and hopes. There is this certainty though, i.e. I must only recount here the high spots, the fallacy of my memory will take me over the minor details of being in Paris.

Somewhere in the back of my mind there runs the knowledge that I registered in the College de La Guilde for French and that I was infinitely weary of hearing so much French and understanding oh so little! Finally, I gave it up—not because I was making a failure of it but chiefly because it consumed three marvelous morning hours and gave so little in return—and there is so much to be done!

I know that the Fourth of July happened! I say "happened" because that's how I feel about it. To have one's National Holiday roll around when one is in a strange land and cant speak the language is an experience never to be forgotten. A homesickness more poignant and aching than anything I can ever imagine held me in its grip. All day long I did not see or speak to a single one of my compatriots . . . nor did I even hear a word of English spoken. There is this marvelous thing about my being here in France. A strange new patriotism has sprung up in me since I've been here in France . . . there are times that I'd give half my remaining years to hear the "Star Spangled Banner" played. And yet even as I feel that way I know that it has nothing to do with the same "home" feeling I have when I see crowds of American white people jostling each other about the American Express.

August 2, [1925]

[. . .] From the shopping tour we rushed home to dress frantically for the tea-dance to which Louis Jones took the four of us. He took us to a delightful place, in the Bois de Boulogne[1] . . . a very chic place that made me feel that I was a dream-girl in a land of dreams. It must have galled the Americans to death to see us there on a par with them. As Louis and I danced together I heard a group of them saying among themselves, "They dance nicely, dont they? You know they have that native rhythm!" Whoa!

And then to home to drop the girls at their hotel and then Louis and I quickly to a little restaurant in the heart of the Quarter for supper. It was real jolly for us to eat together at this cheap little Prix Fixe place for 6 francs . . . Louis and I have eaten together at so many chic, expensive places that this was a lovely novelty.

And then, mirable dictu [sic], to the opera with Dr. Waller and Miss Alexander, a school teacher from Cleveland and a friend of Louis' and oh! such a pill. [. . .]

Today we went to Mr. [Edmund] Jenkins' office where Louis played the violin and a Mr. Callilaux [*sic*] accompanied him. It makes my heart swell with pride to know these musicians who are black and yet so wonderful. [. . .]

August 8, [1925]

I am alone! In every sense of the word. The Garlands and Elizabeth and Charlotte left for Italy today at four oclock. Now I know how little I have been hardened to loneliness . . . I had been gay all day and then we came to say "good-bye" and like the fool that I am I cried. It seems that with their going they take with them the last vestige of America. I felt again for a "devastating space" the same emotion that fairly tore my soul in twain when they pulled up the gang-plank at New York. Then the band played some sort of rousing tune as we put off to sea . . . and with the same sort of irony today the "garcons" and "femmes des chambres" were rushing about chattering like magpies. And tonight, I feel myself again sorely stricken with that "Oh to be in England" feeling.

I know that Thursday night was a night "out." Mr. Jenkins sponsored the party which was made up of Charlotte, Betty, Tellie, Mercer Cook & wife, Harold Jackman, Edwin Morgan, Mr. Jenkins and myself. First to the Chinese Restaurant in the Rue de L'Ecole de Medicine in the Quarter. We stayed there from 11:30 until 1:45 when Mr. Jenkins joined us. Thence to "Le Royal" in Montmartre. There much champagne and many cigarettes and much dancing. I get, in thinking back, a vivid impression of one or two very drunken women and hard, hard faces, and a girl with big baby eyes who affected their over-brilliancy and of Tellie just a wee bit tipsy with too much champagne. For one "charming" moment, Louis [Jones] rushed up from "Florence's" to dance but one dance. Then at 4:15 A.M. to dear old "Bricktop's."[1] The Grand Duc[2] extremely crowded this night with our folk. Lottie Gee[3] there on her first night in town and sings for "Brick" her hit from "Shuffle Along"—"I'm Just Wild About Harry." Her voice is not what it might have been and she had too much champagne but still there was something very personal and dear about her singing and we colored folks just applauded like mad. "Brick" singing as well as ever her hits—"Insufficient Sweetie" and "I'm in Love Again."[4] Louis came in with all the clearing quality of a good gust of fresh air and brought with him Albert [Alexander]

Smith. He liked to have fallen over when he saw me—1st time in about a month. After the first shock of our unexpected meeting he manages to dance with me and we are both agreeably surprised to find the other such a lovely dancer. Louis dances with me one very lovely dance during the which⁵ "Brick" and everybody teases him about how happy he is to have his little brown skin in his arms and he calling me "little lady" and grinning from ear to ear.

And always the inevitable "Hot Cakes and Sausages" at "the Duc."—Home at 6:30 in the lovely grey morning light.

I shall never quite forget the shock of beauty that I get when the door was opened at "Brick's" and as we stepped out into the early morning streets . . . looking up Rue Pigall there stood Sacred-Heart . . . beautiful, pearly Sacre-Coeur as though its silent loveliness were pointing a white finger at our night's debauchery. I wished then that so worthy an emotion as I felt might have been caught forever in a poem but somehow the muse refuses to work these days.

Friday Louis took Tellie, Ed Morgan and me to tea at "Les Acadias." I had one of the best times I've ever had—just dancing my life out for sheer love of movement. As always Louis was the loveliest escort ever. He is without a doubt a real "Prince Charming." Then too, we dance so well together that there is real pleasure in the dance itself. It was not difficult to see the looks of admiration and oftimes envy which followed us around the room. Louis dances like no one else and it would be just "too bad" if I didn't follow him so perfectly.

Such a lovely afternoon. [. . .]

September 27, [19]25
Written at Pontoise Sur-Seine

I have just finished "The Blind Bow-Boy" by Carl Van Vechten. I think back to what Jennie Mustapha¹ said last February when she finished reading "The Tattooed Countess"² by the same author—Carl Van Vechten must be an awful devil. He had put this subtitle to "The Tattooed Countess"—a novel with a happy ending . . . and surely his smile must have been a drawn one. And now just at the close of his earlier book I feel the same way.

All this by way of getting the book's impression off my mind . . .

Life moves so swiftly and now I find myself here where certainly existence is a bit retarded. Pontoise! Things seem so simple here . . . so remote. The smell of trees and grass ought to relieve anything even the human heart.

I wonder will all of my life be this way . . . retreating to some impersonal calm to escape thinking. Always this change of scene to ease the heart.

I have brought one of Gene's pictures with me . . . and with it some memories of him. I wonder if all sadness will be like this . . . some little tangible proof of existing kindliness to help one over the rough spots.

All of this seems to be some one else other than myself. I arise at seven and have now been in Pontoise since ten thirty. A beautiful, little, quaint town.

And I think again of Carl Van Vechten and how I should like to know him.[3] Strange that I dont since all of my friends do. I suppose, though, that I shall meet him when I return to America—that's if his enthusiasm for colored folk lasts. I dont know that it will though—it follows no rule of attraction . . . one being beast the other man. Hell!

September 28, 1925
Pontoise

It is just about ten-thirty in the morning and I have been up now about two hours and a half. It was wonderful to awake to the stinging freshness of country air . . . to the simplicity of the outdoor sounds and to the sound of children's voices in the house.

Last night—quick as a snap—I was the old Gwennie again . . . heart free, head bare and soul for joyousness. I am the only guest here at the Pension. Yesterday being Sunday Madame Raffalli's two sons and their wives and children had come up from Paris for a visit. The big old house was fairly bursting with merriment. Children tumbled over each other screaming with pure animal joy. Mothers discussed the merits and faults of their off-spring. Fathers discussed things of common interest and question[ed] me about American money and prohibition and I was a part of the family. Madame kept saying "Mlle. est bien genteel [*sic*] . . . bons-êtes [*sic*] toute seul, mon petite"[1] and things comme ça.[2]

Before supper we played "Tag" and "Blind Man's Bluff" on the lawn . . . Angel, Uncle Gaston, Uncle Something Else, two aunts, M. Andrés a Swiss friend of the family and myself. And as I said I have recovered my old self again.

We eat supper . . . piles of it and then to bed. At first a deep sleep due to too much wine, then to awaken in the night full of fear because of people snoring in the adjoining rooms and trains passing in the night. The thought struck me as I lay there frozen with fear that snoring is after all the universal language. Then slowly calm began to return to my mind with the thought of how still the air was . . . how remote I was from things that tend to disturb the heart and mind.

Solange, the femme de chambre, awakened me with steaming chocolate. I found to my surprise and delight that I was hungry. Dressed quickly, dashing the coldest water ever unto my face. Then out to a bicycle shop with Angel to rent a "bic" for the day.

Thirteen francs—just that for hours on hours of heaven! I have just come back from riding about two hours. All along the banks of the river over the soft earth with a tune in my heart and my lips whistling gladly. Then I knew that joy was found again like this . . . in old country roads stretching far before one and tunes whistled into the air and tired, tired muscles.

I thought of many people as I rode . . . people I love and miss. But all is very remote and tranquil here.

April 29, 1926

I suppose a night in late April when one has a fire roaring in the grate and the rain comes tapping down on the skylight is about as good a time as any other to catch up a very neglected diary. It does seem a shame to be a student in Paris for one glorious year and keep no consistent record of what one does and thinks. And yet on a second thought having left my record go unwritten until now of necessity does away with all superfluous writing and leaves only the big important things clearly defined in my mind. Fifty years from now I dont suppose it will matter to me or my children's children whether or not I felt alone and woebegone on a winter's evening or whether I thought a poulet cocotte¹ of a Sunday night was the most delicious meal I had ever eaten. It is this sort of nondescript detail with which one is tempted to fill a diary when such is kept with meticulous care and chronological exactitude. When days and months are far removed one can only remember the exact mood of the high and important points in a series of given days. So here goes for the things that have counted during this golden year in "the city of dreams come true" . . .

I came back from Pontoise and started school at Julians and the Acadamie Colorossi on the fifth of October. I started out with an enthusiasm that I reason to be universal with those who come to Paris to study Art. That I later began to feel that French methods in teaching Art are not the best and that the equipment in their schools is poor matters but little. The record of my work as an isolated thing does not come in this chronicle since my sketches and the products of hours of work are in them selves nothing more than a graphic day-book. And so I shall say simply that I started work at these two schools one of which was the old Acadamie Colorossi where I met Norman.

Norman Rolff was a distinct and definite experience like none other that had gone before it and I have every reason to believe that none will come after it that bear it a marked resemblance. I had seen him once before, in July at the same school. I had come there to sketch and upon entering the court-yard had sat on a bench where he was sitting. He was a queer looking chap to me then, very golden hair and blue eyes with an enormous beard the color of which I cannot now remember. It runs in my mind that it was a vivid red but I am inclined to think that I have his appearance confused with that of an American photographer who is here in Paris whose beard is so bright a red that it is scarcely natural. I sat there because that was the only seat available . . . a group of men occupied the other bench and the space directly in front of it. Later I knew them to be dear old Leopold, who had gray hair and did no end of rotten sketches—apparently and [*sic*] old man with a small allowance who spent his days pittling away at what he dared to call Art; Bepo the tall dark Italian who later became Norman's very good friend and finally fell very violently in love with a girl from Finland whom he took home to his people in Florence; and a Spanish fellow whose name I have forgotten but who gave me the nickname of "la belle tete"[2] which lasted through it all. Norman afterwards told me that he had known when I sat down that I would speak to him the which I did asking him some inane question about what time the class began. He replied with the question, "Do you speak English?" That started it . . . He later offered me a cigarette while we exchanged views on the general rottenness of the French ones. Later on in the class when there was a rest he walked over to me and offered me a cigarette. He had advised me to buy a carnet of tickets as paying for the seances was much cheaper that way.[3] After that day I never went to the school again until October fifth. Oh, I forgot—I saw him twice before October fifth . . . I passed him on the street when he was walking with Bepo. He asked me then why I didn't come back teasing me the while for having done such an American trick as to have bought the tickets and then never to use them. And then October fifth . . . I had thought as I went to work that I should see him and was very disappointed when he was not there. However, when I went from the downstairs studio to the upstairs one at four oclock I saw him just as he was coming in . . . he explained that he worked at the Grande Chaumiere[4] until four. He asked me if I wouldn't go up to the Rotunda[5] with him to have coffee and I went . . .

And I feel tired of writing this now so I shall leave it for another time.

○ ○ ○

United States

[April 7,] 1936
Foreword

Despite the fact that the very wise always caution the very foolish against procrastination—it being the thief of time—and in the same breath admonish the unaware virgins to keep their wicks trimmed[1]—despite this I am all for the dear old culprit procrastination.[2] For certainly if dawdling and putting off things steals away time, itself, it in like manner steals away the sting of pain and the exultation of joys that are at best ephemeral. I indulge myself in these philosophical meanderings because since I am starting a diary so late in the year—April 7th to be exact—and so late in life—turning thirty-four to be more painfully exact—I can find no better excuse for my tardiness than that my delay has at least spared me the number of days indelibly written down in their passing fury of joys and sorrow. Had I started this diary yesterday, the day before, last year or any other time than today I would no doubt have put down a rather accurate account of happenings that are passed and somehow very irrevocably over, if for no other reason than that the clock rolls around. I say I'm spared these records of days—yes, spared, for no matter how carefully I remember and retell things that have happened to me the very fact that the emotions attending them have cooled with the minutes, hours and years makes everything that has transpired up to this point a little bit different from what it really is. And so no matter how morbidly I delve into past joys and sorrows they can never quite come alive. As I ruminate over this fact I have a strange, unearthly feeling of suspended time. There are before me pages totaling three months in which to pack the matter of a mere thirty-odd years. There's something of the satisfaction of cheating time in being able to cram so much living in such small space.

Immediately I ask myself why use the pages up to April 7th? Why not just let time remain suspended, unrecorded, unheeded? But such a consideration leads me to the question of why keep a diary at all. And here I really pause to wonder. If ever there were a [the entry abruptly breaks off here]

April 8, 1936

Another day in which I feel nothing will—nothing <u>must</u> happen between Norman [Lewis] and me. And again we quarrel senselessly about such things as fixing a clothesline and whether or not the dog shall urinate in the park. And again we say needless unkind things to each other and Norman again intimates that he's sorry he ever met me or the dog or something—at any rate it all means the same thing. Despite the fact that he again used vile language at me I find myself strangely cold and somehow unhurt at what now becomes a common occurrence between us. However, I say some pretty hard things to him which I sincerely feel are true. When he has left for school I further degrade myself by running to the "El" station after him. Then to school to the Graphic Arts class where I experience a pretty discouraging time what with aimless attempts at cleaning plates and putting on aquatint grounds. And so home pretty well fagged out to meet Norman in the street with Jocko.[1] We then go into the park for another try at it. Rather a sweet session in which I indulge in some more self abnegation and say I'm sorry and only mean I love him. He says little except he is sorry we quarrel. And then home where we try another chess lesson and I manage to remember some of the teachings of the night before. "Lights Out" on the radio and a very mystifying session in bed in which I am desired physically but not spiritually and in which [I] strike real bottom by again doing the asking. Being left by a man at a time most men desire you is heart sickening.

April 9, 1936

[. . .] Home at seven oclock to find Norman aloof, disinterested and prone to start a fight which luckily I am able to circumvent by keeping most of my feelings to myself. Ernestine comes at eight oclock before we have finished dinner at which hour my day ends because this living death I have been through for four hours cannot be called living. What I wonder most at is why I let myself be subjected to the same kind of treatment Jack[1] meted out by someone who doesn't even love me. I finally see Norman and he casually asks me what I've been doing for all the world as some one would ask who didn't really give a damn. Brings up the question of Saturday nite's dance when I ask him to lend me a dollar. Offers to give me a ticket and go alone—how little he seems to understand or care. Going to the dance without him would mean nothing to me. And yet he cares so little about me that he cant understand that it's being with him that really matters. 1:30 and he has a drawing to do and elects to work upstairs rather than in my room—it has always been so sweet to lie in bed and be able to look across the room at him working. And so to bed quite heavy of heart.

And then I go upstairs where he is working only to find Stafford there sketching when Norman knows so well how painfully I've waited to be alone with him and even said, "hurry up with the dishes so we can get out of Stafford's way." And so again I feel very alone when a little thought and consideration on his part would have given me a feeling of togetherness. All thru this very rainy night I have felt a hopeless loneliness when a rainy night at home under the same roof with the man you love should be such a comfort. Makes me think of Frank[2] and how we loved the rains so much together. But I suppose reminiscing is a sign of age so saying I shall emphatically shut this book and its emotions with it and go to bed with the hope that sleep will indeed "knit up the raveled sleeve of care."[3]

April 18, 1936

What a day! I get up fairly early and dash out to buy nitric acid and pans for etching at which I work practically all day. A group of Smith College students come to visit on one of these damned Reconciliation tours which seem sillier with each of their numerous visits. I suppose, though, there's some sense in it in view of the fact that Augusta [Savage] sold $20 worth of the small replicas of "Gamin."[1] Today's most important happenings have to do with my relation to Norman. Together we had planned to arise early and both of us to go out in the morning and then return to work on through the evening. In his characteristic manner he changes his mind and ends up saying bluntly about 6 oclock that he was going out. He was supposed to be going to the tailor's. I ask to go along—he says no et al and the same old arguments ensue. He leaves and I find out later he spent about an hour talking with Augusta about our affairs. He sends her to tell me he has gone to tell Ernestine not to come back again. Augusta tells me that he said had it been left to him to decide he would have chosen Ernestine since she took less out of him and was more restful. It seems from what Augusta said that he left none of it unsaid. So I write him a very nice letter telling him what I expect and what I will give in return. He comes back about 9 oclock and says nothing. While we play chess he says, "This is your night."

May 7, 1936

[. . .] I catch the 3:58 to Hempstead and arrive at the sweet little house I once called home to find Jack asleep after a bad night. When he awoke he seemed glad to see me. [The doctor] came and examined Jack and had a long talk with me in which he advised me that from now on Jack's heart would have a leaking valve. Maje came with fruit and fresh eggs and seemed surprised and glad to see me there. I have the privilege afforded to few wives of reading a letter to Jack from one of his sweethearts recalling past joys and planning a rendezvous with him for June. Leave Hempstead on the 11:34 and arrive in N.Y. very tired but very eager for the welcome of Norman's arms. Before leaving I had written him a note asking that he have Ernestine leave before I returned. I might well have reasoned that I couldn't trust him to consider me this much. I further degrade myself by looking thru the key-hole at them sweetly embracing—nice life we're all living! Lonely and ever so sick of what I consider a dirty mess. Norman is so sweet and loving most of the time that I cant understand how he continues to subject me to such mental torture. I wonder why this had to happen to me of all people—just when I'm trying to live down and forget similar treatment from Jack. I sincerely wish I had never met Norman, altho I love him more dearly, it seems, than I have ever loved anyone. At least I love him with less reason for doing so.

Ernestine and Norman leave together at two oclock.

January 3, 1937

A lazy day in which I do little other than read the Sunday papers. I help Norman get the applications ready for two paintings he plans sending to the Pennsylvania Academy Show. One is called The Yellow Hat¹ a large canvas done very simply in what is generally thought of as Mexican colors—bluish green, white and warm yellows and browns. It was given a very prominent hanging in the last WPA Teachers' Show. It's very lovely in color and very simple in treatment. The other painting is a small canvas of a "Negro girl" done very modernly and having about it quite a mood of mystery. I sincerely hope his paintings are accepted for the exhibition—it will mean so much to him. He deserves success regardless of how unhappy his present actions make me. [. . .]

June 19, 1958

10:40 p.m.

Home from Dorothy West's but a short time, and filled with good feeling at having seen her again after so many years; a charming, bright sharply spoken person. We talk of this and that with an intimacy that was surprisingly at ease after the years that separated our knowing each other. When there is more time, I'd like to rethink the things about which she, Dick and I talked. On first thought, it seems to have been only chit chat, but underneath there seemed the [*sic*] have been something of importance exchanged between us.

What a day we had! Steady rain all morning, and I write post cards while Dick read The Fall by Albert Camus. [. . .]

Then to South Beach where we have the marvelous stretch alone with the waves and gulls. We take a long walk on the wet sand, and seemed to leave all the world behind. Except for the scurrying bit of sea weed that looked like a brown furry animal scooting along the sand instead of dried vegetations propelled by the rising wind, there was no incident during our walk. Just the sea and its waves and occasionally the gulls sailing up and down.

To and from the beach we passed a farmer's field, nicely sown, which was full of a hundred or more gulls with two crows. They were patterned across the dark wet ground eating either seeds or newly grown seedlings, but they made such a pretty picture. Dick told me of the time in Maine when the gulls took a liking to blueberries and ate up the state's entire crop. The following year they returned to eating fish.

Back again to Edgartown and we find a small bookstore—Borrowdale. A nice, friendly place, which made us envy the proprietors' better mousetrap.

On the way back to Oak Bluffs, we found that the wind on the Sound had risen. Then and after dinner, before going to Dorothy's, we watched the waves pounding the rocks and shore. This sea, these waves, this island have stolen our hearts. There seem not to be enough hours for looking, sensing, absorbing and being absorbed by the sea around this wondrous isle.

CORRESPONDENCE

Introduction

Bennett was friends with many literary and intellectual figures throughout her lifetime, including Langston Hughes, Countee Cullen, Harold Jackman, W. E. B. Du Bois, Claude McKay, James Weldon Johnson, and Richard Wright. Her correspondence with many of these individuals provides readers with illuminating snapshots of life inside and outside Harlem, the literary climate, politics, and various other topics. One of the first letters Bennett wrote to a literary mentor or colleague was to Du Bois. In her January 19, 1925, letter, Bennett appears torn about whether she should accept her scholarship and travel abroad to France. She also expresses her wish that Jesse Redmond Fauset would be in France during the same time. While abroad in Paris (June 1925–May 1926) it is clear that Bennett felt isolated from her friends and tried her best to keep alive the connections she once enjoyed in Harlem. Her letters to Hughes, Jackman, and Cullen from France show her actively supporting other writers and reflect her fluctuating feelings about her own ability as a poet. In one of the first letters Bennett wrote to Cullen, on August 28, 1925, she expresses her excitement about him winning the Witter Bynner poetry contest, talks about how ambivalent she currently feels about Paris, and asks after several literary friends, among other things. In a later letter, on December 2, Bennett hopes Hughes will win some of the *Opportunity* prizes, but she also shows her lack of confidence in her own writing with her statement, "I shall try to get some things ready to send off to the Opportunity contest but you know how it is when you definitely set out to do something comme ça."

The longer Bennett stayed in Paris and mixed with young writers the more comfortable she became in her literary talents. In a December 2, 1925, letter to Langston Hughes she expresses her excitement about meeting and becoming friends with Sylvia Beach, who in turn introduced her to literary figures such as Ernest Hemingway, Gertrude Stein, and James Joyce. Mingling with these writers reinvigorated Bennett. Before long she tells Hughes, "I sent some stuff to Opportunity" (1926).

In addition to letters from Bennett's time abroad in the 1920s, we have also included letters from the 1930s and 1940s. These letters show that while Bennett was being hounded by the FBI for her alleged Communist sympathies, she remained steadfast in her dedication to the arts. Two such letters are directed to her colleague and good friend Alain Locke. In one, dated May 11, 1939, Bennett writes of the government scrutiny to which she and the Harlem Community Art Center are being subjected. She asks him if he would consider testifying on her behalf "before the New York committee on one of your trips in town." She also advises him that if he contacts her "records will be kept of such communications coming to me and it would be wise to word anything you send in such a way as to be intelligible only to me." In another letter to Locke, dated November 30, 1941, Bennett writes at length about her suspension from the Harlem Community Art Center, asking "What am I actually guilty of?" The FBI has found "nothing but my most natural connections in things of cultural importance to Negroes." Frustrated by what she has endured to date, Bennett makes fun of the ridiculous claims the authorities are making at her: "With great secrecy I read several poems at the Ford dinner upon the publication of his book on the Negro—so secret, in fact, as to have been announced beforehand and to have appeared with my picture in the Negro press." Though Bennett is concerned that her beloved husband, Dick, might "be drawn into this mess [. . .] for not a single reason except that he married me," she notes that "my sincere interest in the future of Negro arts and letters continues unabated." In the rest of her letter Bennett details her plans to begin work for the School for Democracy in the New Year and asks that Locke will "agree to speak as one of my guest speakers during the term." As part of Bennett's commitment to African Americans advancing in numerous fields, including the arts, Bennett also wrote to her friend Langston Hughes to request that he, too, appear as a guest speaker at the school.

Bennett also offers congratulations to her literary friends Claude McKay, Richard Wright, and James Weldon Johnson. Her letter to McKay, from February 25, 1937, informs him that she hopes to review his autobiography, *A Long Way from Home*, and suggests that they consider collaborating on a book project. It is exciting to hear in her March 3, 1940, letter her comments on Wright's *Native Son* while she is in the midst of reading it while also, on a personal note, congratulating him on his recent marriage and hinting at plans for her own upcoming nuptials. Her January 4, 1938, letter to James Weldon Johnson concerns not a recent Johnson publication, but his earlier autobiography, *Along This Way*. While complimenting Johnson for this work, Bennett segues into a host of other topics, including asking him if he would consider speaking at the Harlem Community Art Center, if he could help arrange a position for her at Fisk University, and if he would think of writing a book on anti-lynching legislation.

In addition to letters to her literary colleagues, Bennett also corresponded with her family and other personal acquaintances. A small sample of these highly personal letters has been included because they reveal the sometimes-tortured relationship Bennett had with her parents. The letters show the love as well as the palpable hurt and anger that existed within this fractured unit. The letter to her father and stepmother dated January 5, 1925, for example, concerns a recent trip home from Howard University. She is apologetic about how little she has written her parents while away and the lack of time she spent with them on her visit. Still, she wants them to know of her gratitude toward them and remind them of her love.

The May 27, 1925, letter to her father is more disturbing. In it, she informs him that the mother of one of her former students has written to her about the relationship Bennett's father is carrying on with the young co-ed. Despite her love for her father, she chastises him forcefully for causing such shame to the family. Even worse, she remarks, "this is the second instance I have had of what your ill-conduct can bring upon me."

As mentioned in prior sections, Bennett's kidnapping as a child disrupted her relationship with her biological mother, Mayme Pizarro. Her mother tries to rekindle the relationship, introducing herself as a close family friend and not Bennett's mother. When she soon discloses the true nature of their relationship, Bennett is overwhelmed and does not respond for some time. In her letter to her long-estranged mother, from August 31, 1938, she apologizes for not contacting her sooner upon discovering who she really was. Bennett tries to explain the significant events that have taken place during their years apart and promises that she will "do everything I can" to reestablish their broken relationship. Although the sentiment seems sincere, both women were never truly able to make up for all the time that they were apart or the wounds each woman suffered because of that forced absence.

It is interesting to compare Bennett's letter to her biological mother to letters to her stepmother, Marechal Neil. As she bluntly stated in an interview with Sandra Govan, "The very fact of being my mother [Mayme] did not make her my mother because the mother to me was the stepmother" (qtd. in *Gwendolyn Bennett*, 182). Gwen is able to be much more relaxed with her stepmother, gossiping over things and calling her "Mumsey." In her July 27, 1928, letter she is even open enough to confess potential marital problems with Alfred Jackson: "Now Mumsey, draw up close to me and look into my eyes. You have always been everything to me—don't fail me now. I want to feel that if ever a time comes that I cant be happy in my married life that I can call on you to lend me carfare to come home. You are always my mother—dont feel you have lost me."

Bennett's October 6, 1947, letter to her Aunt Flora Dugan is important for providing our most detailed description of Dick Crosscup, whom she describes as "handsome" and "well educated." She also advises them that "a finer person you've never met." Bennett goes on at great length about how happy the two of them are and what "a wonderful life [they have] together." With great poignancy she expresses her hurt over her Uncle Len's refusal to let Crosscup into his home because Dick was white. Bennett's delicate balancing act between love of and anger at her aunt and uncle is quite powerful.

The September 9, 1937, letter to James Vernon Herring, her former supervisor at Howard University, helps to explain Bennett's resignation from her teaching post. Her pain over the situation is still palpable some ten years later, and she expresses her thanks to Herring for his support of her at the time. Bennett also provides a good amount of explanation of her work situation after leaving Howard, filling in gaps in her life, as she requests a recommendation letter from Herring for a teaching position in the New York City public school system.

The final letter that has been included in this collection was dated September 27, 1968, and designed as a "farewell" to her many friends.

After years of being hounded by the government for reported Communist activities Gwen and her husband, Dick, decided to move to Kutztown, Pennsylvania. Gwen's marriage to Dick was a true partnership in every way, and each was the other's strongest supporter. There the couple opened up an antiques shop and lived a quiet life away from the hustle and bustle of New York—and they were able to do so with none of the residents of the small rural town knowing anything of Bennett's remarkable place in the development of the Harlem Renaissance.

Literary Friends

To W. E. B. Du Bois
January 19, 1925
[Howard University letterhead]

Dear Dr. Du Bois:—

May I presume upon your friendship to ask for any advice you might have to offer me about my going abroad.[1] I find myself floundering hopelessly.

I am still walking on air about the whole thing . . . it seems that it cant be true. I wish Jessie [Fauset] were going to be there when I go over.

I realize that a typewritten letter is a misdemeanor. Wont you forgive me? Love to Yolande[2] and Mrs. Du Bois.[3]

Sincerely yours,
Gwendolyn B. Bennett[4]

To Countee Cullen
August 28, 1925
Paris, France

Countée—dear friend,

Needless to say that my heart is fairly bursting with pride and joy to hear of your winning this year's Witter Bynner Contest.[1] A less staunch heart than yours would have been content with two second prizes. Speaking of aiming at stars, you have virtually disarranged the entire stellar system. I get infinite courage out of being in the same race with you and inward glow at being able to call you "friend."

I haven't had a just chance to find out whether I like Paris or not. My first impressions were of extreme loneliness and intense home-sickness . . . this and incessant rain. My second impressions were of home-ties, stirred by my American friends who were visiting Europe this summer. And now . . . through the hazy veil of memories I see that Paris is a very beautiful city and that people here are basically different from those I have always known. I feel that I shall like being here bye and bye [*sic*].

I am so happy to hear that Langston Hughes is to have a Vanity Fair page to match yours. Good for the Writers' Guild. Also glad to hear that

Eric [Walrond] is to be Opportunity's new business manager. He needs something like that. It will give him money and also a chance to write.

It's too bad about Dr. [Alain] Locke's ejection from Howard.[2] It seems a shame to do away with so much brains at a stroke.

What are you going to do next year? Going to Harvard? I hope so!

Tell me, what's happening in "the only city"? Literally and other-wisely. Are the Crisis-ilk still sitting on their golden egg of publications. Is Gene [Jean] Toomer writing? When does your book come out?

Harold [Jackman] and I spent many wonderful hours trotting around Paris together and equally as many hours saying to each other, "Who'd a thought it!"

I have joined a very interesting little, private library here—"Shakespeare and Co" by name. It features the newer writers. Harold and I both have ordered "Ulysses" from them. The copies weren't ready when Harold left and hence I am to send his copy to him. I'm kind-a fearful that he wont get it . . . they're certainly strict about that book. Those of us who are a-kin to Croesus[3] can also get a copy of Frank Harris' "Life and Loves"[4] for 300 francs or fifteen dollars. The "Ulysses" only cost 60 francs. I should love to have them both to add to my library of pornography. Oh yes, there is such a thing!

Please write to me . . . I'm starved for both news and companionship. Every item is of worlds of interest to me.

Doesn't it seem ages since we danced so joyously about together at Easter-time? How de world do move, Honey!

Best love,
Gwennie[5]

To Langston Hughes
December 2, 1925
Paris, France

Dear Langston,
This will no doubt be counted as one of the two letters you have asked me to write you . . . do you feel that you couldn't stand any more than that? I ask because I am quite willing to answer as many letters as you will send me, so there!

Life flows along all too evenly here. I begin to meet some new people and know some new things. Chief among them Sylvia Beach and George

Antheil[1] and incidentally the crowd that goes with them. You know "Shakespeare and Co." in the Rue de l'Odeon, dont you? If not, the next time you are here you must go there tout de suite.

Paul and Essie Robeson were here the first week in November. That was a happy break for me. Incidentally I horned in on all the wonderful places to which they were invited. Chief among them were the teas at Sylvia Beach's at which none other than James Joyce, Arthur Moss,[2] Lewis Galantiere,[3] Ernest Hemingway and George Antheil were present along with several other celebrities whose names I do not remember; the tea at Gertrude Stein's and of course every body was there; and the tea at Matisse's home; and I almost forgot the tea and luncheon at the millionaire's home in the Bois du Bologne. It gave me an interesting little peep into things as the great see them. After it was over I was very much the Cinderella sans slipper.

Sylvia Beach is the proprietor of Shakes. and Co. She very sweetly invited me to have Thanksgiving dinner with her. It made me more than happy as you might well guess. Now the only other terrible thing to be gotten past is Christmas alone and in a foreign land. I suppose that by some sort of crook I shall make the grade.

Do send me some of your poetry. And never you mind about whether the colored people like the Covarrubias cover nor the Van Vechten introduction . . . you're not writing your book only for colored people. And if they who chance to have a kinship of race with you dont like your things . . . well, let them go hang!

I have not seen Claude McKay. I know several people who know him, though. At present according to a letter I just received from the Robesons he is in the neighborhood of Nice. Do you know him? If so please send me a letter of introduction to him in the event that he does come to Paris . . . I should like to have your label on me when I shake his hand.

I have not seen Countee's book[4] but I am praying that it will find its way across here to me before long. Everyone agrees with you that is a beauty. I had a long, lovely letter from him about the time I received yours.

I shall try to get some things ready to send off to the Opportunity contest but you know how it is when you definitely set out to do something comme ça. I hope you'll win some of the prizes, though, even if I do like I did last year and send nothing in. With all of my friends behind me I ought to try to send in something. You make no mistake when you say that any money I might win would no doubt come in good about May . . .

and before that. I have sent Countee some stuff for Palms. I hope some of it finds favor in his sight.

You give me a very hard choice to make . . . "if I am not able to get back in college this February, it's down to the seas again for me." Of course, I am strong for higher education, if there is any such animal but I am not so sure that you're not the sort of person who is complete in himself. I envy you your romance of the seas and wish poignantly that I could "hit the wave" with you. I hope we meet in Paris someday. Countee expresses the hope that he will be able to come here next spring. Wouldn't it be marvelous for the three of us to strike here at the same time? It makes me tremble with joy to even think of it.

I haven't gone to the Dome.⁵ I haven't seen the Sinclares.

I shall try to make it to "La Vie Boheme." I wont let Paris down me nor the rains drown me . . . although I'm a-longin' for home.

Write me, boy!

Gwendolyn⁶

P.S. Typewriter is built on an angle like its owner!

To Countee Cullen

January 14, 1926

Paris, France

Dear Countee,

I received your letter of Christmas-tide. Thanks—although it was most painfully short. Pretend to yourself that you are writing copy at so many hundred dollars a page . . . that might do the trick.

The party at the Van Vechtens' sounded marvelous to me. That talking of it should shunt you into a near proposal is appalling. "Does it smack of conceit to say that I thought we would make an admirable alliance?" No, and then again does it smack of conceit for me to tremulously call this a proposal? Allow me that poetic license, wont you?

I like Donald Angus¹—what little I saw of him here. Did he say he had met me?

Unless you get here by the last week in June you wont see me for another space of months. At present I dont think I shall stay through the summer. Money is scarce and I am dreadfully lonely for home and friends.

I <u>do</u> like your book! I fondle its covers at times being glad that it is you who have done this beautiful thing and wondering a bit wistful-eyed whether or not I shall ever have a book published . . . and when? Thanks for the lovely words you wrote in the front to me. I am glad to hear that your first edition is exhausted. I hope you sell a billion of them.

I read and like your poem to Amy Lowell in Poetry.[2] I have sent them two things which they have very kindly returned to me. I am about as convinced as I can be that I cant write. I feel so close to real discouragement. If I could only have one thing accepted, I might feel better. Damn! It's a long road and a rocky one.

I am glad you kept some of my things for Palms.[3] That helped to keep up my spirits a great deal. When will your issue of Palms come out? Send me a copy, won't you? It isn't sold anywhere over here.

I sent several things in to the Opportunity contest. If neither you nor Langston nor Frank Horne send anything in, I might be able to take about tenth place in the race. As it is I simply say to myself that it is something to have entered some stuff. Did you enter anything this year? Langston writes me that he didn't get what he was planning to finish completed in time.

I had a long, wonderful letter from him with much amusing gossip in it about himself and other people. I resent very much his being hailed as "the bus-boy poet." Isn't he rather the poet bus-boy?

By the time you get this letter Opportunity will be out with my cover on it.[4] How do you like it? The truth now.

It's a shame for anyone to be as nice as I am. You wrote me a tiny little note and here I am writing you a young book . . .

Au revoir, Countee. Write me soon, fellow.

Love,

Gwennie[5]

To Harold Jackman
February 23, 1926
Paris, France

Dear Rosebud,

I received your letters of January 30th and Feb. 7th. Thanks so much for such long cheery ones with so much news and expression of opinion therein . . . I get such a kick out of your letters. Do write oftener.

So you think that Sylphine is a clever child, eh? Why, [of] course. I could have told you that much ages ago. I feel that that bit of smuggling entitles me to the Hall of Fame, don't you? So glad you got "Ulysses."[1]

Please tell me at once more about this Albert and Charles Boni prize for the best Negro novel by a Negro. I am really interested so shoot the dope over to me at once.

I dont know the work of Alfred Stieglitz[2] but I too like the moderns although I dont feel that I myself am one . . . at any rate not in painting. My batiks are more so. This year in Paris has been a revelation to me so far as modern work is concerned. Our American modernists are about a thousand years behind the Europeans. Why even interior decoration here has a decidedly modern twist to it. That was plainly visible through the exhibits at the Exposition des Arts Décoratifs[3] this summer. I never saw such furniture. It was rather like the modern poet who says this sound of soft wind is love and its turnings are my darling's lips . . . it was rather impressionism. They said here is bulk and we will call it desk or here is slimness and we will call it a clock . . .

You know too, that I was entertained at the home of one of the most outstanding modern painters while Paul and Essie [Robeson] were here . . . Matisse. It was like going to a holy shrine. His daughter[4] is charming and after that I had tea with her at a very swank place. She is herself a recognized painter among the women of France.

I should have liked to have been in New York to hear Langston read . . . bless him! He has written me lovely letters since I have been here.

Now about my cover on January's Opportunity . . . Of course, I wont get mad about what you said nor about anything that you might ever say. What's a friend for if he cant say what he pleases about you and your work too? But by way of rebuttal—why should my madonna (and you notice that I spell it with a small letter) be "spirituelle," if I dont want her to be? Do you think that immaculate conceptions are such spiritual things as all that? About the swollen jaw I cant say much because I haven't a copy close at hand . . . perhaps you are right, I dont know. I hadn't noticed the fact that my mother of Christ needed her teeth looked after. Now, please dont have "the church" on my trail. [. . .]

Write me soon, H'old.
Just
Gwen[5]

To Langston Hughes

1926

Paris, France

Dear Langston,

Your letter and card came a long time ago and you know as well as do I that I meant to have answered it long ere this. First there came Christmas and a loneliness and longing for home that was kin to desolation. Then came the mad whirl into which I flung myself in order that I might deaden the hurt of my first Christmas away from home. And as always there comes after a tempest a moment of quiet so came my post-Yule lethargy . . . Voilà.

Your recital of places and people made me green with envy and not a little glad with pride for you and of you. Tell [me] more about the proposed Harvard fellowship? Your new book? Vachel Lindsay and others . . .

Raquel Meller[1] is not singing now and I failed to hear her when she was. La Vie Boheme has not played since summer. When it does, I shall go.

I dont like the idea of your being styled a bus-boy gone poet.[2] I'd rather have it . . . "Negro poet finds melody in clatter of dishes." I know some of what you feel although I have not reached the famous stage yet. (Twixt you and me my heart just stops beating for fear I never shall.) I used to wait on tables. Sometime when we meet I shall swap yarns with you about the trials of young artists and especially black ones. But somehow I wouldn't take a seat in heaven for my experiences with and for life.

Glad you liked my pictures. It feels much as though some one had seen my ghost when friends write that my picture looks out at them from Scurlock's window.[3]

And now I have tried for almost two whole pages to talk about this and that just as though I weren't bursting with the loveliest new piece of news ever . . . I HAVE A STUDIO!!!!!! After seven weary months of knocking about here and there I had at last come to the conclusion that finding a studio was an utter impossibility. And then just swish and I had one. I shall move in for good on Saturday next. It is a lovely place and I am so happy. It is just like a nice homely stable and I feel confident that I should be able to do some good work there. The past week has been spent in rushing around and carrying suit-cases. I am worn to a frazzle but tickled silly at the opportunity to wear myself out in this cause. Why, I am so excited about it that I cant even talk about it.

Please send me a copy of your book[4] as you said you would. I got Countee's just before Christmas . . . he had such a lovely autograph and greeting in the front. Wonder what your fly-leaf will say to my kindred spirit. Yes, I, too, think Countee's book is beautiful inside and out. I have read it from kiver to kiver [cover to cover] several times. One doesn't usually do that with poetry but I think I am justified this time. I wish you all the success that you could possibly have with its sale as well as its reviews. Let me know about some of them.

Paris has at last "gotten" me. I feel as tho' I never want to leave . . . These next few months will be so precious and so short. I have never loved any city the way I love this—rain and all. It took me many a day to get at this affection but here it is at last. It's so mellow and dear!

The Konrad Bercovici's[5] are here and have a beautiful apartment. I spend much of my time with them. They insist that I eat a meal at their place every other day. I grow more and more fond of them.

I am giving English lessons to Frans Masereel[6] who is quite a recognized French artist. Have you seen his wood-cuts in Vanity Fair?

I sent some stuff to Opportunity's contest. Pray for my success—a nice heathen prayer.

Please write me again soon. Did you get your prose ready by the end of January? Hope so. My work goes well—

Gwennie.[7]

To Claude McKay
February 25, 1937
321 West 136th Street,
New York, N.Y.

Dear Claude,
Thanks so much for <u>A Long Way From Home</u>!!!!! I received it yesterday and can scarcely contain myself until I can commence reading it. I am just finishing <u>I Write As I Please</u>[1] by Duranty and dont want to lay it aside because I feel that much of it will give me a back-ground for your Moscow experiences.

I am enclosing copies of the letters I am sending to May Cameron on <u>The Post</u> and Irita Van Doren.[2] Here's hoping I get the review from <u>Books</u>.

If not, I shall try places like the Nation or New Republic. Failing all of these, I am certain to get the review for either the Crisis or Opportunity. I wonder if you could possibly come over to the house Saturday or Sunday to talk about this matter of review with me. If not, call me on Augusta's [Savage] 'phone Saturday morning about eleven oclock—the number is Audubon 3-2868.

I need not tell you how much luck I wish you with the sales of this book. Words are inadequate to express how much I wish for you from it! At any rate, let me know what is happening to you about it.

I haven't mentioned to you several ideas I have about books that ought to be written but I'd like to do so. One of them I think you could help me with—we might even do it together.

Since I never seem to be able to find your address when I want it, I am sending this to Furman's[3] with the hope that you will get it speedily. And please get in touch with me.

> Yours very sincerely,
> Gwendolyn Bennett[4]

To James Weldon Johnson
January 4, 1938
250 West 134th Street, Apt. 12 1/2
New York City, N.Y.

Dear James Weldon Johnson,
Let me first wish you and lovely Grace Nail Johnson a happy and prosperous New Year.

Then let me tell you what a thrilling experience I just have had with one of your books, namely, "Along this Way."[1] When the book was published, I not only was marooned out in Hempstead, Long Island, but my doctor husband & I were enmeshed in the bitter depression years that throttled the efforts of the self-employed "little" professional man. The local library did not carry your autobiography nor did my repeated requests that it be purchased for its shelves bring any results. [. . .]

My reading "Along This Way" came in the midst of what practically amounted to a research course in the James Weldon Johnson–ana. As I told you the night of the opening of the Art Center, I had just finished reading "Black Manhattan"[2] for the third time—I was preparing a paper to be read at the Second National American Artists' Congress and also getting together the material for the brochure on the Harlem Community Art Center and I knew "Black Manhattan" to be invaluable source material for anything regarding the historic, social or artistic of the Negro artist or his locale, Harlem. As a logical sequence, I read "Along This Way."

You are wondering, no doubt, why the book, except for its literary merit excited me so much. I dont think you can possibly realize what reading that book means to a young Negro who with one or two talents finds himself lost in the labyrinth of things that must be done and ways to do them and yet live. Mayhap it is because the last ten years have done such terrible things to me—the attempt to make a compatible whole of married life and my artistic talents, my failure to do so; my virtually giving up my own work in order to assist my husband in having his chance—the depression fixed that and he died leaving me out of touch with my own world and penniless; and then WPA and slow, heart-rending steps that falter in the attempt "to get back"—I say maybe this is why your book meant so much to me at this time. I seemed to sense a deep, pervading understanding of what all this mental torture means in what you were telling about your own life. And although I am several years behind time, I want to thank you for having written it.

Having gone through such an emotional experience as a result of having read your book, I find myself full of plans and eager to complete many of those already a-brewing. It makes it all the more necessary that I see you and have one of our old-time talks in which I used to burden you with the role of father confessor. I know you are busy with getting ready to go to Nashville[3] but I would so much like to get a chance to talk to you about so many things.

I see from Claude's [McKay] note that you are meeting a group of us at his house Saturday night. Is there a bare possibility that you have a moment free late Saturday afternoon?

And now on another matter [. . .] I dont know how much longer I can stand the strain of working under the Federal Art Project. It is interesting work and certainly the Art Center should have a real future but it's all so haphazard and insecure. I have a B.S. from Columbia in Fine Arts Education, am a graduate of Pratt Institute in Art, studied abroad for a year, at the Barnes Foundation for another year, and am now at work on my M.A. in History of Art at N.Y.U. I'd like very much to work at a place like Fisk. During the winter I am going to try to arrange to see Dr. Jones on one of his week-ends in New York. I have very definite and special ideas about how art should be taught at a place like Fisk where Music has always played such an important part and now with your work the cycle seems to round out except as to the plastic arts. Ostensibly I shall be seeing Dr. Jones in an effort to have him visit the Harlem Community Art Center and watch it function. Actually, I hope to renew my acquaintance with him and tell him some of my ideas about the teaching of Art. My reason for telling you all this is, first, I should like your opinion on the possibilities of my having a chance to come to Fisk, next, I should like to ask you to put in a good word for me, if the subject is broached to you.

And I want to talk to you about the book on the Negro dance about which you spoke in the restaurant . . .

Please try to make time somewhere in this last week of yours for a talk with me, wont you? I must write now—I have so much to say. Maybe you can help me out of my dirth [*sic*] of too much thinking. And I'd like your opinion on some of my recent poetry.

Just in passing let me suggest that you write a book on the whole neat travesty of the matter of anti-lynching legislation. Your erudition and restraint in writing about it in your autobiography was superb. Now, with what happened in the last special session of Congress⁴ and what is likely to happen in this session, you might add one or two chapters to your own experiences in trying to wipe out this blotch on our country's escutcheon.

I've written a long letter—I only intended a note. Forgive me for "letting down my hair." I've always felt that way about you and Grace, somehow.

I'd like to see her, too, if it can be arranged. She is the most graciously beautiful person I know.

Sincerely yours,
Gwendolyn Bennett⁵

To Alain Locke
May 11, 1939
250 West 154th Street,
Apt. 12/12
New York, N.Y.

Dear Alain,

First let me say that the Harlem Cultural Conference has been held. It was held on May 6h and 7th. I have been feeling pretty miserable because I realized that I was at least partially responsible for your not being here to participate in it. I dont know what happened to the letter I wrote you about the change of dates and what I wanted you to do with reference to the different sessions in which you were undoubtedly interested. [. . .]

And now I want to ask a favor of you. You no doubt are aware of the activities being carried on by the Congressional Investigating Committee, set up to examine the WPA. They seem to be giving especial attention to the Federal Art Projects. Having started on the Federal Art Project with the confiscation of the photograph-book used in the model division, they have turned their attention to the Harlem Community Art Center. Phony telephone calls about union meetings and the location of CIO unions in other parts of the building, questions about the raising of the rent for the Center, special reports et al lead me to think that they are preparing for the consumption of southern senators a juicy bit on thousands of dollars being spent for Negroes to study art with somehow a connection between us and the neighboring unions. It's silly, yes, but entirely possible when we see what they did with the Theater Project and the fact that there are mixed casts in their musical shows. I feel that the Center's nose is eminently clean but you know what it has to suffer from enemies within its own ranks. I know you to be a true sympathizer in the tribulations we have had to bear. I know that you realize as I do that Harlem as a community can not be counted on to see clearly any issues involved when adverse publicity is launched against even as worthwhile a venture as the Center. What I want you to do about it is to volunteer to testify before the New York committee on one of your trips in town. Your testimony need not involve you in any controversial matters. Such statements as you will give about the excellence of the work that has been done at the Center and its value to the community and the need there for will be read into the congressional records as an antidote for whatever twisted impressions the so-called investigators will attempt to voice. There are some real discriminatory issues involved here that should be combatted. I feel that your position as a national figure of importance and judgment in the world of Negro art will add weight to the defense of the Center which I will not be given a chance to give. I am counting on your clarity of vision and our long, fine friendship and your real genuine interest in the Negro artists to persuade you to assist me in this matter.

If you are interested, I shall talk over the details with you on your next visit. If that visit is some time off, I should appreciate a telegram sent to my home address stating that you wish more and explicit information on how to proceed. In the matter of a telegram I shall have to warn you that records will be kept of such communications coming to me and it would be wise to word anything you send in such a way as to be intelligible only to me. [. . .]

Since I have long since given up sleeping at night—so oppressed is my mind with many things—I am able in some of the early morning hours to jot down a poem or two. I look forward to your reading and criticizing them as you have always been kind enough to do. My health has suffered considerably from the lack of rest but I hope a return to the fabulous state of "normalcy" somewhere along the line will allow me a chance to recuperate for another battle along the lines I believe sincerely to by right.

Your friendship is one of the bright spots in what at most times appears to be a pretty dull picture.

Yours sincerely,
Gwennie[1]

To Richard Wright
March 3, 1940

Dear Richard Wright,
Again my hand is extended to you in congratulation and praise!

I managed to squeeze in the reading of about 150 pages of <u>Native Son</u> today even though the week-end catching up had me deeply snowed under. Last night about seven oclock I made such a happy pilgrimage down to Eighth Street to purchase the book, feeling both glad that you had written it and glad that I was one of your friends who happened to have money enough to buy it. Let me say that it has been difficult to lay the tale aside even for the urgent call of work.

Each day I have read avidly the glowing reviews of the book—this comes after the months of waiting for its appearance. My heart swelled with pride when reading of you as Dickens, Dreiser, Dostoevsky, and Steinbeck rolled into one. For me the publishing and acceptance of your book is one of the most momentous points in the Negro's history in America.

This is as good an occasion as any to congratulate you on your marriage.[1] I hope some occasion for me to meet your wife can be arranged. These things interest me mightily these days since I am contemplating a similar step before too long.[2]

Under separate cover I will be writing you about a business matter[3] but for the present let me extend to you my felicitations and hurrahs for the grand thing your book is for all of us who labor on the cultural front.

Sincerely, deeply so,
Gwendolyn[4]

To Alain Locke
November 30, 1941
2 West 120th Street, Apt. 5L
New York, N.Y.

Dear Alain,

So very much has happened since last we talked that I can hardly decide which should be the beginning point. Lucky for me that you are one of the real friends with whom I can skip most of the "in-betweens." I'll presume to jot down highlights, hoping that you know me well enough to fill in the details.

My suspension and the reasons are a matter of public record. I need not tell you who it was that started this attack against me. Finding nothing but my most natural connections in things of cultural importance to Negroes, the investigators then began working with even more irresponsible people than those who first started the attack. What am I actually guilty of? With great secrecy I read several poems at the Ford dinner upon the publication of his book on the Negro[1]—so secret, in fact, as to have been announced beforehand and to have appeared with my picture in the Negro press. I read poems at the Jacques Roumain dinner[2] where the guest of honor advocated the overthrow of our government. I was chairman of the Negro

Playwrights Company where I introduced the well-known Communist, Richard Wright. Together with many other people (no matter that such people as yourself and Jessie Fauset also sponsored) I sponsored these three events. After long questioning of all the people who have worked under my supervision where nothing derogatory to my character could be ascertained nor any indication of Communist activities, the investigators turned to witnesses that either had a grudge against me or were people anxious to give "information," although false. No source of information was divulged. Only because I was up against the same sort of thing for so long a time was I able to read between the lines. The story is a long and horrible one which I shall tell you in detail when next I see you.

I cannot tell you what the present status of the case is. As a matter of experience Mrs. [Audrey] McMahon[3] fired me with fourteen other supervisors on the quota cut. This in itself would be nothing except for the fact that my "case" continues in Washington until something definite is decided. Whether or not the good evidence in my favor is going to outway [sic] that of irresponsible or biased people is something I cannot tell. For a long time my morale was low and I was frankly frightened for fear that Dick, for not a single reason except that he married me, would be drawn into the mess. It's been a pretty sickening thing to me, as you can well imagine. The next time you are in New York I wish you would arrange a moment or two to talk with me about it. I feel certain that even as late as it is you may be able to do something to help me get the record cleared up.

In the meantime my sincere interest in the future of Negro arts and letters continues unabated. My heart has rejoiced at news of your efforts in getting an exhibit of Negro artists' work at the Downtown Gallery. I want to hear first hand from you the story of the exhibit just held[.] [F]or the moment the name of the gallery slips my mind. I want to hear how the sale of the book[4] goes . . . and many other things.

I have decided that I will continue telling the story of the Negro's cultural contribution to American culture, no matter what my enemies have tried to do to me. You know as well as I do how securely the recognized, respectable sources of employment and expression are closed to me. That I have worked hard and maintained an enviable record means nothing to those without courage in their hearts and the will that justice is shown in their acts. And so, beginning in January I am accepting employment in the School for Democracy. I have assured myself that the school is not a

Marxist school; that it is not another Workers' School under a fancy name; that anything I say or do has to be motivated by a particular philosophy.[5] That people on the staff have been the objects of an injustice similar to my own I am convinced. The fact remains that they are interested in my giving a course on the Negro in the various fields of culture in my own way is reason enough for me to accept the job and to be excited about its prospects.

I have made no bones about sespecting your knowledge of this whole field and your sincerity in all your various attempts to advance the thesis that the Negro has made a real contribution to the culture of any land in which he found himself. There are two things you can do to help me out with this new turn in my endeavors: 1) arrange to talk with me and help me plot certain patters of thinking; 2) Agree to speak as one of my guest speakers during the term. The first of these two I am sure you will accede to without a moment's hesitation, since I've always found you a willing listener to all my problems and hopes. The second I dare to hope will bring an affirmative answer, since I know you to be a person of courage and principle. I feel that it is too late for you to begin to be scared off now after all the courageous stands you have made in the past. I will feel that my course is a miserable failure, if I am not able to obtain your consent to speak for me at least once and possibly twice. To say nothing of the personal hurt your refusal will cause me. [. . .]

> Please let me hear from you post haste.
> Sincerely,
> Gwendolyn Bennett

> P.S. Dick sends best regards and says come see us.[6]

To Langston Hughes
May 13, 1942
[School for Democracy letterhead]

Dear Langston,
I just got through calling you only to have Toy[1] tell me that you were "at the studios." Sounded pretty important to me. She suggested that I might be able to get you around dinner time tonight. Since I'm going to have to be catching a train for a lecture in Elizabeth, N.J., I might not be able to get you at just the hour specified. So . . . a letter.

It's nice not to have to go into a long song and dance about what the School for Democracy is and why. Under separate cover I am sending you the staggering catalogue for our just completed successful winter term. At present we are busy planning for our summer school at the same time that we are carrying on a Spring Term. Briefly, the summer school will be at Fishkill, N.Y.—a bit north of Peekskill—on a wonderful "millionaire's estate." In addition to regular classes conducted by members of our staff we are hoping to have a series of single lectures given by people who are well-known in their fields. You've guessed it—we would like to have you be one of those lecturers. The school will be held during July and August and as yet the dates are not set so that you have the whole range of dates to choose from. Please say "yes," Lang.

By the way. I've bought your new book[2] and love it. Furthermore, I've bought one or two (two to be exact) copies for friends. Dick and I as usual are among your most avid fans.

And while we are at it . . . what about the translations you promised me for lending you a book of poetry. Just this debt alone ought to make you agree to come to our summer school for a lecture.

Incidentally, we are pressed for time on this matter of getting our guest lecturers. We were not able to secure the proper place for the summer school until Monday of this week which means that printing etc. must be done in a hurry as people who plan taking vacations are already at work making plans. So please, honey, say yes quick . . . I'll ring you tomorrow for your answer.

Best luck to you.
Gwennie[3]

o o o

Family and Associates

To Joshua Bennett and Marechal Neil Bennett
January 5, 1925
[Howard University letterhead]

Dearest Mumsey and Daddy,
Well, as you requested I am typing a line or two to say I am here all safe and sound. The journey was a long one on a crowded train. It seemed that

everyone under the sun was on the trains twixt here and New York. The train was about three quarters of an hour late making us just barely have time to get in the house, get cleaned up and off to school.

Mr. and Mrs. Glenn were ever so glad to see me and I was most glad to see them. It seemed so peculiar to be in Washington once more . . . Washington with its quiet streets and no elevators nor subways. Strangely enough the streets here are also covered with snow. The weather overhead is beautiful. The campus is really beautiful with the sun shining down on the snow and the trees casting strangely fantastic shadows across all the whiteness.

I know it was awful how little we saw of each other during this my first holiday at home. It came at an unfortunate time. You see it seemed that everything was going on at the same time and if you lived in this God-forsaken place like I do you'd be able to understand why I would want to do a lot of running around. It really would have been wonderful for us to have been a little more with one another. It is so marvelous to be in New York that I just cant go enough. You'll try to forgive me wont you? I know it's kind of hard for you to get my point of view, but try wont you?

I appreciate all the little things you both did for me during my brief stay at home. So often there were little acts of love and thoughtfulness that you might have thought that I did not see nor did I feel the proper grate-fulness therefor . . . I saw, though and I loved you both for everything.

The whole campus is agog with the news of my award[1] and the circum-stances thereof. Every body is congratulating me and wishing me all sorts of luck. The first thing this morning I saw Dr. Scott[2] and he congratulated me upon my award. Mr. Herring[3] and Dean Hatfield[4] are going to help me get a year's leave. I hope their plans work out all right.

Madelienne and I slept most of the way home but we are both crawling around here like two half dead people. Dont possibly see how I am going to teach this afternoon.

Give my best love to all my friends who might ask after me. Keep worlds of it for your own dear selves. Write to me real soon . . . write often even though I may not write you. I am trying to turn over a new leaf about writing.

Lots of love and kisses . . .

Lovingly,

Baby[5]

To Marechal Neil Bennett
March 24, 1925
[Howard University letterhead]

Dearest Mumsey,

Excuse me for writing you on the typewriter . . . it isnt supposed to be done, you know. I happen to be here at school and I can get this letter off to you while I am teaching my class, for I am teaching a class right at this moment.

I am teaching night school now. It's an awful job. Here at Howard you only get paid twenty dollars per pupil for the whole space of twelve weeks. I only happen to have four pupils, which will be only eighty dollars. Do the division in this problem and you'll have just what my salary per hour amounts to. I teach in the evening from five thirty until nine thirty. It leaves me quite tired out at the end of it all. Three days a week I teach all day from nine till five and then return to teach night school at night. The other days I am through at 12 oclock. My work has been so heavy that I have been coming up to school on Saturdays to get every thing in order. [. . .]

My debts are coming along slowly; I hope I shall be able to save something soon. So far it has been an awful struggle. I am planning to leave for Europe almost as soon as school closes. The boat that I plan taking is sailing on June the eleventh. It is a little earlier than I had planned sailing but I have decided to go to summer school in Paris.

Rayford Logan,[1] a friend of Gene's, who was in France all during the World War and just returned this year has helped me tremendously. I loved your letter. Write me again soon.

> Lovingly yours,
> Little Girl

The new picture is lovely according to the proof. Will send it as soon as I get it from the photographers. Going to West Chester for my Easter—only one day besides weekend. Thanks for your dear advice. I shall follow it. G.[2]

To Joshua Bennett
May 17, 1925

Dear Dad,

Enclosed you will find a letter that I received about two weeks ago. The letter came to Howard University and is from Mrs. Norwood, Clara

Hicks's mother.[1] To say that I am surprised and ashamed is to put it mildly. Somehow, I should think that you would scarcely have the courage to look me, your daughter, in the face. As usual I suppose you will say that I dont understand and that the facts contained therein are not true . . .

On Sunday last I was in New York on the excursion from here. While I was there I did some scouting around on my own accord and found out the very shocking truth. Somehow, to have this knowledge come to me just at this time is just like a death blow. Try as hard as I can I cannot fully conceive of your doing this noxious thing.

What do I find? I find that you have given Clara Hicks enough wearing apparel to place yourself in the position of a husband toward her. I find that she has been to and fro in Philadelphia with you and that you have regarded her in the capacity of both a companion and sweetheart. This is the worst blow that I have had in my life.

For years I have done without things that other girls have had. And even while I was teaching at the "Y" and Clara Hicks was my pupil I was poorly dressed while she was garbed like a queen. Is this your idea of working out the Divine Principle of Good? Is this your idea [of] Love[?] How could you have accepted the help and goodness of your present wife while you were doing this infamous thing? How did you have the nerve to look her in the face? Poor, poor woman!

You declare your great love for me. Is this a way to show it? What sort of an example do you set for me? You who have never been an exponent of the "dont-do-as-I-do-do-as-I-say-d" [sic] gospel. It seems that if you cared nothing for your own conscious [sic] you might have cared about my opinion of you. Not only have you laid yourself bare to criticism; you have also endangered my present position in the communities in which I move. One of my sorority sisters gave me a great deal of my information. You might have considered all this. You no doubt can imagine how I feel having this type of letter come to Howard. This is the second instance I have had of what your ill-conduct can bring upon me.

Oh Daddy, I am hurt and ashamed more than you shall every know.

Sadly yours,
[Unsigned][2]

To Marechal Neil Bennett
July 27, 1928
609 W. Jackson St.
Orlando, Fla.

Mumsey dear,

I've been trying to get this letter off to you for a week or more and somehow it seems that I just cant get it finished. I'm determined to send this off today even if I dont finish it.

I want you to know these things about me:—First, I am well. Second, that I made a success of my summer's work and altho I was not asked to stay for the second six weeks' summer school [in Nashville]. They had fifteen hundred students enrolled in the first six weeks session and when they started registration for the second session there were only about three hundred students enroll[ed]. Naturally they had to cut down the teaching force. However, I have been put on the regular roll to return for winter school in October. I am to teach the beginning serving as well as one or two Art courses. I shall tell you more about my work this summer when I write next time. Guess what they have offered me for a salary? One hundred dollars with room and board. It doesn't sound like much up North but it's a pretty good salary down this way. Next I want to tell you how I came to be in Florida. After I had paid seventy-five dollars worth of debts up and was waiting around a day or two to see what the registration would be I decided that it would be cheaper for me to go to Orlando and return to Nashville in October than it would be to go to Brooklyn & return. I didn't have time to think it over nor to write any one. On the spur of the moment I just picked up every thing and came on down here for somehow or other I just felt that Jack needed me. I didn't even write him that I was coming—just telegraphed his mother from Atlanta that I would arrive on train eighty-three. After I got here I surely was glad I had come. He had taken the exam on the eleventh of June and gone on back to Washington to finish out his internship. When he got down here he found that no notice of his exam had come. Well, Mumsey, you know how worried and upset I have been—you see I was positive he would pass because when he took the District Board he received the second highest mark of all those who took [*sic*]. But he has been worried and impatient because the board and everything else down this way are usually so prejudiced. I tell you frankly, Mother darling, I just haven't had the heart to write—so many things have been pressing close to my heart and when I wrote I wanted to be able to write a cheerful story . . . Well, this morning Jack's license came—his mark was 86 and the passing mark is 75. So you know I am relieved and glad to be able to write you some good news. There has been a lot of business to attend to since I have been here. We have driven over to Eustis, Florida to see about Jack's location. It is a good sized town about 32 1/2 miles from Orlando. They have no colored doctor and are sadly in need of one. Jack through the help of his mother has gotten in with the people who count in the town and it looks like he ought to make good quickly. We have been here and there getting acquainted with first this person and then the other—all so that it will be easier for him when he starts. As it is now he is going to Eustis Monday morning for real business. Aren't you glad? Soon we'll have our own home and a nice place so that my darling Mumsey can visit me.

Jack's mother is one of the loveliest women I have ever met. Jolly and so young that I can scarcely believe she has a grown son. She has certainly made me feel perfectly at home. She couldn't have treated me any better had I been her own daughter. She is very well thought of here in Orlando—by the way, it's a dandy town and as pretty as a picture. I shall send you some cards now that the smoke is clearing away. Mrs. Rigell teaches at the high school here and it's one of the prettiest schools I've seen any where.

Now Mumsey, draw up close to me and look into my eyes. You have always been everything to me—don't fail me now. I want to feel that if ever a time comes that I cant be happy in my married life that I can call on you to lend me carfare to come home. You are always my mother—dont feel you have lost me. I shall say more about this some other time.

I rec'd notice that I had passed the New York City [teaching license] exams. Isn't that great? Call up Hank and find out what mark I made and when the oral exams come, wont you please?

Am enclosing money order for eleven dollars. The mules, black with green lining, cost four-fifty. Remember [you] said I'd only have to pay back fifteen dollars. Out of the ten I bought myself two wash silk dresses to wear down here. Sorry I made you wait for the money.

Love to Mitti & Miss Montier.
Your Girl.
A thousand kisses and hugs for your dear self.[1]

To James Vernon Herring
September 9, 1937
321 West 136th Street,
New York, N.Y.

Dear James Vernon Herring,

Yes, it is a long time since you have had word from me! I have kept in touch with you, though, through word of you that has come my way. I am always happy to hear of your continued success. I've talked with James Porter[1] and Lesesne Wells[2] about you during the last few months. When I saw Porter he said that he thought that you were in New York at the time. I busied myself and went around to the Y.M.C.A. in the hope that they had some word of you or that you were stopping there.

My years between have had a full measure of joy and sorrow with a possible preponderance on the latter side. There was much love and many struggles in my married life and just at the time that things seemed to be lifting for Jack and me he died—suddenly and with an irrevocable swoop that has left me desolate. He knew you and liked you—said he came to know you fairly well while you were being treated during his internship. He was an excellent doctor and had just about beaten the depression years when he died. But so much for the sorrow . . . The years for me have had other rich compensations.

The year following my last year at Howard I received the Barnes Foundation Fellowship which gave me a rare opportunity to study what has since become an almost inaccessible collection of paintings and sculpture. Then on to Nashville where I had a successful summer teaching art at A&I State College. Then for two years in Florida with Jack where I taught regular grade school with a little art thrown in on the side. Back then to New York, with Jack practicing on Long Island while I tried my hand at publicity for W. C. Handy, piloting a beginning Y.W.C.A. group as executive secretary in Hempstead, Long Island, free lance book reviewing and anything that came to hand. In January 1934, I started working under the C.W.S. as a journalist for the department of Information and Education of the Welfare Council of New York City. I did a splendid job there as the only Negro on a staff of some seventy-odd people. They allowed me to transfer to the Federal Art Project in December 1935 with a great deal of reluctance. Since that date I have been working as a supervisor in the Art Teaching Division of the Federal Art Project.

I suppose by this time you are wondering why I am telling you all this. The reason is that, if you haven't already done so, you will receive in a few days a form from the New York City Board of Education to be filled out relative to my experience while teaching at Howard. Before you do so, if you haven't already done so, I wanted you to know that I had had a varied type of experience since your last contact with me and also that I have worked in such a manner as to make you feel proud of my record as my first employer.

About the recommendation you gave me way back in 1927—you will never know how much I appreciated it. I was young, inexperienced and bruised by my Howard experience and had expected you to do no more than say I had worked under your supervision two years. When you sent the glowing recommendation of my work in my youthful ignorance I was surprised and began to feel that there was some justice after all.

You will note that the new forms they are sending out are entirely different from the old straight recommendation they used to request. This is the reason that I am writing you asking that you give me a break and in doing so am opening up old sores that time has about healed. It is because I feel you to be a real human being and a person whom I have always liked and admired that I and am speaking quite frankly.

Believe me, Jim, (I used to call you that when we had our off moments), I was not guilty of all the filthy scandal that was put out about me. Dr. Johnson[3] did not request my resignation and I was never brought up on trial nor were any of the students who were mixed up in the scandal with me ever receive any form of punishment since nothing was proven against them. My resignation was a futile gesture made in the stupid heat of youth. I did not know (and have only learned in the experience of years) that one should never resign when there is any form of scandal surrounding one. Fool that I was, I thought that the public would accept the fact that, had I been guilty, I would have been thrown out of the school without further ado.

I never talked over any of this with you—the only reference you, in your extreme decency, ever made to the whole thing was that I didn't have to resign as far as you were concerned and that you would have asked for my reappointment, if I had not resigned. As I said above, I was young and didn't know and since I was angry and hurt I thought the only thing to do was to show my independence. I only mention the whole nasty mess because of sections three, four and six on the Report on Teaching Service you will be asked to fill out. My Howard teaching record can either make or break me and I am particularly anxious that it be as fine as your written recommendation was in 1927, shortly after I felt your aegis.

I often wish I were still teaching with you—I have learned much in the years between. Besides studying at the Barnes Foundation, I have taken my bachelor's degree in Fine Arts Education and done a good bit of the work toward my master's which I hope to get sometime during the next school year. I tell you this so that you will not be afraid to endorse my educational qualifications.

Had I known I would be a widow at such an early age, I would have come back from Florida to take my oral examinations after passing my written tests back in '27 at which time you recommended me. At that time, however, I felt that Jack and I would stay in Florida indefinitely and that by this time the world would be rosy for me. As it is, as interesting as the Federal Art Project work is, I need a job that has more security to it and a really decent living wage as Jack left many debts that I, as his heir, have to pay. You see he was not preparing at his age for death but for life. I, therefore, dont hold the burdens he has left me against his memory.

Jim, I have spoken frankly with you because I know I can trust you and confide in you honestly. You will never be sorry to have given me a good send-off. I need not urge you to extreme secrecy because I am certain you will realize that what I have said has come from deep inside me. I dont believe I have mentioned any of this during the years since I was at Howard.

And now for some things on a little more cheerful plane. I am president of the Harlem Artists' Guild, an organization of some ninety Negro artists. And by the by sometime when you are in New York I should like to have you speak to us. I am also a member of the executive committee of the American Artists' Congress. Maybe sometime when I am in Washington I could meet with a few of your students and tell what's happening in the art world in New York.

Hasn't James Porter grown to be an important person? He was so formal when I saw him that I scarcely realized that I had once taught him.

Where is Dan Reid? Do you have his address?

Please let's pick up our friendship where it left off. And write me.

[Unsigned][4]

To Mayme (Abernathy) Pizarro
August 31, 1938
250 West 154th Street, apt. 12 1/2
New York, N.Y.

Dearest Mother,

I write this letter with fear and trembling in my heart, a prayer on my lips and deep shame filling my breast. I pray to whatever Gods there be that somehow this letter will reach you and that you will find enough pity in your heart to forgive my long, unexplained silence. I am deeply ashamed of my actions and only the fact that you are my mother makes me dare to write even now trying to seek your forgiveness. There is so much in real mother love and understanding that overlooks everything that hurts that I know, if I can find you, you will listen to my plea.

I have only this excuse to offer and as I do so I realize that it in no way explains what I have done to you. I was young and full of silly dreams and fancies when I met you again after sixteen years separation; during those sixteen years I had dreamed of what we would mean to each other, if we were ever reunited. Then when I met you, we started a long series of misunderstandings and incriminations that at that time I could not understand. I couldn't understand some of the things you said and did at that time— some of them I dont understand even now but years of experience and hardship have made me more tolerant of other people's ideas and beliefs.[1] I offer no excuse for my actions, I only ask that you try to forgive me.

In the hope that this letter reaches you I will just give you the bare outlines of what has happened to me during the years in between. I married, went to Florida to live for two years and then returned to Long Island, New York, with my husband. After eight unhappy years of marriage, the last year of which Jack and I were actually separated, my husband died suddenly after just about a week's illness. He left me shouldered with debt but just as you felt with Dad I loved him despite all I felt he had done to me. His passing left me completely at loose ends. He died May 12, 1936.[2] The two years in between have been hard ones with much adjustment, happiness of a momentary character snatched here and there, and many tears and much heart-ache. I am employed in a responsible position as director of the Harlem Community Art Center, a WPA Federal Project that has a reasonable chance of becoming permanent. Briefly, that is the outline which I shall be glad to fill in when I see you and talk to you. I know the story of your suffering during the years between must make what I've been through seem like nothing.

I want to do everything I can to make it all up to you, if it is within my power to do so. Write to me so that I can arrange to see you and talk with you.

Despite the way I have acted please think of me as

Your own daughter,
Gwendolyn
I hope my actions will not make you doubt that
my heart is full of love for you.[3]

To Flora Dugan
October 6, 1947

My own dear Aunt Flora—
If it is possible in a letter, at this distance, let me fling my arms around you and kiss you and kiss you and say again and again "I love you," "I love you," "I love you." Just as I used to do when I was a very little girl, a bigger girl, and then a woman. You used to say, laughing, "Sweetie, you're such a kissing-bug.["] Well, for all the strange reasons people have for feeling one way or the other at a given time, that's just the way I feel at this time. No matter what has happened, no matter what will happen, no matter how my actions have spoken otherwise, the main thing right now is that I love you and Uncle Len truly and deeply and always have.

The sequence of the events of the past few years are simple but tragic. In 1936 I came home to West Chester [Pennsylvania], a woman who had suffered and known many ways of life that were different from those you and Uncle Len had followed; I found sadness and mistrust between you and Uncle Len (you didn't know that I knew the reasons—even though we had always been "pals," you were so hurt and heartsick that you didn't trust me enough to tell me the reasons, nor the recent happenings that had almost broken up the home); in my love for both of you I spoke out to Uncle Len about the inhuman way he was treating you and forced him to have a talk with you and change his way of acting toward you. I feel that in this act I was the main person in bringing about sufficient change in him to make it possible for you to live and rebuild your life and wring some happiness of the days before you. In your new togetherness you and Uncle Len turned on me for bringing Norman [Lewis] home. I know now it was all a misunderstanding and that the hard things you wrote to me were most likely prompted by Uncle Len's dictation. I had done what any young woman should feel free to do—bring to her home any one who was a good friend and who wanted to meet her loved ones. None of that matters now, it was long ago and has no bearing now. All thru the years you have written letters saying "Come home—we love you" without realizing how deep my hurt was or that Uncle Len had again "put his foot in it" (as we used to say when I was a kid) by saying "Don't you bring no white man home." For my husband, Dick Crosscup is white. A finer person you've never met, though. He's handsome, comes from a fine Boston family (his mother says his people first reached England way back with William the Conqueror in the year 1066), he's well educated—a graduate cum laude from Harvard University with a graduate degree from Boston University. I met him during the summer of 1939 when I was visiting the farm of a rich, white from [sic] who had worked on a committee with me—this was in Old Lyme, Conn., and Dick was staying with a neighboring friend. During the ensuing year he came to New York to visit me every two weeks and met all my friends and business associates and introduced me to the friends of his who lived in New York. Twice during the same year I was his guest in Boston, meeting his mother and family and all of his friends. During this year all of his friends, all of mine, once they got over the original shock of his being white and my being colored, came to know and love us together as an ideal couple who loved each other dearly and could make a wonderful life together. That's what it has been a wonderful life together. I don't believe anybody ever stops to think of the difference in our race any more. We go wherever we want for after all he is no whiter than hundreds of Negroes I know. Where people know us they accept the fact that we are an inter-racial couple. Where they don't they just take it for granted that he is a Negro who can "pass." How I longed to bring him to West Chester and have you and Uncle Len know him and put your stamp of approval on him just as every one else had done. But always in my mind and heart was the reaction toward Norman. I who had suffered so in my first marriage—more than you or Uncle Len ever knew—could not take a chance of anything you might say marring this second chance at happiness. On June 25, 1940 we were married at my step-mother's house in Brooklyn with his mother present, his best friend acting as best man—down from Boston with his wife for the ceremony—Negro and white friends present—just twenty— and a Negro minister marrying us. And let me say that never for one single moment have either of us had occasion to regret it. He got a good job in New York and we have lived here ever since. Uncle Len's ice-breaking telephone call made me sad and happy at the same time. How could I bridge the gap between myself and you two whom I loved so dearly[?] I've always known how hard and unbending Uncle Len was but I wouldn't take a chance on his reactions without writing a letter that would explain how hurt I had been about Norman and who I had married. In the meantime the pressure of my work became increasingly hard and the attendant heartaches all the more telling. I loved you and wanted to see you—I have hung eagerly onto every little piece of news of you that came my way either through your letters or through acquaintances. Ralph Brock[t] told me of your coming golden anniversary and I waited hopefully to be invited—This was the occasion I had chosen for putting in my appearance—the invitation never came.

For the past six months the ardors of my work have told bitterly on my mental well-being. I became sick with despondency and discouragement. I had lived so closely with the problems connected with my work that my real self, except for the trend of my life with Dick, had become lost to me. I began to stay in the house to myself, a sense of failure engrossed me to the point of my not wanting to live. This became so acute that thoughts of suicide began to seem to be the only way out. Dick who is in charge of children's work nationally for a Fraternal Order was out of town 32 weeks out of the year's 52 this past year. This allowed long stretches of time for me to struggle vainly with the problems of my work and for me to give myself up to despair that ate so viciously into my morale.

Since early July when Dick returned to New York after a series of trips, his love has sustained me. Bit by bit his loving care has led me from despair to a place where I can see things in proper perspective. One of the needs for rebuilding my ravaged spirit is to get away from New York, from all the people and things that have so undermined my will and self-confidence. The sweetest cure for my wounded mind was to start at some simple beginning, some place of security and happiness. During the years Dick and I have been together he has constantly heard me tell over and over of my wonderful Aunt Flora and Uncle Len and of my happy days in West Chester. He had never heard anything but the wonderful part (and I'm sure you'll agree that the loving family of you, Uncle Len, Louise and myself is a wonderful story to tell!) and had no idea why I had not seen you during the years he had known me—I suppose he thought the pressure of work etc. was the sole reason. Always both he and I had spoken of some time in which he would meet the Dugans and love them as I always did. At any rate one of the main steps (in his mind) toward my complete security was to be with the two people he knew from all I said were the people I loved best in all the world. I, myself, recognized this to be true and in my joy and hope in looking forward to being with both of you and healing my spirit at the warming love in your hearts I forgot how hard and uncompromising Uncle Len can be when he is angry and hurt.

I asked nothing of either of you but your love and the right to be near you. I am beyond the stage where I'd be a burden to either of you and in many ways I might even be a help. Well, you can imagine how I felt when Dick called up and Uncle Len gave his gruff "no." A bucket of ice water poured on one in mid winter was nothing to what this did to my already wounded spirits. Then I remembered how stern and hard Uncle Len could be even to those he loved best. Louise, his father and you—all the forgotten memories of the years passed through my mind. [. . .]

Well, I wont be coming home now. I've forfeited my welcome. I am deeply sorry for this. Whatever I can do in the days or years to come to make up for the past I shall do so. I was trying to say how much I loved you even in the past few neglectful years when I sent greeting cards and when I sent my picture. Perhaps it wasn't enough. I'm sorry, my dear Aunt Flora. I always have loved you and Uncle Len and always will as long as there is breath in my body. Perhaps, even if I am no longer welcome at home, you may find it in your heart to write me a letter. Maybe even some day you will win Uncle Len over to wanting me home again. Even though he feels that denying me is the right thing to do and even if you agree with him which I can scarcely believe possible, I know this final gesture against me has caused you both no end of heartache. For this I am sorry, too. My heart aches to have ever caused you worry or hurt—in the past and now.

Please write to your broken-hearted Sweetie who loves you so very, very much.[. . .]

Sweetie[2]

To Everyone
September 27, 1968

Many of you have expressed an interest in what I am going to be doing when I leave Consumers Union. This seemed to be the simplest and most direct way of letting all of you know at one time.

My husband and I are opening an antique shop immediately after I leave Consumers Union, which will have its base in Kutztown, Pennsylvania, on our farm there in the heart of the Pennsylvania Dutch Folk Country. The shop, itself, will not be finished and ready for the public until Spring 1969. At the rate local workmen go, it takes some months to complete the reconstruction of a small building, which has been intermittently a machine shop, and many years ago, a combination chicken and pig house. Fortunately, the latter use was terminated some twenty-odd years and four sets of owners ago. Until Spring, then, we will be selling by appointment only since we will not be moving to Pennsylvania permanently until June 1970. Meanwhile, we will be participating in Flea Markets, Antique Shows and selling the things we have collected over the years by appointment at our home on the farm. As you travel to the South or the West, I hope many of you will make a point of stopping by to look us over.

The Name: Buttonwood Hollow Antiques

The Address: R.D. 3, Box 147
    Kutztown, Pa., 19530

Telephone: (Hamburg, Pa.) Area Code 215-562-7927
    (NYC) Area Code 212 LE 4-4350

This is my way of saying farewell to those whom I have known for well nigh twenty years, with a hope that we will not lose contact altogether in the coming years.

Sincerely,
Gwendolyn Bennett Crosscup[1]

Notes

Introduction

1. See also "Colored Girls Attend Dance" in the Gwendolyn Bennett Papers, Schomburg Research Center, New York Public Library, reel 2.

2. The letter we are quoting is referenced in Sandra Govan's dissertation. There are three letters from Bennett to Van Vechten that are housed in Yale's Van Vechten Collection, box 2, folder 56.

3. See Jerry Langley, "FOUND! Gwendolyn Bennett Painting," *IRAAA*, n.d., http://iraaa .museum.hamptonu.edu/page/FOUND! -A-Gwendolyn-Bennett-Painting.

4. See Federal Bureau of Investigation, "Gwendolyn Bennett FBI File," *Internet Archive*, n.d., https://archive.org/details /GwendolynBennettFBIFile.

Published Work

Poetry

INTRODUCTION

1. See William J. Maxwell and Joseph Valente, "On 'Heritage,'" *Modern American Poetry*, n.d., http://www.english.illinois.edu /maps/poets/a_f/bennett/heritage.htm.

"Dear Things"

1. A low wall or dam built across a body of water that raises its level and changes its direction.

Short Stories

INTRODUCTION

1. A manuscript copy of the work, titled "Almost True Story," is located in the Bennett Papers at Yale University, Box 2, folder 17.

"WEDDING DAY"

1. A well-known area in Paris around Place Pigalle that attracts many tourists because of its theaters (including the Grand Guignol), cabarets such as the Moulin Rouge, and risqué shows. It was also home to many artists.

2. Montmartre is a large hill in Paris's eighteenth arrondissement. The surrounding district is also known by this name and makes up part of the Right Bank. It became the center of the art community during the Belle Époque (1871–1914). It is also a well-known nightclub district. A famous landmark is the white-domed Sacré-Cœur Basilica.

3. Joe Gans (1874–1910), born Joseph Gant, was an African American boxer who was lightweight champion from 1902 to 1908.

4. A brandy-based liqueur.

5. A derogatory name for whites.

6. "Mr. Jefferson Lawd Play That Barber Shop Chord"—also known as "Play That Barber Shop Chord"—was recorded by Bert Williams in 1910. It was written by William Tracey and Lewis Muir.

7. Slang meaning special.

"TOKENS"

1. Saint Cloud is a prosperous area in the western suburbs of Paris.

2. William Mercer (Marion) Cook (1869–1944) was an African American musician and composer of popular songs and such musicals as *Clorindy; or, The Origin of the Cakewalk* (1898) with Paul Laurence Dunbar.

3. A nightclub.

4. Clocks painted with radio luminescent paint containing radium-226. Those making the clocks, usually women, would often lick their paint brushes (called "pointing") in order to make the lines and numbers on the

dials straighter. Ingesting the radium could cause cancer. As a result, the use of pointing stopped in 1930. However, inhaling the fumes could still cause cancer.

Editorials

"THE EBONY FLUTE" (AUGUST 1926)

1. Sometimes poems, plays, novels, and so forth were cited appropriately in the text (e.g., italicized or underlined text for book titles). Sometimes they were not. We have decided to reproduce these texts as is, without making any editorial changes in this regard.

2. Moses Jordan was the author of *The Meat Man: A Romance of Life, of Love, of Labor* (1923).

3. Maud Cuney-Hare (1874–1936) was an African American musicologist, pianist, and folklorist now best remembered for her book *Negro Musicians and Their Music* (1936). She edited *Six Creole Folk-Songs* (1921).

4. The Boni brothers, who were leading publishers, held a contest in 1926 with a $1,000 prize, given to the "best novel on Negro life written by an American of Negro descent."

5. *Maria Chapdelaine* was a popular novel written in 1913 by Louis Hémon and set in Quebec.

6. John V. A. Weaver (1893–1938), an American writer, authored the poetry collection *In American* (1921). He also co-wrote (with George Abbott) the comedy *Love 'em and Leave 'em* (1926).

7. Hall Johnson (1888–1970) was an African American composer, choral director, and violinist. He was in the orchestra for the hit musicals *Shuffle Along* (1921) and *Runnin' Wild* (1923). He was especially interested in black choral music.

8. The collaboration in question is *Mule Bone: A Comedy of Negro Life*. Quarrels over the play ended the friendship of Hurston and Hughes. It was staged posthumously in 1991.

9. *My Magnolia* was a short-lived production that opened on July 8, 1926, with a book by Alex C. Rogers and Eddie Hunter and music by C. Luckyeth Roberts. The

show, which had only four performances, was set in Harlem and New Orleans.

10. George Ivanovitch Gurdjieff was an American spiritualist and teacher whose followers included Jean Toomer. He created the Gurdjieff Institute for the Harmonious Development of Man in Paris in 1922.

11. Arthur Huff Fauset (1899–1963) was a Philadelphia-born writer, teacher, and historian who was the half brother of Jessie Redmon Fauset.

12. Rudolph Fisher (1897–1934) was a physician and fiction writer.

13. A branch of the New York Public Library opened in 1905 in Harlem. It was renamed the Countee Cullen branch in 1951, and later the Schomburg. It was a major venue for Harlem Renaissance authors to gather and read from their works.

14. Arna Bontemps (1902–1973) was a widely published poet and novelist whose works include *Black Thunder* (1936), about a slave rebellion. In later years, he worked as a librarian.

15. Richard Bruce Nugent (1906–1987), an avant-garde writer and artist, worked with Bennett on *Fire!!* He was one of the few openly gay figures in the Harlem Renaissance.

16. John P. Davis, like Bennett, Hurston, and Nugent, among others, helped to produce *Opportunity* and served for a time as the literary editor of *Crisis*. He was also a lawyer, journalist, and political organizer.

17. Horace Liveright was head of a mainstream publishing firm that bears his name. The company published such pioneering African American works as Jean Toomer's *Cane* (1923) and Eric Walrond's *Tropic Death* (1926). *Black Boy* was a comedy that opened in October 1926. The show—produced by Liveright and written by Jim Tully and Frank Mitchell Dazey—closed the following month after thirty-seven performances. Paul Robeson played the lead opposite Edith Warren (then the stage name for the well-known black actress Fredi Washington).

18. *All God's Chillun Got Wings* (1924), a play by Eugene O'Neill. The white character, Ella Downey, was played by Mary Blair.

19. Clarissa Scott (1901–1927) was married to attorney Hubert Thomas Delany. She was a social worker and published several poems before dying of kidney disease.

20. Bennett says that the line from Hughes is from *The Railroad Blues*, but it is actually from *Homesick Blues*. She also misquotes the lines: "De railroad bridge's / A sad song in de air." She also misquotes the lines from Hughes' "Our Land": "Where the twilight / Is a soft bandanna handkerchief."

21. Lewis Grandison Alexander (1900–1945) was a Washington-born writer, actor, and editor best known for his poetry.

22. These lines are from Jean Toomer's "Georgia Dusk."

23. William Stanley Braithwaite (1878–1962) was a poet and editor of several important anthologies of poetry. He also was a professor of creative writing for many years at Atlanta University.

"THE EBONY FLUTE" (APRIL 1927)

1. Nathalia Crane (1913–1998) was a child prodigy whose collection of poetry, *The Janitor's Boy*, was published when she was twelve. Markham thought she was a fraud, but it was determined she was indeed the author of her work.

2. Charles Edwin Markham (1852–1940) was a poet and prose writer. His work often focuses on the plight of the exploited laborer.

3. *Fine Clothes to the Jew* (1927).

"THE EBONY FLUTE" (JULY 1927)

1. A spiritual also known as "Hold On."

2. Young former slaves from Nashville, Tennessee, who sang spirituals and gave concerts to raise money for their college, Fisk University.

3. Eugene Gordon (1891–1972) was an African American author who wrote fiction and nonfiction and edited the *Saturday Evening Quill*. He was a member of the American Communist Party and was married for a time to African American author Edythe Mae (Chapman) Gordon.

4. Blanche Colton Williams (1879–1944) taught at Columbia University and Hunter College and was a co-founder of the O. Henry Award for short stories. She was one of the judges for the 1924 *Opportunity* awards.

5. Dorothy West (1907–1998) was one of the youngest of the writers associated with the Harlem Renaissance. She wrote two novels, *The Living Is Easy* (1948) and *The Wedding* (1995), and she lived her later years on Martha's Vineyard.

6. Georgia Douglas Johnson (1880–1966) was a much-published poet who also wrote numerous one-act plays. Her home at 1461 South Street NW (known as the S Street Salon) was a gathering place for African American writers and scholars when they were in Washington.

7. Angelina Grimké (1880–1956) was a poet, essayist, and playwright.

8. Edward Christopher (E. C.) Williams (1871–1929) was a social critic and the first publicly trained African American librarian. He is best remembered for the epistolary novel *When Washington Was in Vogue* (2003), originally titled *The Letters of Davy Carr: A True Story of Colored Vanity Fair* (1925–26).

9. Marita Bonner (1899–1971) was an African American writer, musician, and teacher best known for her plays, essays, and short stories.

10. Frank Horne (1899–1974) was a poet and a member of Franklin D. Roosevelt's Federal Council of Negro Affairs (aka his "Black Cabinet"). He was also an optometrist. He was a lifelong friend (and possibly lover) of Bennett's. She became executor of his literary writings, which are contained in Bennett's papers at the Schomburg Library.

11. Helene Johnson (1906–1995) was a poet and cousin of author Dorothy West.

12. Eulalie Spence (1884–1981) was born on the West Indian island of Nevis. Her family moved to New York City in 1902. She wrote fourteen plays during the Harlem Renaissance and went on to be a high school drama teacher. One of her students was theatrical producer and director Joseph Papp.

13. Benjamin Brawley (1882–1939) was a poet and professor at several colleges, including Howard University and Morehouse College. He is best known for his books *The Negro in Literature and Art in the United States* (1921) and *New Survey of English Literature* (1925).

14. The concluding lines of "Yet Do I Marvel" are "Yet do I marvel at this curious thing / To make a poet black, and bid him sing!"

15. Bennett is quoting Herbert George Wells's *The Research Magnificent* (1915), 143.

"THE EBONY FLUTE" (SEPTEMBER 1927)

1. An all-black revue staring Ethel Waters that debuted in 1927.

"THE EBONY FLUTE" (APRIL 1928)

1. The Quill Club (also known as the Saturday Evening Quill Club) published the *Saturday Evening Quill*, edited by Eugene Gordon.

2. The Ink Slingers were a Los Angeles-based group of African American writers. Their members included poet, short story writers and dramatist Eloise Bibb and her husband, journalist, Noah Davis Thompson, who joined the group after moving to California in 1911. *Black Opals* was a Philadelphia-based literary magazine established in 1927 and co-edited by Arthur Huff Fauset and educator and author Nellie Rathborne Bright (ca. 1902–1976).

3. James B. Lowe (1879–1963) was an African American actor best known for playing the title role in the film *Uncle Tom's Cabin* (1927).

4. A popular African American vaudeville team.

5. A religious vocal quartet formed around 1916.

6. Lawrence Brown (1893–1972) was Robeson's pianist and arranger.

7. A chorus founded in the mid-1870s and revived in 1928 by entrepreneur Forbes Randolph.

8. Eva Jessye (1895–1992) was a well-known choral director who collected sixteen spiritual songs in *My Spirituals* (1927). Bennett reviewed the book in the November 1927 issue of *Opportunity*.

9. Clarence Cameron White (1880–1960), a composer, teacher, and violinist, published *Forty Negro Spirituals* in 1927.

10. Nathaniel Dett (1882–1943), born in Canada, was a teacher, composer, pianist, and musical director who helped found the National Association of Negro Musicians in 1919.

11. Albert C. Barnes (1872–1951), a doctor, inventor, and art collector, invited Bennett to study at his famed Pennsylvania art collection.

12. Allan Freelon (1895–1960) was an African American impressionist painter born in Philadelphia.

13. Edmund T. Jenkins (1894–1926) was a composer and jazz clarinetist. Bennett wrote about him in the November 1925 *Opportunity*.

14. Frank Wilson (1886–1956), an actor and playwright, performed the lead roles in such classics as *In Abraham's Bosom* and *Porgy*. He won first prize for playwriting in the *Opportunity* contest for 1927. *Meek Mose*, about an African American preacher who believes that "the meek shall inherit the earth," opened on Broadway on February 6, 1928, and closed after twenty-four performances.

15. Alston Burleigh (1899–1977), son of composer Harry Burleigh, was an actor, musician, and teacher born in New York who taught for many years in Washington, DC, public schools.

16. Laura Bowman (1881–1957), an African American film, stage, and radio actress, was a member of the Lafayette Players. She starred in several films directed by Oscar Micheaux.

17. John Lawrence Criner (1898–1965) starred in *Meek Mose*. He was a member of the Lafayette Players and also appeared in almost thirty films in his career.

18. Lester Walton (1882–1965), an African American journalist and civic leader, was

appointed an American envoy to Liberia from 1935 to 1946. He was the manager for Harlem's famed Lafayette Theatre from 1914 to 1916 and again from 1919 to 1921.

Reviews

"heartbreak and north carolina sunshine"

1. Barrett H. Clark (1890–1953) was a drama teacher, editor, and translator.

2. The play *In Abraham's Bosom* was awarded the Pulitzer Prize for Drama in 1927.

"blue-black symphony"

1. The doctrine of or adherence to prohibition. The National Prohibition Act (informally known as the Volstead Act, after Andrew Volstead, the chairman of the House Judiciary Committee, who managed the legislation.) carried out the intention of the Eighteenth Amendment, forbidding the manufacture, transport, and sale of alcohol in 1919. It was repealed with the passage of the Twenty-First Amendment in 1933.

2. George was a generic name given to African American porters, named after the engineer and manufacturer of sleeping car trains, George Pullman (1831–1897).

"plum-bun, by jessie redmon fauset"

1. *There Is Confusion*, a 1924 novel by Jessie Fauset, was a direct response to the novel *Birthright* (1922) by the white author T. S. Stribling, which Fauset felt was unrealistic in its depiction of African American life.

2. Often attributed to Lord Byron from his poem *Don Juan* (1823): "[. . .] for truth is always strange; / Stranger than fiction."

"the emperors jones"

1. Edward H. Sothern (1859–1933) was an American actor known for his romantic leads. He partnered with Julia Marlowe in such plays as *Romeo and Juliet*, *Much Ado About Nothing*, and *Twelfth Night*.

2. Walter Hampden (1879–1955) was an American-born stage and film actor as well as theater manager.

3. Julia Marlowe (1865–1950), originally Sarah Frances Frost, was an English-born American actor best known for her roles in Shakespeare's plays.

4. Helena Modjeska (1840–1909), a Polish-born American actress, gained international fame for her portrayals of Shakespearean heroines as well as more modern figures like Nora in Ibsen's *A Doll's House*.

5. Bennett likely means the American stage and film actor and screenwriter Jane Cowl (1883–1950), born Jane Bailey. She starred in (and co-authored) the hit *Smilin' Through* (1919) as well as performing in Noël Coward's *Easy Virtue* (1925).

6. Ira Aldridge (1807–1867) was the best known-African American actor of the 19th century. He toured internationally and may perhaps be best known for his portrayal of Shakespeare's *Othello*.

7. Charles Gilpin (1878–1930) was an African American actor, singer, and dancer. In 1920, he took the title role in *The Emperor Jones*, performed at the Neighborhood Theater in New York's Greenwich Village. Illness led to his replacement by Paul Robeson in 1924.

8. Broad Street station, located at the intersection of Broad and Market streets in Philadelphia, opened in 1881 but closed in 1952. At its peak, over a million passengers a month used the station.

9. An area in northwestern Philadelphia long linked to the abolitionist movement. In the 1920s a large number of African Americans from the South began to migrate to Germantown.

10. New York–based actor and director Jasper Deeter (1893–1972) founded the Hedgerow Theatre in 1923, which is still in operation today.

11. A Cockney character in *The Emperor Jones*.

12. Abriea "Abbie" Mitchell (1884–1960) was born to an African American mother and a Jewish German father. She starred in such musicals as the Bert Williams and George Walker production *In Dahomey* (1903), the

music for which was composed by Mitchell's husband, William Marion Cook.

13. Jed Harris (1900–1979) was an Austrian-born American theater producer and director. *The Coquette*, produced in 1927, ran for 366 performances.

Cultural and Social Articles

INTRODUCTION

1. Bennett calls him Albert Alexis Smith, but his correct name is Albert Alexander Smith. He was an African American musician and illustrator whose work appeared in *Crisis* and the *Brownies' Book*, among other venues. He traveled throughout Europe for over twenty years.

"THE FUTURE OF THE NEGRO IN ART"

1. Paul Guillaume (1891–1934), a well-known French art dealer, was one of the earliest to organize African art exhibitions.

2. Władisław T. Benda (1873–1948) was a Polish-born graphic artist, book illustrator, mask maker, and costume designer.

3. Phidias (ca 490–430 BCE) was a Greek architect who directed the construction of the Parthenon.

4. Henry Ossawa Tanner (1859–1937), a native of Pittsburgh, won international acclaim in part because of his religious paintings. He resided in Paris for many years.

5. Laura Wheeler Waring (1887–1948) was an artist and a teacher. She traveled to Paris in 1924–25, where she met Bennett. She created landscapes and still lifes, but she is best known for her portraitures of such famous African American subjects as James Weldon Johnson and Jessie Redmon Fauset.

6. Elmer Stoner (1897–1969), a graphic illustrator who originated the art for the Planters logo Mr. Peanut, was the first African American illustrator of U.S. comic books.

7. Augusta Savage (1892–1962) is known for her sculpture *The Harp*, created for the 1939 New York World's Fair. She also worked as an art educator and was a close friend of Bennett's, until they had a falling out over

leadership at the Harlem Community Art Center.

"THE AMERICAN NEGRO PAINTS"

1. The Harmon Foundation was established in 1922 by the white philanthropist William E. Harmon. It is best known for its support of Negro artists beginning in 1926. In addition to providing awards to individuals, it sponsored traveling exhibitions from 1927 to 1931 and again in 1933 and 1935. The foundation ceased operating in 1967.

2. Palmer C. Hayden (1890–1973) was known for his depictions of black life in New York City and in the rural South.

3. Sargent Johnson (1888–1967), a painter, potter, graphic artist, and sculptor, was known for early modern and abstract figurative styles.

4. Hilyard Robinson (1899–1986) designed the historic Langston Terrace Dwellings in Washington, DC, between 1935 and 1938, only the second federally funded housing project in the United States.

"THE PLIGHT OF THE NEGRO IS TRAGIC"

1. Civil Works Administration.

2. St. Philip's Episcopal Church is located at 204 East 134th Street in Harlem. The present site was built in 1910–11, but the congregation itself was formed in Lower Manhattan in 1809. It is the oldest Episcopal parish in New York City. Thurgood Marshall, Langston Hughes, and W. E. B. Du Bois were among its parishioners.

"I GO TO CAMP"

1. Civil Works Service.

2. A normal school was designed to train teachers.

3. One of the seven main lakes in Harriman National Park in Orange County, New York.

"THE HARLEM ARTISTS GUILD"

1. Likely Mary Marvin Breckinridge Patterson (1905–2002), a photojournalist and philanthropist.

Unpublished Work

Poetry

INTRODUCTION

1. All of the unpublished poems are held at the Schomburg Research Center, New York Public Library, Gwendolyn Bennett Papers, reel 1. A copy is also housed at the Amistad Research Center. Many of the poems at Amistad have dates written or typed by Bennett.

"TRAIN MONOTONY"

1. A handwritten note in Bennett's papers indicates the poem was written in 1928 "on a train going from New York to Philadelphia—feeling blue and aware of life's emptiness at times."

"I BUILD AMERICA"

1. A rushing, murmuring sound.

2. Bennett handwrote the date she composed this poem in the copy she sent to Frank Horne at the Works Progress Administration (Amistad Research Center).

"WISE GUYS"

1. Hundred-dollar bills.

2. Derogatory name for someone of Irish descent.

3. Detectives.

4. A street on the Lower East Side of Manhattan where many immigrants lived.

5. Cash.

6. Derogatory term for a Jewish person.

7. Promiscuous woman.

8. Dancers.

9. Cocaine users.

10. Derogatory term for an Italian.

"THRENODY FOR SPAIN"

1. Silver.

2. At the end of the poem is a handwritten note: "On March 28th the *New York Times* carried the story of the surrender of Madrid—listing the history of the Spanish War the battle names were those of Spanish towns—their sound was so beautiful but so sad because of a lost cause—1939."

Unfinished Novel

INTRODUCTION

1. The name is given as Edmunds in the outline but Edwards in the rest of the manuscript.

CHAPTER OUTLINE FOR THE CALL

1. Most likely Révolte "Rada" Bercovici (1906–1993), daughter of the Romanian American author Konrad Bercovici. Bennett became friendly with the family while living in Paris.

2. The novel outline and excerpts are held in the Beinecke Collection, Yale University, Gwendolyn Bennett Papers, box 2, folder 18.

EXCERPTS FROM THE CALL

1. Jean-François Millet (1814–1875) was a French painter known for his paintings of peasants such as *The Sower* (1850), *The Potato Harvest* (1855), and *The Gleaners* (1857).

2. Haunt, a ghost.

Essays

INTRODUCTION

1. All unpublished essays are in the holdings of the Schomburg Research Center, New York Public Library, Gwendolyn Bennett Papers, reel 2.

"MY FATHER'S STORY"

1. Now called Prairie View A&M University, a historically black university established in 1876. It is located in Prairie View, Texas, about fifty miles northwest of Houston.

"[WARD PLACE]"

1. A handwritten note indicates this piece was written on October 29, 1941.

2. From William Blake's poem "London": "I wander thro' each charter'd street."

3. From a traditional folk song, "Make Me a Pallet on the Floor."

"LANCASTER, PA."

1. "My Beautiful Lady," from the musical *The Pink Lady* (1910), composed by C. M. S. McLellan and Ivan Caryll.

2. "My Hero," from the German operetta *The Chocolate Soldier* (1908), based on George Bernard Shaw's play *Arms and the Man.*

3. A popular song written by Percy Wenrich and Edward Madden in 1911.

4. A silent film released in 1912.

5. Elie Sheetz founded the company in Lancaster in 1892, for which he obtained a trademark on the name in 1906. The company folded by the 1940s.

"LET'S GO: IN GAY PAREE!"

1. A musical performance originated in Paris in 1925 starring Josephine Baker.

2. Louis Douglass (or Douglas) (1889–1939) was a dancer and choreographer who starred in *La Revue Nègre* in 1925.

3. Miguel D. Covarrubias (1904–1957), a Mexican artist and writer known for his stage designs, choreography, lithography, and caricatures, whose sketches have appeared in many prominent publications.

4. A popular song written in 1925 by Walter Donaldson and Gus Kahn.

5. Dark brown and light yellow skin complexions.

6. Bennett probably intends the song "Cake Walking Babies from Home," composed by Chris Smith, Henry Troy, and Clarence Williams ("Strut your stuff, they're the cake walkin' babies from home").

7. The Claridge Hotel is a luxury hotel on the Champs-Élysées where celebrities such as Coco Chanel, Edith Piaf, and Marlene Dietrich were once guests. Ernest Hemingway often frequented the hotel bar. The novelist Colette lived in the hotel for several years.

8. The Dolly Sisters—Jenny and Rose—identical twins born in Budapest in 1892, had great success in the 1920s throughout Europe and the United States.

9. Mistinguett was the original stage name of Jeanne Florentine Bourgeois (1875–1956), a French actress and singer.

10. *Tea-dansante*—or *thè dansant*, literally a "tea dance"—refers to a late afternoon or early evening dance.

11. *Mirabile dictu*, borrowed from Latin, means "wonderful to relate."

25

1. Skirts with narrow hems that hindered the wearer's gait, popular from about 1905 to 1915.

2. The Washington Senators baseball team won the American League pennant in 1924 and 1925 and the World Series in 1924.

3. The University of Pennsylvania was victorious in their annual football games against Harvard in 1927, 1928, and 1929.

4. On May 20–21, 1927, Charles Lindbergh made the first solo transatlantic flight, from New York to Paris, in his plane *The Spirit of St. Louis.*

5. The ability to reproduce sounds accurately.

"[LIFE AS A JAVANESE]"

1. Pieter Mijer's *Batiks, and How to Make Them* (1919).

2. Spencerian script, developed by Platt Rogers Spencer, was considered the standard from about 1850 to 1925.

"[KU KLUX KLAN RIDES]"

1. *Lagerstroemia*, a genus of around fifty trees of deciduous and evergreen trees and shrubs, largely native to certain parts of Asia and Australia.

2. It is also known as the Confederate Rose, perhaps one reason for the Klansmen's fondness for it.

"LAST NIGHT I NEARLY KILLED MY HUSBAND!"

1. The name Bennett used for her real home, Hempstead, Long Island. Brentwood is in the borough of Queens.

2. President Franklin D. Roosevelt issued Proclamation 2039 declaring the "holiday" from March 6 to March 13, 1933, to prevent hoarding. During this period, banks were prohibited from making any transactions other than issuing change.

3. This alludes to Esau's sale of his birthright to his younger brother, Jacob, for bread and a stew of lentils (Genesis 25:29–34).

4. Perhaps Bennett is alluding to the Barbizon Hotel for Women, opened in

Manhattan in 1927, which did not admit men above the first floor.

"[HARLEM REFLECTION]"

1. Cullen translated Euripides's Greek drama *Medea* in 1935.

2. In 1934 Douglas was commissioned by the Public Works of Art Project to paint a large murals for the New York Public Library's 135th Street Branch (now known as Schomburg Library). Arna Bontemps's novel was *God Sends Sunday*.

3. Founded by W. E. B. Du Bois in 1926, the Krigwa Players (the Crisis Guild of Writers and Artists) was a Harlem theater company.

4. Bennett probably intends Regina Anderson Andrews (1901–1993), a librarian and author closely involved with Du Bois and co-founder of the Krigwa Players.

5. Bennett's note: "Look up what was happening in Music. I really don't think much was happening except small bands but Paul Robeson was giving one or two successful concerts in Carnegie Hall each season and startling the dramatic world in the English production of *Othello*."

6. The article, "The Plight of the Negro Is Tragic" (1934), is included in this anthology.

7. Civil Works Service Section.

8. A philosophical approach to reality. It is derived from the teachings of Karl Marx and Friedrich Engels, who maintained that thoughts, emotions, and ideas could only arise as products and reflections of material conditions. It is the theoretical basis for Marxism.

9. From Hughes's poem "My People" (1923).

10. The essay was clearly left incomplete. Bennett gives a sense of where she intended to go in her notes at the end of the piece: "Tenants League—Recent rent strike at 409 Edgecom[b]e Avenue. The whole uprising of Harlem against the rent situation . . . The Race Riot [of 1935]—I want to have the race riot and the fact that all these doctors and lawyers and [illegible word] were drawn into such things as the

Mayor's Committee and Commissions against Conditions in Harlem and lead up to the most recent which is Lester Granger's Commission [Granger worked for the National Urban League and fought for worker rights]. Mention that the artists no longer painted alone but in groups. The Krigwa players were no longer the only theatre, there was a new theatre in Harlem, there has been an organizational change among all Negroes, lower and higher up until now there is a different type of community entirely . . . Workers Alliance. Prominent Negro teachers who were formerly Society belles now actively working in the Teachers Union . . . Ask Selma Day [an artist who created a mural at Harlem Hospital] what the name of the man who is starting all the business about Buy Harlem."

Diaries

INTRODUCTION

1. All the unpublished diaries are held at the Schomburg Research Library, New York Public Library, Gwendolyn Bennett Papers, reel 1.

2. Norman Lewis (1909–1979) was a notable African American painter. He studied under Augusta Savage from 1933 to 1935 and helped co-found the Harlem Artists Guild in 1935. Although he is now known mostly for his abstract expressionistic work, Lewis was painting in the social realist style in the 1930s when he was involved with Bennett.

JUNE 26, [19]25

1. The Foyer International des Étudiantes, founded in 1906, was the first student residence located in Paris's Latin Quarter.

2. The third street on the left.

3. Eugene Davidson (1896–1976) was a Washington-based lawyer with whom Bennett had a brief romantic relationship. He worked in real estate and was the president of the Washington branch of the NAACP between 1952 and 1958. There is a letter from Genie (June 21, 1935) in the Bennett papers, Box 1, folder 1.

AUGUST 2, [1925]

1. Bois de Boulogne is a large public park in the sixteenth arrondissement of Paris.

AUGUST 8, [1925]

1. Ada "Bricktop" Smith (1894–1984) was an African American singer and dancer. Her club in Paris, Chez Bricktop, operated from 1924 to 1961.

2. The Grand Duc, located on 52 Rue Pigalle, in Montmartre, opened in 1924. It was a central hub for African American artists and musicians as well as such white celebrities as Charlie Chaplin, the Prince of Wales, Cole Porter, and F. Scott Fitzgerald.

3. Lottie Gee was an African American entertainer best known for her starring role in the hit musical *Shuffle Along* (1921).

4. "Insufficient Sweetie" was from the musical *Lady, Be Good!* in 1924, written by Gilbert Wells and Cliff Edwards (Ukulele Ike). "I'm in Love Again" was written by Cole Porter in 1924 for the show *Greenwich Village Follies*.

5. An archaic form of "which" generally used as a sentence connection.

SEPTEMBER 27, [19]25

1. Jennie Mustapha (1898–1992) graduated from Howard University in 1919 and taught English at DC's prestigious Dunbar High School for many years.

2. *The Blind Bow-Boy* (1923) and *The Tattooed Countess* (1924).

3. Bennett would soon meet Van Vechten, who became one of her close friends.

SEPTEMBER 28, 1925

1. Should be *vous-êtes*: Madame is very nice . . . you are all by yourself, my little one.

2. Things *comme ça*: things like that.

APRIL 29, 1926

1. Chicken cooked in a pot.

2. Literally "the beautiful head."

3. carnet: A book of tickets. séances: French meaning sessions.

4. The Académie de la Grande Chaumière is an art school founded in 1904, located in the Montparnasse district of Paris.

5. The Café de la Rotonde, founded in 1911 and located in Montparnasse, is notable as a gathering place for writers and artists.

[APRIL 7,] 1936

1. A reference to Matthew 25:7 "Then all the virgins arose, and trimmed their lamps."

2. It is difficult to give exact dates for the entries as Bennett sometimes ran one day into another day in her diary. We have given the dates listed on the tops of the pages.

APRIL 8, 1936

1. Lewis and Bennett's dog.

APRIL 9, 1936

1. Bennett's first husband, Alfred Jackson, whom she often called Jack.

2. Likely Frank Horne.

3. "Sleep that knits up the raveled sleeve [or sleave] of care." Shakespeare, *Macbeth*, 2.2.

APRIL 18, 1936

1. A 1929 sculpture of a small black boy that won Savage a scholarship to travel to Europe. *Gamin* is French for "street urchin."

JANUARY 3, 1937

1. *The Yellow Hat*, one of Lewis's best known works, was completed in 1936 and is now held in the Architecture, Urban Planning, and Visual Arts collection at MIT.

Correspondence

TO W. E. B. DU BOIS (JANUARY 19, 1925)

1. Bennett's journey to France.

2. Nina Yolande Du Bois Williams (1900–1961), who was briefly married to Countee Cullen.

3. Du Bois's first wife, Nina Gomer, to whom he was married from 1896 until her death in 1950.

4. This January 19, 1925, letter is held at the University of Massachusetts, Amherst, W. E. B. Du Bois Papers, reel 14, folder 1153.

TO COUNTEE CULLEN (AUGUST 28, 1925)

1. Cullen won the $125 undergraduate prize in 1925.

2. Locke was dismissed from Howard in 1925 because of a controversy over his fight to secure equal pay for black faculty, but was reinstated in 1928.

3. King of Lydia from circa 560 to 547 BCE who was believed to have possessed great wealth.

4. Frank Harris (1856–1931) was born in Ireland but became a U.S. citizen in 1921. He was an editor and fiction writer. His *My Life and Loves*, published privately in four volumes between 1922 and 1927 and then collectively in 1931, was a graphic account of his own (and other well-known people's) sexual adventures. The scandalous nature of the book caused it to be banned in the United States and Great Britain for forty years.

5. Held at Tulane University, Amistad Research Center, Countee Cullen Papers, box 1, folder 10.

TO LANGSTON HUGHES (DECEMBER 2, 1925)

1. George Antheil (1900–1959) was an American-born avant-garde composer, author, and musician.

2. Arthur Moss (1899–1969) was an American expatriate poet and magazine editor.

3. Lewis Galantière (1895?–1977) was a translator of French literature, a playwright, and a journalist.

4. *Color* (1925).

5. Le Dôme Café, which opened in Montparnasse in 1898, was from its beginnings a frequent gathering place for writers and artists. Today it is a seafood restaurant.

6. Held at Beinecke Library, Yale University, Gwendolyn Bennett Papers, box 1, folders 7–8.

TO COUNTEE CULLEN (JANUARY 14, 1926)

1. Donald Angus (1900–1982) was the longtime companion of Carl Van Vechten.

2. "An Epitaph" (1925).

3. "Dear Things," "Dirge," and "Song" ("Oh My Sweet . . .") were all published in the *Palms* October 1926 issue.

4. Bennett is referring to the January 1926 issue of *Opportunity*.

5. Held at Tulane University, Amistad Research Center, Countee Cullen Papers, box 1, folder 10.

TO HAROLD JACKMAN (FEBRUARY 23, 1926)

1. James Joyce's novel was first published serially in *The Little Review* (1918–20) and then in its entirety by Sylvia Beach in Paris in 1922. It was banned in the United States until 1934 on charges of pornography.

2. Stieglitz (1864–1946) was a well-known American photographer and promoter of modern art.

3. The Exhibition Internationale des Arts Décoratifs et Industriels Modernes, which exhibited works from twenty-one countries, was held in Paris in 1925.

4. Marguerite Duthoit (1894–1982), Matisse's only daughter, and his manager, muse, and model.

5. Harold Jackman (1901–1961)—a teacher, writer, model, actor, and patron—was close friends with many Harlem Renaissance figures, particularly Countee Cullen, who may have been his lover. This letter is held at Beinecke Library, Yale University, James Weldon Johnson Papers, box 1, folder 19.

TO LANGSTON HUGHES (1926)

1. Raquel Meller was born Francisca Romana Marqués López (1888–1962), a Spanish singer and dancer.

2. There is a famous story that American poet Vachel Lindsay (1879–1931) "discovered" Hughes while the latter was working as a busboy at the Wardman Park Hotel in Washington, DC.

3. Addison Scurlock (1883–1964), founder of the Scurlock Photographic Studio, took portraits of many prominent African Americans. It was seen as a mark of distinction to have your portrait hanging in his store window.

4. *The Weary Blues* (1926).

5. Konrad Bercovici (1882–1961), a Romanian-born American writer, is best

known for his short fiction with Gypsy themes.

6. Frans Masereel (1889–1972) was a Flemish painter and graphic artist who worked primarily in France. His paintings of Paris street scenes and his woodcuts brought him international fame.

7. Held at Beinecke Library, Yale University, Gwendolyn Bennett Papers, box 1, folders 7–8.

TO CLAUDE MCKAY (FEBRUARY 25, 1937)

1. Walter Duranty (1884–1957) was a Pulitzer Prize–winning journalist best known for his controversial writing on the Soviet Union, including *I Write as I Please* (1935).

2. Irita Van Doren was the editor of the New York *Herald Tribune*'s book reviews for over thirty-seven years.

3. Furman's, a small, New York–based publisher active in the 1930s, put out McKay's *A Long Way from Home* (1937).

4. Held at the Beinecke Library, Yale University. Claude McKay Papers, box 1, folder 9.

TO JAMES WELDON JOHNSON (JANUARY 4, 1938)

1. Johnson's autobiography published in 1933.

2. *Black Manhattan* (1930).

3. Johnson accepted a teaching position at Fisk University in 1931. He taught classes in creative writing and literature in the fall and spring semesters.

4. Anti-lynching legislature had been attempted for several years with little success. On February 21, 1938, the Wagner–Van Nuys Anti-Lynching Bill was defeated by a Senate vote of 58 to 22, largely due to pressure from Southern states.

5. Held at the Beinecke Library, Yale University, James Weldon Johnson Papers, box 3, folder 44.

TO ALAIN LOCKE (MAY 11, 1939)

1. Held at Moorland-Spingarn Library, Howard University, Alain Locke Papers.

TO RICHARD WRIGHT (MARCH 3, 1940)

1. Wright married Dhimah Rose Meadman in August 1939. The union lasted only a year.

2. Bennett married Richard Crosscup on June 26, 1940.

3. Bennett is inviting him to read at her school (as in the Locke and Hughes letters).

4. Held at the Beinecke Library, Yale University, Richard Wright Papers, box 3, folder 1208.

TO ALAIN LOCKE (NOVEMBER 30, 1941)

1. Nick Aaron Ford published *The Contemporary Negro Novel: A Study in Race Relations* in 1936.

2. The Haitian-born poet and novelist Roumain (1907–1944) was a friend of Langston Hughes, who translated some of his work. He was a communist fiercely opposed to the United States' occupation of Haiti (1915–34).

3. Audrey McMahon (1898–1981) was the director of the Federal Art Project from 1935 to 1943.

4. *The Negro in Art: A Pictorial Record of the Negro Artist and of the Negro Theme in Art* (1940).

5. Unfortunately, the School for Democracy was also seen as having Communist links, and she left her position in 1942.

6. Held at Moorland-Spingarn Library, Howard University, Alain Locke Papers.

TO LANGSTON HUGHES (MAY 13, 1942)

1. Hughes met Toy and Emerson Harper, an elderly couple, in the 1930s. He had a close relationship with them and bought a home with them at 20 East 127th Street in Harlem in 1947, where he lived until his death in 1967.

2. *Shakespeare in Harlem* (1942).

3. Held at the Beinecke Library, Yale University, Gwendolyn Bennett Papers, box 1, folders 7–8.

TO JOSHUA BENNETT AND MARECHAL NEIL BENNETT (JANUARY 5, 1925)

1. In December 1924 Bennett was awarded a $1,000 scholarship from Delta

Sigma Theta Sorority for continued study of art abroad.

2. Emmett J. Scott (1873–1957) worked as Booker T. Washington's secretary for eighteen years. He served as treasurer-secretary at Howard University from 1919 to 1932.

3. Mr. Herring (1887–1969) was an artist and teacher at Howard University. He founded the school's Art Department in 1922.

4. Dean Harold De Wolfe Hatfield: Director of the School of Manual Arts and Applied Sciences.

5. Marechal Neil Bennett was Bennett's stepmother. Letter held at the Beinecke Library, Yale University, Gwendolyn Bennett Papers, box 1, folders 2–3.

TO MARECHAL NEIL BENNETT (MARCH 24, 1925)

1. Rayford Logan (1897–1982), an African American historian who taught at Howard University from 1938 to 1965, wrote *The Betrayal of the Negro: The Nadir, 1877–1901* (1954).

2. Held at the Beinecke Library, Yale University, Gwendolyn Bennett Papers, box 1, folder 4.

TO JOSHUA BENNETT (MAY 27, 1925)

1. Anna Hicks Norwood, who wrote a scathing letter on May 3, 1925, to Bennett complaining about the abuse of her daughter by Joshua Bennett. Gwendolyn wrote an equally cutting letter back to the woman on May 15, 1925. Both letters are in the Bennett papers at Yale University (box 1, folder 2).

2. Held at the Beinecke Library, Yale University, Gwendolyn Bennett Papers, box 1, folders 2–3.

TO MARECHAL NEIL BENNETT (JULY 27, 1928)

1. Held at the Beinecke Library, Yale University, Gwendolyn Bennett Papers, box 1, folder 4.

TO JAMES VERNON HERRING (SEPTEMBER 9, 1937)

1. James Porter (1905–1970), an African American artist and art historian, taught at Howard University for over forty years.

2. James Lesesne Wells (1902–1993), a leading graphic artist and art instructor, taught at Howard University from 1929 to 1968. He was awarded the Harmon Gold Medal for his expressionistic painting *Flight into Egypt* (1931).

3. Mordecai W. Johnson (1891–1976) was a pastor and Howard University's first African American president from 1926 to 1960.

4. Letter held at the Beinecke Library, Yale University, Gwendolyn Bennett Papers, box 1, folder 5.

TO MAYME (ABERNATHY) PIZARRO (AUGUST 31, 1938)

1. Mayme was passing for a white at the time the two were reunited. When Gwen came to the hotel where Mayme worked, she was very upset.

2. Bennett would give differing opinions of Jackson and her relationship with him depending on whom she was writing. None of her letters to Jackson seems to have survived, but there is one from him in the Bennett papers at Yale (box 1, folder 9).

3. Bennett's biological mother. Letter held at the Beinecke Library, Yale University, Gwendolyn Bennett Papers, box 1, folders 10–11.

TO FLORA DUGAN (OCTOBER 6, 1947)

1. Bennett is possibly referring to Ralph Brock (1881–1959), who graduated from Pennsylvania State Forestry Academy (now Penn State Mont Alto) in 1906 and is considered the first African American forester.

2. Held at the Beinecke Library, Yale University, Gwendolyn Bennett Papers, Box 1, Folder 12.

TO EVERYONE (SEPTEMBER 27, 1968)

1. Bennett handwrote the message "Hail and Farewell" on the letter, which is held at the Schomburg Library, New York Public Library, Gwendolyn Bennett Papers, reel 1.

Bibliography

Bennett, Gwendolyn. Letter to attorney Louis L. Horowitz. 21 May 1939. Bennett's personal papers, Schomburg Library, reel 1.

Churchill, Suzanne W., and Adam McKible, eds. *Little Magazines and Modernism: New Approaches.* Burlington, VT: Ashgate, 2007.

Conrad, Earl. "A Lady Laughs at Fate." *Chicago Defender,* 5 Jan. 1946, 9.

Dolinar, Brian. *The Black Cultural Front: Black Writers and Artists of the Depression Generation.* Jackson: UP of Mississippi, 2012.

Dutrieuille, Bernice. "Art Weds Science." *Pittsburgh Courier,* 28 Apr. 1928, 6.

"Eastern Social Circles Agog over Bennett's Suicide (?)." *Pittsburgh Courier,* 28 Aug. 1926, 2.

Fabre, Michel. *From Harlem to Paris: Black American Writers in France, 1840–1980.* Urbana: U of Illinois P., 1991.

Goeser, Caroline. *"Not White Art Painted Black": African American Artists and the New Primitive Aesthetic, ca. 1920–35.* Dissertation. Rutgers University, 2000.

Govan, Sandra Y. "After the Renaissance: Gwendolyn Bennett and the WPA Years." *MAWA Review: Quarterly Publication of the Middle Atlantic Writers Association* 3.2 (1988): 27–31.

———. *Gwendolyn Bennett: Portrait of an Artist.* Dissertation. Emory University, 1980.

Griffin, Farah J., and Cheryl J. Fish, eds. *A Stranger in the Village: Two Centuries of African-American Travel Writing.* Boston: Beacon, 1998.

"Gwendolyn Crosscup Dies." *New York Amsterdam News,* 20 June 1981, 22.

Herring, Scott. "Du Bois and the Minstrels." *MELUS* 22.2 (1997): 3–17.

Hofmann, Leonore. "The Diaries of Gwendolyn Bennett." *Women Studies Quarterly* 17.3–4 (1989): 66–73.

Honey, Maureen. *Aphrodite's Daughters: Three Modernist Poets of the Harlem Renaissance.* New Brunswick, NJ: Rutgers UP, 2016.

Howsam, Leslie. *Old Books and New Histories: An Orientation to Studies in Book and Print Culture.* Buffalo: U of Toronto P, 2006.

Hughes, Langston. *The Big Sea: An Autobiography.* New York: Hill and Wang, 1993.

Johnson, Charles S. "Editorial." *Opportunity,* Aug. 1926, 241.

———. Letter to Ethel Ray. 24 Mar. 1924. Johnson Papers. Special Collections, Fisk University.

Johnson, James Weldon, ed. *The Book of American Negro Poetry.* New York: Harcourt Brace, 1922.

Langley, Jerry, and Sandra Govan. "Gwendolyn Bennett: The Richest Colors on Her Palette, Beauty, and Truth." *IRAAA* 23.1 (2010): 6–15.

Levering-Lewis, David. *When Harlem Was in Vogue.* New York: Penguin, 1997.

Levine, June, and Gene Gordon. *Tales of Wo-Chi-Ca: Blacks, Whites, and Reds at Camp.* San Rafael, California: Avon Springs Press, 2002.

Maffly-Kipp, Laurie F. *Setting Down the Sacred Past: African-American Race Histories.* Cambridge, MA: Belknap Press of Harvard UP, 2010.

Mao, Douglas, and Rebecca L. Walkowitz, eds. *Bad Modernisms*. Durham, NC: Duke UP, 2006.

Maxwell, William J. *F.B. Eyes: How J. Edgar Hoover's Ghostreaders Framed African American Literature*. Princeton, NJ: Princeton UP, 2015.

Maxwell, William J., and Joseph Valente. "Metrocolonial Capitals of Renaissance Modernism: Dublin's 'New Ireland' and Harlem's 'Mecca of the New Negro.'" Quoted on *Modern American Poetry Site*. MAPS. Urbana: U of Illinois, 2001. https://www.english.illinois.edu/maps/.

McHenry, Elizabeth. *Forgotten Readers: Recovering the Lost History of African American Literary Societies*. Durham, NC: Duke UP, 2002.

Nadell, Martha Jane. *Enter the New Negroes: Images of Race in American Culture*. Cambridge, MA: Harvard UP, 2004.

Nelson, Cary, ed. *Anthology of Modern American Poetry*. Vol. 1. 2nd ed. New York: Oxford UP, 2015.

Sanders, Mark A. "American Modernism and the New Negro Renaissance." *The Cambridge Companion to American Modernism*, edited by Walter Kalaidjian, 129–56. New York: Cambridge UP, 2005.

Sharpley-Whiting, Denean. *Bricktop's Paris: African American Women in Paris Between the Two World Wars*. Albany: State U of New York P, 2015.

Stott, Richard. Review of *Love and Theft: Blackface Minstrelsy and the American Working Class* by Eric Lott. *Journal of Southern History* 61.2 (1995): 377–78.

Tanner, Martha. Email correspondence. June 2016.

Walrond, Eric. "Cynthia Goes to the Prom." *Opportunity*, Nov. 1923, 342–43.

Wells, Herbert George. *The Research Magnificent*. London: Macmillan, 1915.

Wheeler, Belinda. "Gwendolyn Bennett: A Leading Voice of the Harlem Renaissance." *The Blackwell Companion to the Harlem Renaissance*, edited by Cherene Sherrard, 203–17. West Sussex, UK: Wiley-Blackwell, 2015.

———. "Gwendolyn Bennett's 'The Ebony Flute.'" *PMLA* 128.3 (May 2013): 744–55.

Index

A&I State College (now Tennessee State), 219
Académie Coloressi, 9, 176, 185
Académie de la Grande Chaumière, 9
Académie Julien, 9, 185
Africana, 60, 71
Alexander, Lewis, 66, 69
Allen, Frederick, 11
All God's Chillun, 66
American Artists' Congress, 221
American Artists' Guild, 221
American Life Magazine, 63
Anderson, Regina, 10
Antheil, George, 198–99
Art Front, 89–90
Austin, Texas, 5

Baker, Josephine, 9, 37, 72, 143, 156
Barnes, Albert C., 73, 92
Barnes Foundation, Albert C., 9, 72, 160, 207, 219, 221
Bartlett, Walter, 11
Batik, 160–62
Beach, Sylvia, 9, 193, 198–99
Bearden, Romare, 14
Benet, William Rose, 59–60, 62, 171
"Harlem," 59–60, 62
Bennett, Joshua, 4–5, 7, 11, 194, 213–16
Bennett, Marechal Neil, 6, 7, 11, 195, 213–15, 217
Bennett, Mayme Abernathy, 5, 194, 222
Bercovici, Konrad, 204
Best Short Stories of 1927, 68
Better Times, 89, 173
Black Opals, 1, 71
Blake, Eubie, 72
Bond, F. Fraser, 64
Boni and Liveright, 11, 63–64
Boni Prize, Albert and Charles, 202
Bonner, Marieta, 69
Bontemps, Arna, 65, 69
"Golgatha Is A Mountain," 65

Book and Bench, 71
Books, 204
Boston, 68, 71
Boulogne, Bois de, 180, 199
Bowman, Laura, 73
Braithwaite, William Stanley, 1, 67
Anthology of Magazine Verse for 1927, 1
Brawley, Benjamin, 70
"The Negro Literary Renaissance," 70
Briarwood (Long Island), New York, 168
Broadway, 60–61, 73
Brooklyn Girls' High School, 7
Brooklyn Urban League, 91, 99–100
Brooklyn YMCA, 10
Brown, Lawrence, 72
Burleigh, Alston, 61, 73
Buttonwood Hollow Antiques, 16, 227

California, 71
Cameron, May, 204
Camp Normana, 98–100
Camus, Albert, 190
The Fall, 190
Carolina Magazine, 59, 69
Century, 11
Cezanne, 92
Charleston (dance), 156–58
Chicago, 69
Cinema, 72
Civic Club, 10, 22
Clark, Barrett H., 77
Columbia University, 7, 206
Teachers College, 7
Communism, 16
Communist, 14, 193, 196, 211
Congressional Investigating Committee, 208
Consumers Union, 16, 227
Crane, Natalie, 67
Creole Folksongs, 63
Criner, J. L., 74
Crisis, 1, 10, 12, 22, 35, 36, 198, 205

Crosscup, Richard (Dick), 16, 177–78, 190–91, 193, 195–96, 211–13, 224–27
Cubism, 92
Cullen, Countee, 1, 3, 4, 10, 37, 65–66, 70, 107, 172, 174, 192, 197, 199–200, 204
  A Brown Girl Dead, 66
  Caroling Dusk, 1
  "Heritage," 37
  "Yet Do I Marvel," 70
Cullen, Reverend, 65
Cummings, E. E., 64
C.W.A. (Civil Works Administration), 97, 174
C.W.S. (Civil Works Service Section), 174, 219

The Daily Chronicle, 72
Davis, John P., 43, 65
Deeter, Jasper, 87–88
Delta Sigma Theta Sorority, 9
Department of Education, 173
Depression, *See* Great Depression
Dett, Nathaniel, 72–73
Dickens, Charles, 210
The Dixie Jubilee Singers, 72
Doren, Carl Van, 11
Doren, Irita Van, 204
Dostoevsky, Fyodor, 210
Douglas, Aaron, 9, 10, 12, 43, 63, 69, 95, 172
Douglass, Louis, 143, 156–57
Dreiser, Theodore, 210
Du Bois, W. E. B., 4, 10–11, 58, 192, 197
Dugan, Flora, 16, 195, 223–26
Dunbar, Paul Laurence, 22
Duranty, Walter, 204
  I Write as I Please, 204

École de Panthéon, 9, 176
England, 72
Epiphany, 37
Ethan Frome, 64
Europe, 65, 69
Eustis, Florida, 13, 217–18

Fauset, Arthur Huff, 65, 69
  "Symphonesque," 65
Fauset, Jessie (Redmon), 10–11, 25, 63, 67, 76, 84–86, 192, 197, 211
  "From Venice to Vienna," 63

Plum-Bun, 76, 84–86
There is Confusion, 25
FBI (Federal Bureau of Investigation), 16, 109, 193
Federal Art Project, 208, 219, 221
Federal Writers Project, 108
Federation of Artists' Unions, 102
Fire!!, 1, 12, 43–44
Fisher, Rudolph, 65
Fisk University, 194, 207
Florida, 2, 13, 142–5, 162–65, 167
Fontainebleau, France, 65, 69
Fort Valley, Georgia, 69
The Four Harmony Kings, 72
France, 11, 44–45, 65–66, 76, 90, 93, 142, 175–76, 180, 192
Franco, Francisco, 109
Freelon, Alan, 73
Fuller, Meta Warrick, 9

Galantiere, Lewis, 199
Garvey, Marcus, 58, 83
Georgia, 163, 165
George Washington Carver School, 15, 108
Giddings, Texas, 5
Gilpin, Charles, 76, 86–88
The Glasgow Bulletin, 72
Gordon, Eugene, 68
  "Rootbound," 68–69
Govan, Sandra, 1–2, 7, 14, 17, 35, 37
Great Depression, 14, 89–90, 107, 109, 145, 176
Great War, 43
Green, Paul, 76–77
  In Abraham's Bosom, 76–77, 87–88
  The Lonesome Road, 76–77
Gregory, Montgomery, 11
Grimke, Angelina Weld, 69
Guillaume, Paul, 92
Gurdjieff Institute, 65, 69

Hare, Maude Cuney, 63
Harlem, New York, 1, 3, 11, 13–15, 58–59, 63, 75, 79, 89–91, 96–98, 142
Harlem Art Center, 14, 108, 221
Harlem Artists Guild, 14, 102–4
Harlem Community Arts Center, 103, 193–94, 207, 222
Harlem Cultural Conference, 208

The Harlem Poets, 69
Harmon Foundation, 72, 90, 94
Harper's, 11
Harrisburg Central High, 7
Harrisburg, Pennsylvania, 7
Harris, Frank, 198
   Life and Loves, 198
Harvard University, 16, 159, 198, 203
Hayden, Palmer C., 95
Hayes, Roland, 72
Hedgerow Theatre, 76, 86–87
Hemingway, Ernest, 9, 193, 199
Hempstead, New York, 14, 145, 189, 205
Hempstead YMCA, 14
Herring, James Vernon, 195
Hicks, Clara, 11, 215–16
Home Relief Bureau, 97
Honey, Maureen, 2, 9, 11, 16
Hoover, J. Edgar, 109
Horne, Frank, 69, 188, 201
House Un-American Activities Committee, 14, 108
Howard University, 5, 7, 9, 66, 93, 143, 159–60, 194–95, 215, 219–20
Howard University Record, 89
Hughes, Langston, 1, 3, 4, 10, 22, 43–44, 59, 63–66, 68–70, 109, 174, 192–93, 197–98, 200, 202, 212
   The Big Sea, 10
   "Brass Spittoons," 65
   A House in Taos, 68
   "Let America Be America Again," 109
   The Midnight Blues, 65
   Mother to Son, 64
   "Pale Lady," 63
   The Railroad Blues, 66
   Song for a Banjo, 65
   Weary Blues, 63, 70, 174
Hurston, Zora Neale, 1, 3, 43–44, 65, 69
   Color Struck, 44
   "Muttsy," 69

The Illustrated Graphic, 72
Information of the Welfare Council of New York City, 173, 219
Ink Slingers, 71

Jackman, Harold, 181, 192, 198, 201

Jackson, Alfred J., 2, 9, 13–14, 143, 176–78, 189–90, 195, 217–22
Jenkins, Edmund T., 73, 181
Jessye, Eva A., 72
   My Spirituals, 72
John Keats Prize, 68
Johnson, Charles S., 10, 12–13, 65, 69
   Ebony and Topaz: A Collectanea, 12
Johnson, Georgia Douglas, 11, 58–59, 69
Johnson, Grace Nail, 205
Johnson, Hall, 64–65
   Goophered, 64
Johnson, Helene, 69
Johnson, James Weldon, 11, 23, 192, 194, 205
   Along This Way, 194, 205
   Black Manhattan, 206
Johnson, Sargent, 95
Jones, Louis, 181–82
Jordan, Moses, 63
   The Meat Man, 63
Joyce, James, 193, 199
   Ulysses, 198, 202
Jubilee Singers, 68
Julliard School of Music, 97

Keep Your Head Upon the Plow, 68
Kellogg, Paul, 11
Krigwa players, 172
Ku Klux Klan, 144–45, 162–65
Kutztown, Pennsylvania, 16, 196, 227

Lafayette Players, 74
Lancaster, Pennsylvania, 7, 153–54
Larsen, Nella, 1, 3
Lawrence, Jacob, 14
Lewis, Norman, 16, 175–78, 187–90, 224–25
Lindsay, Vachel, 203
Liveright, Horace, 11, 65–66
   Black Boy, 65
Locke, Alain, 1, 4, 10–11, 35, 67, 69, 193, 198, 208, 210
   The Negro in Art, 35
   The New Negro, 1
London Pavilion, 72
Lowell, Amy, 201

A Magazine of the Middle West, 69
Mansfield Theater, 65
Marie Chapdelaine, 64

Markhan, Edwin, 67
Marseilles, France, 67, 76, 82–84
Marxist, 212
Masereel, Frans, 204
Matisse, Henri, 89, 92, 199, 202
McKay, Claude, 1, 3, 4, 37, 67, 75–76,
    79–84, 192, 194, 199, 204, 206
  Banjo, 75–76, 82–84
  "Harlem Dancer," 37
  Home to Harlem, 75, 79–81
  A Long Way from Home, 194, 204
McMahon, Audrey, 211
Mediterranean fruit fly, 14, 145, 167
Meller, Raquel, 203
Merion, Pennsylvania, 9, 72, 160
The Messenger, 12, 35
Michelangelo, 93
The Midland, 69
Miller, Nina, 10
Moore, Charles, 73
Moscow, 204
Moss, Arthur, 199
Mount Vernon, 150–51, 153
Musical Observer, 63
My Magnolia, 65

NAACP (National Association for the
    Advancement of Colored People), 10
Nation, 205
National Negro Congress, 15
National Urban League, 13
Negro Playwrights Company, 211
Nevada, 5
New Masses, 110
New Negro, 10, 58–59, 65, 172
The New Negro, 64
New Republic, 205
New York, 4, 6, 7, 9, 14, 35, 66, 69, 71–73,
    94, 171
New York Amsterdam News, 17
New York Artists' Union, 103
New York Herald Tribune, 75
New York School of Fine and Applied Art,
    179
New York Times, 64, 74, 160
New York Times Book Review, 64
New York University, 207
Nugent, Bruce, 43, 65

O'Brien, Edward J., 68–69
October Theatre Arts Magazine, 62
*O. Henry Memorial Award Volume of Short
    Stories for 1926*, 69
Old Spirituals, 68
135th Street Library, 10, 65, 174
O'Neill, Eugene, 76, 86–88
  The Emperor Jones, 76, 86–88
Opportunity, 1, 3, 10, 12–13, 22, 35, 36, 37,
    58–59, 65–66, 68–69, 75, 89, 171,
    192–93, 198–200, 202–205

Palms Magazine, 68, 200
Panama, 69
Pamphlet Poets, 67
Paris, France, 3, 9, 12, 43, 45, 72, 93, 143, 156,
    173, 175, 184, 192, 197–98, 215
Pennsylvania, 6, 76
Philadelphia, Pennsylvania, 71
Piccadilly Circus, 72
Picasso, Pablo, 92
Pittsburgh Courier, 13
Pizarro, Mayme (Abernathy), *See* Bennett,
    Mayme (Abernathy)
Poetry, 201
Porgy and Bess, 87
Porter, James, 219, 221
Prairie View College, 147
Pratt Institute, 7, 161, 206
Princess Theatre, 73
Publisher's Weekly, 63

The Quill Club, 71

Rag Tang, 60
Randolph, Forbes, 72
  Kentucky Jubilee Choir, 72
Ray, Ethel, 10
Reading, Pennsylvania, 16
Reid, Dan, 221
Reynold's, 72
Richardson, Willis, 69
Robeson, Paul, 65, 72, 76, 86–88, 199, 202
Robinson, Hilyard, 95
Rolff, Norman, 176, 185
Rose, Ernestine, 10
Roumain, Jacques, 210
Rudd, Wayland, 76, 87–88

Sand, George, 64
Sadburg, Carl, 67
Saturday Nighters, 58–59, 69
Savage, Augusta, 89, 189, 205
Sawyer, Alta, 63
School for Democracy, 193, 211, 213
Scott, Clarissa, 66
    Solace, 66
Scribner's, 11
Shakespeare and Company, 9, 198–99
Simon and Schuster, 67
Sissle, Noble, 72
Smith, Albert (Alexander), 89, 93, 181–82
Smith College, 188
Social Work Today, 75
Sorbonne, France, 9
The Southern Workman, 70, 89
Spanish (language), 13
Spence, Eulalie, 69
Stein, Gertrude, 9, 193, 199
Stieglitz, Alfred, 202
Stoner, Elmer, 93
St. Phillip's Episcopal Church, 97
Strunsky, Simeon, 64
Survey Graphic, 11

Tanner, Henry O. (Ossawa), 9, 89, 92
Teachers College, *see* Columbia University
Texas, 4
Theatre Arts Magazine, 67
The Three Eddies, 72
Three Kings' Day, 37
Thurman, Wallace, 43–44
    "Cordelia the Crude," 44
Toomer, Jean, 65–66, 69, 198
    Cane, 65
The Town Crier, 68

Valente, Joseph, 21
Van Doren, Mark, 68
Vanity Fair, 70, 74, 197, 204
Van Vechten, Carl, 7, 58–59, 63, 70–71, 74,
    76, 79, 182–83, 199–200
    The Blind Bow-Boy, 182
    Nigger Heaven, 58, 63, 70, 74, 76, 79
    The Tattooed Countess, 182

Walrond, Eric, 7, 10, 11, 63, 69, 174, 198
    Tropic Death, 63

Walton, Lester, 74
Waring, Laura Wheeler, 9, 89, 93, 95
Washington, DC, 5, 6, 7, 9, 12, 58, 66, 69,
    142, 148, 151–52, 168, 211, 214
Waters, Ethel, 60, 71
W. C. Handy Music Publishing Company,
    14, 219
Weaver, John V., 64
Welfare Council of New York City's
    Department of Public Information
    and Education, 14
Wells, H. G., 71
Wells, Lesesne, 219
West, Dorothy, 1, 3, 69, 190–91
    The Typewriter, 69
Westminster's Flood Relief Fund, 72
Wheeler, Laura, *See* Waring, Laura Wheeler
White, Clarence Cameron, 72
White, Walter, 10
Williams, Blache Colton, 69
Williams, E. C., 69
Williams and Walker, 73
Wilson, Frank, 60, 73
    Meek Mouse, 60, 73–74
Workers' School, 212
Works Project Administration (WPA),
    103–4, 110, 206, 208
Works Progress Administration Art Project,
    14
World's Fair, 35
Wright, Richard, 4, 192, 194, 209, 211
    Native Son, 194, 209